WALK LIKE A MAN

MANI HAYRE & AMO RAJU

TABLE OF CONTENTS

EVERYBODY HURTS

"Nurse! Nurse! I need the toilet."

A young male nurse marched right past his little room, then took two steps back and peered through the door. "You're next on my list, Mr Rai, just two ticks," he said with a heavy Australian accent and walked off.

"Two ticks my arse," AJ muttered under his breath, knowing it meant at least half an hour. "I'll do it alone."

He tried shuffling to get out of bed but the morning shift had pretty much shrink-wrapped him in sheets and blankets with no room to move. After three attempts, he gave up and just gazed at the ceiling. He counted three cracks, remembering they had already been counted the day before and the day before that.

He looked across to the mirror on the adjacent cabinet and caught sight of himself for the first time since his arrival at the hospital. He seemed to have aged two decades. His hair was dishevelled from lying in the hospital bed and his face looked pale and withdrawn.

"You're still as handsome as ever, AJ." A soft, familiar voice suddenly lifted his spirits. He smiled internally and said under his breath so she could still hear.

"Liar."

She ignored him, smiling slightly. Sonia was a couple of years older, in her late fifties, but looked a decade younger. Standing in the doorway, her straight jet black hair had the thinnest strip of grey running through it and fell to her shoulders over her navy suit. AJ turned with a half-smile, which he immediately reversed.

"Three days in this place and I can't go to the toilet on my own." He noticed the same nurse from earlier walk past his room again.

"I'm so pleased to see you too!" Sonia's tone was sharp but her face couldn't hide her happiness and relief at seeing him. He had always had a habit of ignoring social etiquette and talking about himself first and foremost.

In a much softer tone, so as not to stress him, she said, "You missed your appointment, vanished without trace, and I hear from the florist that you've had a heart attack." That's when he noticed the yellow roses, his favourite, which she had in her hand.

"You're a doctor, I'm sure you can find me if you wanted to." AJ instantly realised how absurd that sounded but nevertheless committed himself to the statement. He stared back at the ceiling and fruitlessly continued to try and push the sheets off. Unsuccessful, he gave up, visibly exhausted from the effort.

"What are you trying to do? Do you want me to call someone?" Sonia walked into the room, put the flowers down on the table next to him, and looked around the bed for the assistance buzzer. It was hooked to the side of the bed. Instantly realising why he hadn't pressed it, she let out a deep frustrated sigh.

Her voice filled with anger. "They should know better. How ignorant."

She looked into AJ's eyes — it was clear he didn't want her to say anything to them. She knew he was proud in spite of his disability and that asking for help didn't come naturally. Born with Diplegia, he knew from an early age that his parents had been told not to hold out too much hope for a "normal" life for him. It was a constant shadow that had always followed him his whole life and made it all the more difficult to ask for and seek out help, especially when his limbs were tired.

She grabbed the buzzer and pressed it.

"I can't wait anymore, I need to go now. They're not going to come. Pull these damn sheets off me." He looked at her with a desperate, helpless look.

"Are you allowed out of bed? Where's your care plan?"

She checked his notes on the table in front of his bed. She was a doctor but didn't have the clearance to intervene in his medical care. Sharing his frustration, she lifted the sheets to expose his legs and let out an audible gasp.

"What happened? The bruises? How?" AJ's left leg was covered in bruises and what looked like small cuts. She looked up and noticed that his left arm was in a similar mess. Sonia recalled part of their last conversation before he went AWOL. She had told him to use his walking stick, which he had filed away with his painkillers. Realising he was still desperate to go, she helped him to his feet and walked with him to the en-suite. He locked the door behind him.

Sonia turned around and dropped onto the bed; tears started flowing effortlessly. She had known him a long time and not seen him as physically broken as he was now.

A few minutes passed, then the sound of the flush interrupted her thoughts and she gathered herself to hide her tears; she sat upright, ready for some answers.

The door opened and AJ stood there with a cold but confused stare. He looked paler and even more frail than when he entered the bathroom. Something else was wrong. His mouth was open but no words came out as he collapsed to the floor.

Within seconds, the room was filled with blue and white uniforms. Now crying uncontrollably, Sonia was marshalled to the waiting room at the end of the corridor, which didn't actually seem to end, by a nurse who she thought looked like a school leaver.

"Have a seat here, someone will come and talk to you in a little while. Are you next of kin?"

Stuttering, Sonia said, "No. No. I'm his ther…"

"The doctor will be here shortly, there's a coffee machine in the corner, help yourself," the nurse said kindly and walked away leaving Sonia to wait.

Sonia glanced across the room at some kind of contraption, which didn't look like it would give her the caffeine shot she needed. She sat down and cried some more. She mumbled, "Get a grip, you idiot. He's just like any other patient. Get a grip."

For some completely unknown reason, she recalled the song playing on the radio on the way to the hospital: *Everybody Hurts* by R.E.M. That didn't help as the tears continued to flow.

Just over an hour had passed when she heard footsteps approaching. A tall man who appeared to be in his thirties came in. "I'm Dr Ash Kumar. Are you with Mr Amraj Rai?"

"Yes, Yes I am. Is he all right? Sorry, my name is Dr Khan, Sonia—Dr Sonia Khan." She fumbled, instantly realising her cringe-worthy habit of introducing herself as a doctor when meeting her peers. She asked again, "AJ, I mean Mr Rai, attends my clinic for counselling. Is he all right?"

"Initial results indicate another heart attack, which doubled up with his episode a few days earlier, doesn't put him in a strong position. He's sedated and resting at the moment." Dr Kumar had a kind and empathetic tone that reassured her. "His emergency contact has been alerted."

Sonia didn't feel professional at all and asked "Can I see him? I won't disturb him." She wanted to be with him before his family arrived.

"Yes of course. I'll walk with you." Dr Kumar walked at a pace she couldn't match and kept falling a few steps behind. Sonia couldn't for the life of her get that song out of her head.

They walked into AJ's room. It seemed eerie but warmer for some reason. "Please try not to wake him." His voice suddenly softened. "I'll be on the ward if you need me. The nursing staff are at their station too."

She looked at him and felt an urge to correct him about the availability of the nurses but that could wait. He walked out across to the ward opposite and she turned to AJ.

AJ was now attached to a respiratory pipe, an ECG monitor and other equipment not necessarily recognisable to a psychiatrist, bleeping in the background. The chair beside the bed looked appealing. She sat down feeling spent and looked at her watch. She would wait until his siblings arrived and make her leave then. AJ's family, including his siblings, never knew of their relationship and that AJ had been having therapy and she would never want to make it awkward for him now.

She looked towards the door as if to keep watch of anyone approaching. Compelled to grab hold of his left hand, she felt the tears commence. She could hear her own heart, which was loud and beating fast. She turned to AJ once more.

Composing herself and holding back tears, her voice wavering, she said, "I remember the first time I met you."

CHAPTER 1:

PILLS

"Mr Rai? Amraj Rai?"

She looked across the small waiting area to see a man pacing up and down with a nervous energy; he looked toward her at the sound of his name.

He was unshaven and looked to be in his early- to mid-twenties. His mullet hairstyle was still the rage among his community, a remnant of the 80s that hadn't disappeared in the early 90s. His hair had clearly been left to its own devices. It was wild and looked like there hadn't been any attempt to tame it. He was wearing nondescript clothes, plain stonewashed jeans, and a dark brown shirt with black shoes in need of a good polish. It was almost as if he chose colours that would camouflage him.

Peering down through her glasses, which were balancing on her thin nose, in a comforting tone she asked him to follow her into the room. He stopped pacing and made his way reluctantly towards her.

Her eyes immediately zoned in on his walk. The gait was different. He looked steady but the right leg swerved outwards with each step. The foot appeared to miss the floor. She realised she was staring and even though it lasted no longer than a few seconds, she pretended not to have noticed and walked ahead into her room.

He followed her, having noticed the slight stare, an all too familiar occurrence. He forced himself to move forward and reminded himself why he had agreed to these sessions. His GP would only prescribe him antidepressants if he attended six appointments with Dr Khan, who was a counsellor.

"Please take a seat," she carried on even though he had not yet entered the room.

It wasn't what he had expected. The room resembled a living room he had once seen in a wealthy couple's house in Nottingham years earlier. Bright coloured walls, a soft shag-pile carpet, with ample daylight streaming through. Very homely indeed. There were a number of certificates in dark frames strategically placed around the room, ensuring that no patient escaped a reminder of her many qualifications.

He stood there unsure and a bit awkward and looked across at her for some direction. She could read what he was thinking and said. "It's not like in the films — you can sit on either the chair or the sofa. No need to lie down either," she added with a soft smile, hoping to start on a light note to make him feel comfortable.

The indecision was written all over his face, and it took a second or two before he headed for the most comfortable looking chair and sat down. Once seated, he noticed Dr Khan properly for the first time. She was an attractive woman who seemed to be a few years older than him. Her hair was dark and tied in a loose knot at the base of her neck. She pushed the glasses further up her nose and he noticed her hazel eyes.

"How do you like to be known?" she asked, "Amraj? Mr Rai? Or do you have any other nicknames or preferences?"

He hadn't realised he had been staring, and answered, "Whatever, I'm not fussed, but most people call me AJ." His voice was soft and deep but it sounded withdrawn. His eyes looked sad and in sync with his troubles.

Her training pushed her past being affected by this initial observation and she knew better than to become overly familiar with him. Calling him AJ could go one of two ways, over-familiarity which he might resent, or he might open up but not in a way that she needed in order to help him.

"I'll stick with Amraj, if that's okay?" He just nodded slightly so she continued. "I just need to go through a few details with you and I'll explain how these sessions work. You can ask me anything at any time if you need clarification. My only rule is that you remain seated at all times. Our conversation ends when you stand. I'll be taking notes throughout, and you can have a look at them at any point should you wish."

She paused in case he had any questions at this point. His eyes seemed to be vacant but she could sense he was taking in what she had said. She continued, "Dr McKleish has sent me the referral and given me some information but I really want to spend this first session getting to know you. Tell me a little about yourself."

He paused, unsure where to start. "Erm," he mumbled, "I'm twenty-four, born and raised in Derby. I live just down the road in a one-bedroom flat. No job. I'm on benefits. I have no money and I'm the eldest of three. You want me to go on?"

She sensed some hesitation to continue although he had volunteered more than others at the first question. It sounded mechanical; he was just reciting facts, nothing too personal until the end. There was the chance he might not open up too much, and for a millisecond she recalled her previous patient who had sat silent for at least ten minutes before engaging.

Dragging herself back to the present, she asked, "Let's go back to your childhood; what's your earliest memory?"

CHAPTER 2:

NO ONE WILL MARRY HIM

Sonia was surprised when he immediately answered her question, his eyes glazed somewhat as if he was reminiscing. For AJ, the past wasn't always the problem: he'd had a happy early childhood; he was here for the present but was happy to deflect from that and answer the doctor's question.

"My granddad came to the UK in 1963, and my dad followed him in '65. My mum, grandma, and her other children came over two years later. We all lived together."

Sonia probed a little further, his voice had softened with the mention of his grandparents, "Were you close to your grandparents?"

He smiled, "As a child, I sat with them for hours and hours listening to stories about their struggles. They had nothing, absolutely nothing. They lost everything, their house, cattle, and belongings in 1947, during partition."

For a second, they both fell silent, picturing the scenes their ancestors would have faced. He suspected that her family were from Pakistan due to her surname, but asking her directly felt rude and intrusive and he wasn't sure she would answer if he did ask.

AJ broke the silence first, "When granddad had a shot of rum, the painful memories would flow, followed by a stern lecture about how we should be ready to uproot at a moment's notice. The fear of losing everything was still there. He would tell us to carry enough cash so we could buy a ticket to India at any time. When dad bought us our own home, I'd stay with them every weekend. I never got tired of listening to them."

She had left him to speak uninterrupted; he paused in his story as he remembered weekends at his grandparents' house. She asked, "Are they still with you?" She had to be careful how she asked the question. Some patients could become quite irate when asked something so personal and painful.

His expression changed from smiling to sombre and his response was a little solemn. "Yes, but I don't see them much these days."

She noted the change in expression during the conversation and made an initial assessment that he'd had a happy early childhood.

"And your parents?" she probed with a little caution.

He looked directly at her, "They're fine. We don't need to talk about them or my siblings."

She noted the steely response and jotted it down on her pad.

"I know you've said you don't want to talk about them but I want to know about your childhood, with your parents and siblings." A few years earlier, her mentor had advised her to probe once and only once after such a response. With a little hesitation, it worked.

"They were great and loved me dearly," he continued. "I know they still love me. There's no complaint there. I caused them a lot of problems and they still loved me." A small pause, then AJ continued, "I was a burden to them you see, because of this." He pointed to his leg, "Dad had to take so much time off work to take me to appointments with doctors, physios, and even charlatans who claimed they could *heal* me. The other two were neglected because of me."

She sensed guilt and with it, a lot of internal pain and suffering. There was a longer pause this time and whilst she was pondering whether to continue this line of discussion and shift the topic, he carried on.

"I tried not to let them know how I was. I was always in pain, you see. I was so hurt by my leg. They were terrified for me and the lack of prospects. Mum was always saying that the world won't let me be. Whenever dad had a drink, he'd get emotional and lecture me that my only hope was to gain an education, be a doctor. I was six when I first heard this."

Clearing his throat he ended with, "They loved me."

Sonia let him have a moment before carefully wording her next question, "And your siblings?"

"I'm the eldest. I was supposed to watch over my brother and sister. Instead, I stole their attention. All my extended family and friends ever wanted to do was talk about me and my *condition*. It was years later when I realised how unfair that was to them. They were good kids. But I won't be talking about them much — it's an elder sibling thing, the need to protect them, even now."

She scribbled some more and looked across at him; his eyes had misted over. There was a box of tissues within his reach on the coffee table. He knew where they were if he needed them.

"Do you need a moment?" she asked.

"No."

"You talked a little about your dad, how about your mum?"

Genuinely pleased to move on, he forgot that this was an equally uncomfortable subject but felt the need to smile. "Now that is a tad Hollywood, hey? It has to be mummy issues if it isn't my dad?"

Months earlier, when Dr McKleish had suggested these sessions, AJ had mocked him with, "Let's skip to the part where we conclude that all my problems led to my mother like in the movies and then you can give me those pills!"

Realising Sonia was still waiting for an answer, he said, "Mum was just fine. She was the stereotypical housewife. I only recall her working for a very short period—for most of my childhood, she was at home."

"She cooked, cleaned, and kept us in order. We never went hungry, although she insisted I learn to be independent. I recall her saying to me that I needed to learn how to cook basic food and wash my own clothes by hand. I knew how to cook a mean omelette and how to get rid of shirt stains by the age of 10." He looked quite proud of the recollection, but soon switched back to his sombre stance.

Listening and writing, Sonia was fascinated by this mini-revelation and wanted to know more. Before she could ask further, he continued, lost in memories of his mum and his earlier childhood. He had been happy and he had never been made to feel any less happy because of his disability.

He could sense a rising anger, however, the more he talked to Dr Khan. It was bringing up some memories he had learned to suppress. When he next spoke, he could hear it in his voice.

"I pulled a sickie from school once." Sonia noted the hardness of his voice and could sense his anger. The sudden change in topic and mood made her question where this was going but his eyes were staring off into the distance and she let him speak uninterruptedly.

"A few of mum's friends came to see her on this particular day. I suppose that's what housewives did: finish their chores and then have tea with their *sisters*. They would chat, gossip, and revel in their miserable existences. Oh, let's not forget how much they missed their motherland!"

He paused before continuing. "The truth is I realised much later in life that mum had never really left India in 1967. Her settling in the UK was a massive inconvenience and all her friends shared that view."

"You see, my dad worked all manner of hours and with the advantage of being able to speak English, he understood the issues facing my generation. Women in my mum's position who just stared at the TV trying to guess what was happening understandably had a nostalgic view of how we should be as kids." He looked up and asked, "Is your mum like that?"

Sonia cleared her throat. Her code of conduct was to ensure that her sessions with patients didn't get too personal. She had to play it safe so as not to give too much of her own life away. "Amraj, I should have made it clear that you can't ask me questions about my private life in these sessions, but I empathise with what you have told me."

He sensed a slight rebuttal but appreciated her honesty. He noticed a picture behind her, on a shelf, showing her standing next to a tall, handsome man, his arms around her and two small children, all smiling wide, toothy grins at the camera. He wanted to ask about them but sensed she would be less forthcoming to a second question about her life.

"I'm sorry, I'm not used to talking. I spend most of my days alone. That was the first time I'd felt angry at my own culture. I don't think I've ever admitted that out loud before." He went quiet, contemplating these long-dormant feelings. "Where was I?"

She gave him a prompt and he continued, "Oh yes, her friends, one in particular, Kamala Aunty, came round and mum disappeared into the kitchen to make some Indian tea." His mouth went dry as if indicating his yearning for his mum's tea. There and then, he decided he would make a cup when he got home.

Realising he had drifted in thought, he said, "Anyway, I was watching TV and I realised they were talking about me in Punjabi. I didn't want them to think I was eavesdropping so I pretended to carry on watching *Rainbow*. I caught the tail end of the sentence, which led to one of them saying to the other *'It's such a shame, no one will marry him. Who is going to give their daughter to him?'* "

She put her pen and paper down, and the movement broke AJ's thoughts. It was in her training not to show emotion when patients were talking. Sonia knew how the Asian community could be openly blunt in its assumptions. She was surprised at the lack of emotion in AJ's voice as he told the story. He was clearly masking the pain from overhearing this and had never dealt with it as a child or a young adult.

"I carried on watching *Rainbow*, which was normally a source of joy and laughter, but the songs and funny exchanges between the characters had no effect. I was only ten years old and was now introduced to worrying about marriage and life in general as a disabled child."

He looked into her eyes, "You know, years later during a disagreement with mum, I recalled that incident and she wouldn't believe me that those women would say something like that. It fucked me up. Really fucked me up."

CHAPTER 3:

SPICY TEA

He left the counsellor's office and popped in quickly to pick up some yellow roses from the florist next door. The walk home seemed a little quicker than usual today. No real interaction with anyone apart from the cashier at the shop who he asked about the masala tea bags he'd just purchased.

"Do they taste like the real thing?"

After the session, talking about Indian tea, the original plan had been to make some from scratch. It had been more draining than he realised and chose the easy ready-mixed tea bags.

"No, but it's the next best thing." Not overly happy with his answer to the question, AJ took his change and made an exit, thinking the verbal exchange would have been shorter with a simple yes or no.

The journey home continued with his natural head-down stare at the pavement all the way to his front door. "*Don't make eye contact with anyone*" was his usual silent mantra. He lived in a predominately South Asian area and being stared at for his walk and disability had been a staple in his life for as long as he could remember, especially from his own community—a community he was angry at after his session. A flood of emotions and memories had been suppressed but brought to the surface by Dr Khan.

He had found out at quite a young age that even his orthopaedic surgeon had told his father not to hold out too much hope for his son. There was little prospect of doing well at school, let alone getting a job, learning to drive, or settling down and having his own family. That had been his professional opinion.

AJ smirked. "Well I guess he was onto something with a lot of those predictions. Who knew doctors were also fortune tellers?"

The ground-floor flat he called home was just off the high street and was within walking distance of the counsellor's office and local shops. All he needed for basic amenities.

The flat served a very basic purpose. It had one bedroom with a single plain bed in the corner, a bathroom, and a kitchen-diner. It represented his internal struggles and even though each item of furniture was spotless and aligned at perfect right angles, there was very little colour except the yellow roses that he kept in a vase on the table to one side, which doubled as a dining table.

There wasn't a speck of dust to be seen on the hardwood floor, and the cream curtains hung without a crease in sight. The kitchen was worthy of a 5-star hygiene award. The only item that looked out of place was the mug placed upside down having being left to drain after his morning cuppa.

He walked over to the kettle and switched it on. Once the water had come to a boil, he added a splash of milk and a brown sugar cube to his tea and sat down to taste the past. It was too hot to drink so he placed it on the table next to his two-seater sofa. The only personal item was just in front of him, a very finely hand-drawn, detailed picture of a woman with three young children in a wooden frame. The picture was the only connection in his flat to his family. He had left a lot behind when he moved out to make it on his own.

The day had tested his emotions more than he had planned. Deciding to kill some time by having a nap, he lay his head down and stretched. He had at least two during each day to break up the silence. Looking across at the picture, he smiled, closed his eyes, and began his daily visit to his other world.

"Hey baby, did you enjoy the concert?"

He woke up an hour later with tears streaming down his face.

CHAPTER 4:

THE GESTAPO

It took a minute or so to straighten his arm and leg, which had tensed and were now numb from his siesta. This was a usual occurrence after sleeping yet still took him by surprise. He stood and stretched to relieve the stiffness, then glanced out of his window overlooking the main road. With a sharp intake of breath and a feeling of anxiety weighing on him, he saw that his parents were heading slowly towards his front door.

The key turned; it was one of the areas he had negotiated with them in order to leave home. "We want a key to check on you." He often felt angry with himself for giving in to such a demand, which would end in a half-smile when he realised it meant they still wanted to look after him.

He immediately started to position himself, choosing a chair in the centre of the room, and sat down trying to look in control. It was the usual weekly visit and he knew the drill.

When they entered, his mum headed straight towards the kitchen and then did a U-turn through to him. She was followed a few seconds later by his dad. She was a tall woman, which was unusual in Indian families, and she had a good few inches on his father who followed behind. He was a little more rotund and stout in appearance.

His mum was dressed in the traditional Punjabi salwar kameez. Her hair was perfectly parted in the middle and scooped back into a bun, no grey hair in sight. Recognising the familiar strong smell of Imperial Leather soap, the smell of every Punjabi mum, he giggled without moving a single muscle.

"Where you go?" Her voice was stern, strong, and comfortably inquisitive. She often started sentences with a question in her broken English. After an unsatisfactory response, she would switch to her mother tongue for the supplementary follow-up. Her powerful voice didn't affect him too much these days. He had grown up with it and knew it was backed by love and concern.

AJ wasn't going to volunteer his movements for the day. In Indian culture and particularly for his generation, counselling and mental health were taboo subjects and very rarely understood.

"Leave him alone," his dad responded, as always jumping in to save the day. "He went to the shop." His facial expression hinted that AJ should play along.

Rai Senior was by contrast a much more reserved character, with a softer voice, even if he did sound a little tired. AJ resembled his dad in appearance — his father was a good-looking man and was ageing well. He had more of his mother's height and some of her temperament; there was no mistaking that he was their son. His mum would always joke that the blend of the two was successful.

"Yes, I wanted some masala tea bags," AJ responded by playing along with his dad; it felt like a plausible semi-truth, which could very easily be proven if the Gestapo, his secret name for her, wasn't satisfied.

"Are you okay son? Your back okay? Do you need anything?" Three consecutive questions with more emphasis placed on the last one as if she was desperate for AJ to say he needed her help.

"I'm fine, both of you, I'm fine." He beamed an almost perfect Hollywood smile at them. He wasn't fine but he wasn't going to divulge that to them.

A silence followed where AJ tried to conceal his face and the fact that there were continuous aches and pains in his knees, feet, and lower back as well as the never-ending lethargy. He would often wake up during the night feeling like a lorry was parked on his chest. It wasn't a heart attack but would almost always be an oncoming anxiety attack. He hadn't been eating well, and even though the fridge was stocked with curries cooked by his mum, he ate the bare minimum on most days.

"If you want them, you come home. It is your house, you know. I your mother you know. Nine month I carry you, change your nappy, look after you. Look." She pointed at her fingernails, "Still got your shit from nappy in there. I your mother." By now, her voice was quivering and her eyes were starting to well up.

Mrs Rai knew he wasn't going to come home for tea. He hadn't been home since he left more than two years ago. She walked across to him and tried to wipe his dry face, which she was hoping would also be flooded with tears. Rai Senior just looked at them both, shook his head slowly, sighed, and muttered, "Same bloody drama every time."

"He said he was fine," he stated, knowing too well his intervention was not going to reassure her. It never did.

31

Mrs Rai was having none of it, "Look at his eyes, they swollen. He been cry."

AJ was about to correct her when he remembered he had shed a tear or two after his nap. A usual occurrence following on from a dream of another life. Nevertheless, he needed to shift the subject back to tea.

"No, I had a nap earlier, that's why my eyes seem puffy and I only woke up when you came," he tried to reassure his mum.

"Stop lying. You been cry." She then followed tradition by bursting into Punjabi insisting that he wasn't over that heartless girl from college. He should stop pining over her by getting married to a nice girl from India.

"You want some tea. I'll make some Indian tea." The ball was back in his court and he walked swiftly to the kitchen leaving his parents in a muffled conversation that he had no intention of joining.

In the kitchen, he noted a carrier bag with a couple of curries and a handful of chapattis. The bag was still warm and he could see a little condensation; his stomach lurched slightly.

"Here, try this." He handed them both a mug and commented, "I think they're great." Knowing full well he had no idea about the authenticity of the taste, he had committed to the product and wanted to keep talking about tea to avoid his mother's further line of enquiry.

"A little weak but can pass as Indian tea, right?" He kept a straight face but knew there wasn't a chance in hell she would agree.

She ignored him.

Rai Senior piped up with, "Not bad, not great but not bad."

They both looked at her again for approval. She gave a half-smile and said, "Mine is better."

The conversation continued about her health, as it always did. She would list every ailment she had heard about from her friends and was convinced she had them too. Father and son would listen attentively and nod at the right moments, but were secretly relieved that there were no more tears.

An hour or so later, they departed and the circle of life continued.

CHAPTER 5:

THREE LITTLE GIRLS

AJ was in two minds about the second session with Dr Khan and had reversed his decision six times before arriving at her clinic the following week. The last session had been draining, and he wasn't keen to repeat the process.

"Come on through," she motioned. "How have you been since our last session?"

He didn't want to say out loud how he was really feeling. Like he constantly had a dark cloud following him and could feel the rain hitting him even when it was blazing hot outside. To describe that out loud, with your chest tightening, when you were in a haze of mist and darkness, was not a conversation he wanted to have with anyone. He hesitated, "I'm okay. I wasn't going to come, you know."

She nodded. She could empathise with how hard these sessions can be, especially for young men who aren't accustomed to therapy and talking about how they feel. It was still rare to have men attend the sessions, especially those from ethnic minority backgrounds. Her field of work was unorthodox, even for her family.

She gave him a minute to settle, so he opted for the same chair as the first session; her patients were creatures of habit. She let him have a moment before prompting, "Shall we pick up where you left off from last week; we discussed your family and relationships, and I wanted to know what school was like?"

It was important to focus on his early years, as this would unearth the feelings that he was going through now and pick up on traits and patterns that could improve his current state of mind.

AJ was transported back to his secondary school with that question. A small nondescript two-storey building in Derby, which served as the backdrop for the hell he suffered there.

Realising he hadn't answered, he said, "I was an introvert, I tried to blend in and did well at school, so my grades were always top-mark," he said with a little pride and then fell silent before continuing.

"It was uneventful for a short period, and when the bullying started, it was so subtle at first that I didn't immediately notice it. It began with three little girls who were a year younger than me."

Dr Khan was making more notes on her pad. She was saddened but unsurprised to hear he had been bullied.

"Children can be so cruel," she mumbled and her eyes fell on the photograph of her own boys in the frame on the shelf beside her. AJ followed her gaze. "As a mother, I worry about my own children being bullied, or something like that happening to them."

Noticing him staring at her, she coughed and refocused her attention from her back on him. She prompted him to continue.

"There was one particular day when I heard giggling behind me. I didn't pay attention to it at first but I soon became aware that the giggling was aimed at me. When I looked behind me, I noticed that the one in the middle was imitating my walk with the other two giggling at her. I'd always been stared at but this was the first time it was aimed directly *at* me."

The scribbling stopped. Dr Khan wanted to interject but she took stock and realised that as a professional she must allow him to continue his story, even though she was experiencing a rising sense of anger.

"What did you do when you found out?"

"I ignored it. I assumed it was a one-off and I would be left alone." Sighing heavily he continued, "I was wrong. The next day, walking the same route to class, they were behind me again, mimicking my walk and laughing until we got to class. As the days went on, the giggling was sometimes replaced with strange noises, almost imitating an injured animal, and the noise coincided with their mocking my walk."

She could feel her anger and indignation at his suffering as a small child from bullies but again remained composed. She noticed he sounded pensive, so she let him have a moment before asking, "Did you report what the girls were doing?" Her voice wavered with suppressed outrage. Hoping he hadn't noticed, she coughed and waited for his response.

He looked up at Dr Khan and replied, "I told my friend. I confided in him as I needed someone to believe that it was aimed at me. He laughed it off, telling me that it was three little girls and to not take it so seriously."

"The bullying had started to take a toll on my grades at school. Having confided in my friend and teacher to no avail, I didn't want to bring it up again. I started taking longer routes to classrooms to avoid them finding me, which caused me to be late to class. I would make up fake illnesses to avoid going to school so I could escape the subtle taunting that was starting to affect me."

"Did it eventually stop?"

"No, the bullying continued for years. The taunting and mocking. I never challenged them, which probably gave them confidence to continue. After a while, it carried on past the corridors and classrooms."

"When I took the issue up with a teacher, the advice I was given was to put up and shut up, that I was being too reactive and sensitive. It was something I should get used to because of my disability. I suppose we have to remember, it was a different era. Kids were expected to be tougher, as were teachers. I remember one of the geography teachers being quite insensitive to my needs too."

AJ began to gaze out of the window. Sonia looked in the same direction wondering what made him stop part-way through his recital. After a few long seconds, he continued.

"I'd just had major surgery at the age of 11. I had to learn how to walk again. My dad felt I was missing out on my education and so he hurried me back before I was ready. It meant I was walking slower."

"All the teachers allowed me to finish each lesson a few minutes early, which gave me ample time to walk to the next. This one teacher felt the need to single me out at the front of the class to say I was always late to her lesson."

Sonia tutted slightly. She knew it was unprofessional but she found it hard to hide her disapproval of the teacher's behaviour.

"I didn't really have a reply and just let her have her moment of power. I remember thinking 'maybe I should try walking faster' despite being told by the physiotherapist to build my strength back slowly. I simply apologised and decided to sit back down without a fuss. Some of my classmates told me afterwards how they felt disgusted with her comments but I played it down."

Becoming aware of the silence, she looked up.

"Amraj, I'm sorry you had to endure this so young and it's taken a lot of courage to share that so openly with me." For a second or two, he found himself thinking it was finally good to talk and not be told to forget about it or just deal with it.

She found herself reaching forward, subconsciously wanting to comfort him. His story was making her angry and she wanted justice for what he had to endure. She caught herself and pretended to straighten up her notes from the session.

AJ had noticed her reaching forward and wondered what that meant.

CHAPTER 6:

PUTTY IN HIS HANDS

He arrived home after his session with Dr Khan, not stopping en route. He contemplated going to the florist but his roses were faring quite well from last week.

It had been a more taxing session than the first and even though he had anticipated it, the hour had completely drained him. Lost in thought as his frustrations began to rise, he just wanted the anti-depressants; the charade of therapy didn't seem to be helping. If anything, it felt like he was getting worse.

He was also perplexed by Dr Khan — her reaction towards the end of their session had been out of character for what he was expecting from a therapist. Was she really just sorting through her notes? It had looked like she was reaching out to touch him, console him after reliving a painful memory. He shook the thought away. Surely he was just over-thinking this? The movement had been so quick he could have misread her.

He let himself into the flat and lay down, with numerous thoughts spinning in his mind. He knew he should get some food but found himself drifting off into a slumber.

*

The crowd was cheering and he was getting ready to go on stage, the room reverberating with his name, "AJ! AJ! AJ!"

The sound of his name being screamed by a few hundred people was such a buzz! He gave himself a quick once-over before heading out.

His permed hair was slicked back. He was wearing a dark denim jacket over a white t-shirt and denim jeans. He could feel his confidence and swagger become more pronounced as he entered the stage.

The crowd was still chanting.

He was warming them up before his performance. Being on stage made him forget everything. It was just him and the crowd waiting for him to start singing and entertaining them for the night.

Tonight felt electric. He was gearing up to start singing when everything froze. That's when he spotted her at the back of the room. His mind went blank, only vaguely aware of the crowd waiting to hear him perform.

Who was she? he asked himself; he hadn't seen her before.

Not realising he'd been staring for a good couple of minutes, he was brought back to reality by the band getting louder. Shaking his head but keeping his eyes on her, he started performing. It was like the crowd didn't exist and it was all for her.

His confidence took over as he was performing; it was what made him come alive. He wanted her to notice him and pay attention, to not just dismiss him as the entertainer for the evening. He wondered if she had noticed the way he had walked onto the stage and noticed his disability. He shoved that thought to the back of his mind as he didn't need to think about that right now.

As he was performing for the crowd, who were showing off their best Bhangra moves to each track he was singing, he made a mental note to find her quickly once he was done.

He was a different man on stage. Everything he had endured at school was from a lifetime ago and tonight he was in control. They were like putty in his hands, moving because he commanded them to move with the music and his singing.

His set lasted a couple of hours, and he was sweating from the performance, with his confidence making him feeling bolder. Throughout the show, he had kept an eye on the girl at the back, smiling to himself because he knew she was also dancing to the music and his words.

He knew the set was coming to an end and didn't want to get bombarded by those in the crowd, a usual occurrence after a gig. He loved to mingle but he had to find the girl at the back before they swamped him.

Once finished, he slid off stage and to the side of the dance floor so he could manoeuvre to the back as quickly as possible. He caught up with her before she had noticed he was there.

As he approached, he tapped her on the shoulder and she turned round. With a huge smile, she introduced herself, "Hey, I'm Esha."

*

AJ woke up with a start. He could feel his heart pounding loudly in his ears. He felt disoriented and it took him some time to understand where he was and why he was lying down.

As his senses caught up with him, he noticed it was starting to get darker outside — *how long had he been asleep?* The dream had brought up a lot of memories he was avoiding. As he shook his head to clear the images of the crowd, the stage, and the woman, he stood up.

"No," he muttered to himself. "No."

He picked himself up slowly from the sofa, and he could feel his agitation rising. The need to occupy his mind was overwhelming. He spent the next few hours clearing, dusting, rearranging furniture, and tackling his small flat like his life depended on it.

Anything to distract himself from the dream that had made him spiral into despair at what he had lost.

CHAPTER 7:

THE SINGING DEPRESSIVE

The dream had left him feeling agitated all week. He had found it hard to do anything productive apart from his cleaning binge. But it also came with headaches. He couldn't shift the dream as after-images were lingering in the back of his mind. His parents had been over but he'd been too distracted by his own thoughts to engage with them.

They stayed a while as his mum dropped off more food for the week and engaged in generic chit chat that he gave non-committal answers to. For once, they didn't push him to engage in conversation, and he sensed they wanted to say something important but were holding back.

As if he wasn't already irked by having to attend these sessions, the dream had heightened how he was feeling. All he wanted were the pills from Dr McKleish so they could cure his depression. Why persist with these sessions, which were bringing up memories he wished to keep buried?

"Amraj? Amraj?"

He was so caught up in his own thoughts and despair, he hadn't heard Dr Khan summoning him.

"AJ?" she said a little more softly. The use of his nickname filtered through and broke his thoughts.

"Sorry? Yes I'm ready."

He walked into the room behind her and sat down in his usual spot. His eyes drifted to the picture of the man and two children and his curiosity peaked. These sessions were just to get the drugs, he reminded himself.

"How have you been since our last session, AJ?" Sonia asked as she gathered her notes and pen towards her. She had switched to his nickname to connect further with her patient.

"Fine."

A little taken aback by his abrupt response, she pressed further, "What have you been up to this week?"

He didn't want to admit he had done nothing but compulsive cleaning. The dream had left in its wake a feeling of lethargy and even more inactivity than usual as he was so consumed in his own thoughts and depression.

"It's been okay." He just wanted to get through the hour and go home, thinking he should have cancelled and stayed away. The only driving force bringing him to these sessions was that the anti-depressants could be prescribed to him.

"AJ," Dr Khan said softly and her professional tone dipped slightly. "Remember this is a safe space to talk to me. You have been making such good progress — tell me what's on your mind. I'm here to help, listen, and not judge."

Her tone seemed to penetrate through the cloud of despair he was feeling. There was something about Dr Khan that made him want to share everything and open up. He was fighting an internal battle between wanting to offload to someone listening to his woes and not wanting to say too much. He realised she was still talking. "We left our last session with you talking about school. Did you go on to college? You said your grades had dropped?"

"I did actually. I managed to scrape high enough grades to get through. Did I ever mention that I was the lead singer in a Bhangra band?"

She was taken aback — that was not the response she was expecting. She smiled at him and said, "No you didn't. What was that like?"

He noticed her smiling and felt the icy demeanour thaw slightly. The dream had brought up some painful memories. He had to admit, even if just to himself, that the one thing he did miss was performing. The cheers of the crowd, before he noticed the woman, were still ringing in his ear.

"The girls I mentioned last time didn't follow me into college. Those six weeks of summer were like heaven. I could finally get rid of the fear of seeing them, and trying to avoid them when back at school. Knowing that I was starting afresh, I gained a sense of freedom and became overly confident. I was no longer the subdued child I had been during those years at school, and college offered a respite as a place to start again. I was popular, you know, and had friends in abundance, even female ones!" His eyes lit up. He looked up to see whether this might be a shock to her. It wasn't.

"Anyway, as a joke, my friends entered me into a talent show the college was organising for Diwali," he started, reminiscing. "I had a good voice." Dr Khan was still smiling so he continued. "I wasn't the best but could carry a tune and being Punjabi was suddenly cool, especially with the Bhangra scene becoming a bit mainstream. To compensate for years of being an introvert, I became such a loud character. People knew when I entered a room as I was larger than life, and for the first time, my disability was no longer a prominent part of me."

Dr Khan was making notes whilst still smiling. She couldn't quite picture this man who she had known for three weeks, with his quiet demeanour, singing in front of people. She was very tempted to ask him to sing a few lines for her but she reminded herself to remain professional.

She let him continue uninterrupted and was enjoying listening to him speak. He was coming alive, reliving his moments in the limelight, and she didn't want to disturb him at this point.

"The first time I performed, I felt so high! The handful of people I performed to before the talent show always made me feel in command and now here I was commanding a full room! The boost to my ego was something," he finished with a half-laugh. The idea that he could command a room that way felt like a very distant memory.

Dr Khan noticed how his face had lit up and he was beaming, a contrast to the man she had been meeting every week. He was reminiscing about a time where he was truly happy.

"I was fast becoming the most popular guy on the college campus," he continued, still beaming. "It was definitely a much better feeling than what I had at school. I didn't want to lose it," he ended, sounding a little dejected; he hadn't realised how much he missed being the centre of attention for something other than his disability.

"Do you still sing?"

"No, I'm an old-hat now. There are singers popping up all over the place. Much better than me too. People still remember me but I can't compete with the talent out there. I feel my singing days aren't completely over yet but, yeah, no one is interested in me these days."

Dr Khan could hear the despair creeping back into his voice. She wanted him to remember the good times. He was speaking so passionately about singing — she wanted to reassure him that if it brings him joy, he shouldn't let the idea that he wouldn't make a living out of it stop him from the activity.

"AJ, it's well-documented that singing is a good method to release emotion. You should find a way to continue, even if it's just in the shower." She looked directly at him, he had clearly drifted into another time zone.

"Tell me about your friends at college, the ones who entered you into the talent show."

He was smiling now as he spoke. "My best friend was Jags, I mean, he still is I guess. He's just busy at the moment, you know what it's like after college. People start to get jobs and girlfriends... life happens. To some of us anyway."

The smile and the beam of light when he was talking about his singing were slowly disappearing. She noticed the painful sarcasm and a bitterness to it, as he clearly longed for those elements in his own life. She saw an almost physical change come over him as he came crashing back to the present day.

"It certainly sounded like you were in demand at college, did you happen to befriend any girls?" AJ looked a little perturbed, as it seemed too personal a question. *Why was she asking?* The dream was still lingering in his mind. He didn't want to talk to Dr Khan about the woman.

"No, plenty of mixed friends including females. Maybe one of them was nice but nothing ever materialised." He left it vague; this particular subject was off-limits, even to Dr Khan.

She made a mental note to pick up on this throwaway comment, which may be of interest, in a future session. To really understand, she needed to get to the heart of why he was here, and usually past events triggered what was happening to her patients in the present.

"AJ, I'm curious, it's important that you work on yourself outside these sessions. What do you have planned for the rest of the day?"

She wanted to bring him back to the present. They could revisit college and his friends in the next session; he might be more willing to open up later if she didn't press too hard today.

"Oh, just the usual, a bit of food shopping. My parents will be coming to visit today so I'll spend some time with them. What are you up to?" He hadn't meant to ask the question but it was just a natural response to ask in return.

A little taken back, she decided to answer; she wanted him to trust her and she had been a little curt the last time he had asked her a question.

"Oh me, just the usual, a few more patients and paperwork before I head home. Shall we look at a time for next week?" Her tone indicated that she would not like to be asked further questions about her personal life.

CHAPTER 8:

THE PART-TIME MOTHER

Sonia was just finishing up her notes from the day when there was a knock at her door. It was Carole, her receptionist, popping her head in to see if she would be much longer.

"You go on Carole, I can lock up. See you tomorrow."

Sonia set her notes aside, next to the picture of her husband and her two young boys. She leaned back in her chair and closed her eyes. A few minutes later, she jerked her eyes open. Her thoughts drifted to AJ. She was thinking about her sessions with him and how she really wanted to get him to open up about his depression. She had to help; there was an urgency within her that needed to do this right.

Noticing the time, she got her things together to go home to the boys. She let out a little groan as she knew her mother-in-law would moan at her for coming home late again.

As she pulled into her drive, she was steeling herself for the disapproving tone and look from her mother-in-law. She walked through the front door, dropping the keys into a bowl in the spacious hallway, and made her way through to the kitchen at the back of the house. She couldn't hear the boys and realised they must have gone to bed. That was another evening she had missed their bedtime. A pang of guilt went through her. She vowed to make it up to them tomorrow.

Mrs Khan Senior was at the dining table with a book and a cup of tea. An elderly widow, she was short and stout with sharp hazel eyes that pierced through you even with her glasses on. She didn't look up immediately as Sonia went to the sink to refill the kettle. As she made herself a drink, she could feel the icy tension building and didn't know if she had another fight in her.

She sat down opposite her mother-in-law and stayed quiet. Mrs Khan Senior would break the silence eventually. She always did. Sonia rarely spoke first these days and decided to delay the inevitable for as long as possible if it meant a few more moments of peace.

"The boys are asleep. They were asking about you." Mrs Khan Senior didn't look up from her book as she spoke.

Sonia responded, biting her tongue to stop herself from rising to the bait, "I had a lot of patients today and paperwork to catch up on. The boys understand, and I will make it up to them over the weekend."

"Hmph," she exhaled. "They do not deserve a part-time mother," she retorted. "Make sure you lock up everything before you go to bed." There was a pause and Sonia knew her mother-in-law couldn't help but get the last word in each night.

"Don't let them down like you did my son." And with that, she left the kitchen and proceeded to her own room.

Sonia was too numb to allow words to affect her much these days, but they still stung and she felt her eyes welling up. She shook her head and forced herself to breathe deeply and calm down for fear she would run after her mother-in-law and slap her hard. She cleared the dishes and made sure all the doors were locked before heading upstairs. She checked in on the boys, guilt shooting through her again. They were fast asleep. She stood staring at them for a few minutes, just listening to them breathing. They were so young and peaceful.

"I must do better," she muttered to herself as she closed the door to their room behind her. With tears forming in her eyes, she made her way to her own room and got ready for bed.

She couldn't sleep; she never really could these days. Her thoughts were scattered unless she was at work, and she found it difficult to switch off and sleep. After tossing and turning for half an hour, she decided to do some work. As she was reading through her notes from her session today with AJ, she knew she had to do all she could to help him out of his state of mind. She couldn't afford to lose another disabled person to his own mind.

CHAPTER 9:

DAMP AND SHIT

AJ was returning home from the local shop when he saw a woman heading towards him. It often happened that they would stare and eventually move out of the way at the last minute. He carried on and would swerve to avoid her if he had too. As they got close to each other, there was something familiar about her. "Amraj?"

He stopped in his tracks. "Oh shit," he mumbled under his breath; it was one of his mother's mafia gang, Kamala Aunty.

She was around 5 feet tall with grey streaks in her scraped-back hair and covered in a pale shawl, which matched her equally pale traditional salwar kameez.

He was in no mood to deal with her today, yet politeness was so inbred within him that he couldn't ignore her. He had no choice but to be polite and stop. "Hello Aunty Ji, how are you?"

"Yes, yes. I am well. How are you, puth?" AJ internally cringed at *puth* (meaning son); he really should have ignored her.

"I see your mother the other day. I tell her that you should be home with them, puth," she continued, not really expecting a response from him. He just mumbled and nodded and did his best not to be rude. After a couple more awkward moments of chit chat, he said he had to get going and get home with his shopping as he didn't want the food spoiling.

"Okay, puth. I tell your mum she is not feeding you enough; you look too thin." And with those parting words, they went their separate ways. He could feel her eyes on him as he continued to make his way home.

As he reached home, he was still seething from his interaction with Kamala Aunty, who was committed to lifetime service as a busybody. She was the one he had overheard about his marriage prospects when he was a child. He hated her interfering nature, thoroughly convinced that she should focus more on the antics of her own children than on his life. "I'll say that out loud next time," he said angrily to himself, knowing only too well he wouldn't.

He heard footsteps behind him. "Where you been?" he heard his mum demand. He bit his tongue and said as calmly as possible, "Shops mum. I needed some milk." He felt like they had sprung themselves upon him and wished they came with a bell as a warning to prepare him for their arrival.

They followed him indoors and as per normal, his mum made her way to the kitchen, taking the bag of shopping off him. She had her own supplies and started to empty the groceries and homemade curries she always brought into the cupboards and fridge. He heard the kettle being filled and switched on and realised she had started to make a cup of tea for everyone. AJ, calming slightly, had to smile — she just couldn't help herself. She couldn't sit still for a minute even as a guest in his home.

He let her carry on and sat down in the living room with his dad. The usual small talk followed, enquiring about each other's health in the generic almost awkward way that fathers and sons did. AJ sensed something different today. His dad seemed a little on edge but he couldn't quite put his finger on why. He realised he could be reading too much into it as he wasn't in the best place either.

Mrs Rai came into the living room with some snacks and three mugs of tea. "How are you mum?" He asked just to be seen as polite and accommodating. There was an odd energy around them and he thought that acting normal would get them to confess what they were really doing here.

"Nothing. Same, same. My knees are hurting more but it's okay. But what can you do." She stopped to take a sip of tea and continued. "You know Kamala Aunty?" AJ internally recoiled. 'Here we go!' he thought. "She was asking after you. Said you should come home, eat properly, and be with family."

AJ looked at his dad in disbelief, hoping for some support, but his dad was fixated on his own drink and avoiding eye contact with him. "She know a social worker, so we made a meeting for you to see him at the centre." She paused. "We come with you. Be good for you to leave house, see other people."

AJ felt blindsided, but he could feel his fight leaving him. Caught between day-to-day living, his therapy sessions with Dr Khan, and now this — he said, "Okay mum". Within an hour, AJ and his parents had been picked up by the day centre they were going to visit. They had organised a taxi as his parents didn't drive and he no longer had a car. *Thanks Kamala Aunty for interfering so much!* he thought angrily to himself.

He got out of the taxi when they arrived and his heart sank; the Ryegate Day Centre was a huge, square, white building and nothing about it was inviting. He followed his parents towards the main entrance where they were greeted by a receptionist who asked them to sit after signing them in. A few minutes later, an Asian man came towards them.

"Mr and Mrs Rai?" he asked. "I'm Riz, we spoke on the phone." Riz was a stocky man around 5 foot 7 and looked to be in his early forties. He was wearing a two-piece suit and a blue tie, which looked out of date and a little out of place at the day centre, along with his long beard and thick-rimmed glasses.

They stood up to greet him and AJ waited before standing. He didn't have a good feeling about this. It didn't seem the type of place where he belonged.

"You must be Amraj." Riz turned to AJ with an extended hand and a large slightly condescending smile. AJ reluctantly stood up to shake the outstretched hand, more out of good manners than any desire to engage with him. He shook his hand firmly, wanting this over with and to get away from Riz's smile. He was already annoyed and it had only been a few minutes since they met.

"It's good to meet you. Your parents mentioned that you would be interested in our day centre. Follow me, I'll show you around." He motioned for them to follow him. He glanced at his parents; his mum was smiling — she looked pleased with herself — and his dad was avoiding any eye contact with him as they followed Riz down a long corridor. He was talking about the day centre and the work they did with others in the community and "those with disabilities".

He couldn't quite place his discomfort at being there; the tone and way Riz was speaking was slow and deliberate. The same way an English person would speak to his mum, slow and clipped so they could be understood. He wanted to scream, *"I have a disability, I'm not stupid."*

When they arrived at a set of double doors, Riz took them inside and AJ's feeling of discomfort was justified. "This place smells of damp and shit," AJ mumbled.

"Chup," his mum scolded him in a loud whisper; it was Punjabi for '*quiet*', and it always seemed more threatening than in English. AJ hadn't realised she'd heard him and continued the rest of his thoughts silently.

He looked around in disbelief at the residents. Some were staring into space, others appeared to be basket weaving, and another in a corner was banging wooden blocks on the table.

"We like to keep them here. It's a place to escape for them and their families."

Keep them here? AJ thought angrily; *they were certainly being kept. Kept to be left in a mindless vegetative state because they had a disability? Is this why he had been made to come here, was this all he was capable of?* His thoughts wandered back to the orthopaedic surgeon from his childhood who had told him he wouldn't amount to much, and that would be the case if he came here.

They walked around the room with Riz pointing out the "activities" they were doing to keep them active. Mrs Rai was making suggestions that this would be good for AJ, and that he should attend regularly. He had nothing to say to either his parents or Riz as he talked about the activities. In his mind, he was thinking about how basic it all was. They seemed to just be left there all day. *He was only twenty-four, and he was dealing with his depression and joblessness, but he wasn't a vegetable.* AJ could feel himself getting angrier that they thought he belonged here!

They spent another half an hour checking out the rest of their facilities before they left. AJ couldn't wait to get out of there and as he left with his parents, his anger was reaching boiling point.

He turned around to Riz before storming off and said out loud, "Is this all you think I'm capable of? You want me to come here each day and stare at the walls? Just you wait and watch. I'll prove to you I'm going to be someone special and not what you think I should be."

CHAPTER 10:

A SAFE SPACE

The trip to the day centre had left him feeling empty and tired. Riz encapsulated everything that was wrong with society and the system, which was slowly eating away at his confidence. Riz was less obvious, but the tone and condescension he had shown was the same.

AJ was used to being stared at because of his walk but the implication that he belonged in a day centre made him feel angry all over. The burning flame of anger would then die out and be replaced by disbelief that his parents thought this is where he belonged. But he was more annoyed at the interfering aunty who had instigated the whole charade.

All these thoughts were whirring in his head as he made his way down the road to Dr Khan's offices for his next session. He was still lost in thought when his name was called to enter her room, which was becoming a theme every time he came here.

As he settled into his usual chair, he looked up and realised that Dr Khan was asking how he was. "I'm okay," he muttered. "What are we digging deep into today?" he asked sarcastically.

Sonia smiled. She felt they were making progress and would accept the jibe at the obvious lack of desire to commit to these sessions, but she refused to give up on him or rise to his sarcasm.

"I wanted to know more about your singing. It was fascinating. Why did you stop?"

AJ felt an ego boost, but was reluctant to share too much about his singing as it might lead back to the woman from his dream. Even in therapy, it was a conversation he was not ready to have. She may have been one of the reasons behind his need for antidepressants but he'd be damned if he let Dr Khan dig into that part of his life, no matter how well-meaning her intentions were.

"My granddad. He was one of the reasons I stopped. For him, my being an entertainer was a hobby but it wasn't a real job and one day he asked if I was done with it. It felt like a bit of a punch to the stomach as I was gaining traction — I was known and was going to be recorded. But my granddad wanted me to get a *proper* job. I'm such a disappointment to them for not doing anything and being on benefits."

She felt a little of his disappointment. As a teenager, she had her own dreams and desires, which were shelved due to societal expectations. She hadn't realised she was nodding in agreement until she heard him ask, "Do you get that pressure from your family?"

Sonia felt that he was opening up to her more when she gave a little of herself. She contemplated this whilst answering, "Yes, therapy isn't normal for a lot of people, especially in *our* community, so they don't fully understand or support what I do."

He felt comforted by her answer. "Singing gave me the chance to forget about my life and disability. My family didn't understand that. Nobody noticed it when I was singing. I was popular and commanded a room. There's power in that — how could I give that up?"

AJ was taken back to the days of driving his peers around at college, "I was encouraged by my friend Jags to buy a car without a licence, you know. It was in keeping with my new *'he's a singer'* image," he reminisced as he told Dr Khan about the yellow Ford Escort Mark 2 he had ended up buying with just £30 to his name.

"Because of my popularity and the bright car, I ended up being the designated driver. It gave me the freedom to do my own thing and not just be AJ the guy with a disability and funny walk. Nobody at college or during the gigs I did ever discussed it. I was popular."

Sonia noticed the use of past tense when he was speaking. She wanted to find out why had he stopped doing the gigs and singing if it was clearly something he loved. Sensing a reluctance to speak about a major factor he was concealing beyond the comment of his granddad wanting him to stop, she was confident that was only half the story.

"That sounds fun. During these times of popularity and all the singing you did on such a public platform, you must have caught the attention of the ladies; did you ever meet anyone?" she probed. Her instincts were telling her that there was something or someone else he was omitting from his story.

He internally sighed. He thought he had done a good job of creating a story without mentioning the woman but his stomach was tied in knots. He wasn't ready for this. He felt his cloud starting to form above him and the first sprinkling of rain drops on his face, even though he was inside. His chest felt tight and he could feel acid rising in his stomach.

"AJ?" She noticed he had become withdrawn and tense in his chair; she didn't want to push him too far and decided to delay questioning him too much until he was ready.

"Sorry." He was trying to keep his black cloud and acid reflux from overwhelming him. "If you must know, there was someone I did like and saw for a short period of time." This was much as he was willing to give her.

Dr Khan hadn't expected him to admit that there was someone who meant something to him romantically so quickly and felt professional pride at this breakthrough. She waited for him to say more, not wanting to break his cycle of thoughts.

AJ was internally berating himself for allowing his guard to drop and even mentioning the woman from his dream. Dr Khan had a comforting way about her and he hadn't realised he was opening up so much until now.

"She isn't relevant to our sessions, Dr Khan. I did meet someone and we were dating whilst we were at college but we broke up. Nothing more to it really." He shrugged, as if that would fool her into thinking that was all there was to it.

She didn't believe him and knew that digging deeper into this person was key to unlocking and healing him, to helping him move past his current state of mind. She would try to encourage this conversation in their next session.

AJ stretched and got up to leave. Noting the time, he heard her say quietly behind him, "AJ, don't forget this is a safe space." She was now staring at the picture of the man and two children and finished with, "I know how painful it can be to have someone hurt you after you've lost them."

CHAPTER 11:

SLEEPING PILLS

Sonia made her way home not long after AJ left. She wasn't in the mood for a lecture and was making a conscious effort to get home to cook and spend some time with the boys before they went to bed.

As she got to her car, she spotted AJ outside the florist next door to her office staring at some yellow roses. She fought the urge to go over and see if he was okay after their session and simply continued to watch him until he disappeared inside. She wondered what he was thinking.

She could sense that he was keeping something from her. The pain and hurt in his eyes were palpable when she had asked about there being someone he was involved with at college. She recognised the pain as she saw the same look in her own eyes. There was no way to hide the sort of heartache caused by another human being. It left a mark of its own.

She pulled into her drive fifteen minutes later and made her way inside. "Mummy," shouted Avi, who came running towards her. The delight at her being home was evident all over his young face, and she felt guilt flood through her at not being more available to him and his brother.

She scooped him up and put her face into his neck, holding him tight. He started squirming as she hadn't realised how hard she was hugging him. She let him go and they made their way into the kitchen where her mother-in-law and her eldest, Amir, were sitting at the table.

As per usual, Mrs Khan gave no sign that she had noticed Sonia walking in, but Sonia ignored her too and made her way to her first-born. He was colouring and started to lift up his artwork to show her, with a smile on his face. "Mummy, look what I made," he showed her proudly. "That's beautiful," she said beaming; it looked like a dinosaur in a forest. She took it from him smiling, declaring she would pop it on the fridge so they could always see it.

They spent the evening just being together, playing games, and eating. From the outside looking in, they were a happy family. When she had finally bathed them and put them down for bed, they seemed content. Her own sense of guilt heightened — she had neglected them for far too long. They'd already lost a father; they didn't need to be abandoned by their mother too.

The last eighteen months had been the hardest in their lives. Sonia had the whole world before her when she married the love of her life five years earlier. She was still at school studying to become a therapist, and he had been so supportive of that journey for her.

It had been a challenging and emotional day. Not just with AJ reluctant to disclose his pain but the evening with her family was flooding her with emotions that she had fought so hard to keep at bay. The wall she had built to protect herself was starting to crack and leak, and she didn't know if she had the strength to hold it up anymore.

As sleeping was not easy, her GP had given her sleeping pills to help her get some rest. They seemed to be taking an age to kick in today as she was still wide awake and alert an hour later — her thoughts racing into each other as she remembered the trauma her family had gone through in the last couple of years.

It wasn't just Taj leaving them; it was the pain he left behind. Why, why couldn't he find the strength to be there for them like they were for him? Why did he have to leave them? They could have made it work after his accident. He didn't have enough faith that they could get through this and still live the life they had dreamt of. Her boys, her poor beautiful boys.

Unable to sleep, she decided to speak to her GP in the morning about upping the dosage on her sleeping pills. She took out her notes from today's session and her thoughts drifted to AJ as she wondered who had hurt him.

CHAPTER 12:

WILD HAIR AND CREASED JEANS

AJ had popped into the florist next door for his usual purchase. He was in there so often the proprietor, Vanessa, was now on first-name terms with him. She knew his favourite flowers and always had some prepared for him. It saved on small talk when he wasn't in the mood, especially lately, after his sessions with Dr Khan. He sometimes asked her to keep them to one side.

Today, he'd had to make a detour to the job centre and didn't want to be carrying flowers around with him.

He had been unemployed for six months and was on the council's Training for Work Programme so he could claim and get an extra tenner. If it meant more benefits, he didn't mind popping in to see them.

He was called forward by a woman he knew. She was his regular employment coach and made it quite obvious she didn't enjoy the fortnightly questioning about his efforts to seek work. However, today she seemed happy to see him. AJ was intrigued by the smile of his nemesis and cautiously took a seat in front her.

"Mr Rai, there is an opportunity I think would be good for you to start as a volunteer position with a charity for those with..." She paused awkwardly before finishing, "your condition."

"You mean for disabled people? It's okay to say it out loud; it's not a dirty word." His tone was sharper than he had intended, but he didn't care if he sounded rude, especially after the incident a few days earlier at the day centre. *Why am I being pigeon-holed like this again?*

Before he could respond, she pointed out that this was a good opportunity to help him build some experience and structure in his day as well as ensuring he continued to receive the extra income as part of the programme. It was his only incentive, as he had nothing else to do and the extra pennies were always welcome.

"Okay, fine. I'll volunteer," he conceded. She gave him the information he needed and told him to report to the office first thing on Monday morning.

As he was leaving the florist, he heard his name being called, "AJ!" He kept his head down and ignored it as he made his way home. He could do without the interfering Kamala Aunty today, especially after she had coerced his family into taking him to the day centre.

"AJ! AJ?"

Wait a minute, he thought, Kamala Aunty sounded a little masculine.

He turned around and came face to face with a man his age, panting slightly, red-faced, and sweating. He had clearly been running to catch up to him. It took him a second before he recognised Jags, his best friend from college.

AJ noticed how well-put-together Jags was, despite the sweaty face. AJ became very aware of his own oversized shirt, wild hair, and creased jeans. Jags had always dressed well and kept his appearance in check. He was wearing a dark green suit and shirt with the collar open. AJ would never say it out loud but Jags was your stereotypical 5 foot 11, good-looking Punjabi friend. He was chiselled and could easily have made it as a model, according to Jags himself, having been approached by an agency a few years ago.

"Jags?" he said, still a little stunned at seeing him.

"Yeah, didn't you hear me calling you?"

"Sorry, I thought you were an aunty." Jags smiled at that. "What are you up to these days, AJ?" He spotted the flowers he was holding and winked. "Oooh, who are the flowers for?"

Blushing slightly, he ignored the questions, "It's good to see you man. What are you doing here?"

"I've got a shop down the road, selling CDs of all the greatest classics in Bhangra and Bollywood. I thought I recognised you coming out of the florist, but wasn't sure it was you at first until you started walking." He was smirking, because he knew he could get away with comments like that.

AJ smiled, same old Jags.

"I'm off work today, you fancy a pint? It's been a while! You've been off the grid." AJ really didn't want to go for a drink, not in the state he was in, but seeing Jags was making him reminisce about their escapades at college and he could never say no to drinks with him. "Sure," he responded, a little surprised at himself.

A local they used to frequent quite often was a ten minute walk away. It was on the corner of the street not far from where they lived as kids. The Sun Inn was their favourite jaunt every Thursday; they'd get a drink and move on for a curry. The staff and pub landlord had been on first-name terms with them.

As they entered, they spotted Rob, the same landlord from the previous decade. He looked up and noticed them; it took a couple of seconds but he smiled once it dawned on him who had entered. "All right lads," he said with a nod.

Still feeling self-conscious having been caught off guard by Jags at the florist and his scruffy demeanour, AJ smiled and nodded in response; he wasn't in the mood for a catch up with the landlord today.

His old friend insisted that he would get the first round in and headed towards the bar as AJ found a seat for them. He set their drinks down a few minutes later. AJ picked up the beer glass and took a nostalgic sip, immediately realising he had broken etiquette.

"No cheers?" Jags put him at ease with a giggle. There was a moment of awkward silence. AJ had not only moved out of his family home and cut ties to an extent with them — he had also cut off his friends after his singing days stopped, Jags being one of them. He cleared his throat and sheepishly looked at AJ before saying, "You look like shit man."

There was a split second of silence before they both burst out laughing. The rest of the afternoon and early evening was spent sharing memories and talking about college escapades.

"It's been good to catch up man. Truth be told, I've been worried about you. You went all weird and disappeared after you quit singing at gigs. Hell, you look exactly the same! It's like time has stood still," he laughed, staring pointedly at AJ's hair.

He knew he was being made fun of as per usual with Jags but perhaps he had a point on this occasion. He pretty much wore the same outfit all the time and he couldn't remember the last time he'd gone to the barbers. He used to care so much about his appearance, but it was not something he thought much about these days.

"I mean, for someone who used to be such a dude, what happened? Why are you wearing trainers with your trousers?" he asked.

"Well, thanks mate," he replied sarcastically.

As they finished the last dregs of their drinks, Jags asked what he was doing for work. "I start a new job in a few days," AJ responded. He wasn't about to admit to Jags it was only voluntary so he could claim his benefits. He hadn't really given it much thought since he said he'd give it a go, and it dawned on him talking to Jags that he didn't have a decent mode of transport to get to work.

"Do you need wheels?" Jags asked as if he could read AJ's mind.

"Yeah, they would come in handy, you know anyone selling anything cheap and cheerful?"

"Don't worry mate, I'll sort you."

As they left the pub, they agreed to meet over the weekend to get together. "AJ!" Jags shouted, "Pick up a fucking razor on the way home, you bum!"

CHAPTER 13:

BATTERY ACID

AJ felt a shift in his mood after his spontaneous encounter with Jags. He had a bit more of his swagger back. He knew he hadn't been completely honest with him about what he was going through but for a few short hours, his mood was lifted.

They had arranged to meet the next day and AJ was encouraged to meet Jags at the barbers, which he used to frequent regularly in his heyday as a singer. Jags' comment about wild hair had echoed in his mind and was just the nudge needed to take action.

The comment had stung but he let it slide, as the alternative meant admitting to Jags he was on the verge of a nervous breakdown.

Over the years, he had been tempted on a number of occasions to tell Jags his troubles but he just couldn't appear weak. The world showed no kindness or empathy for his physical weakness — it might totally destroy him if it became aware of his mental illness. *It's not worth the gamble*, he had always thought, and reverted to his default position of invisible suffering.

Jags had it together in comparison to him. Still smart and popular and married not long after they'd finished their studies, his life was the textbook good Punjabi boy. By contrast, AJ felt like he was spiralling down a dark hole with the best of his days behind him.

Snapping himself out of these thoughts when he saw his friend walking towards him, he greeted him with a "Sore head?" It had been a while since he'd gone to the pub and drunk.

Jags smiled, "Nah, I'm not a lightweight like you," he joked and they made their way inside the barbers.

Chris, the same guy who gave AJ the best cuts throughout his singing days, looked up as the bell tinkled above them. As his long-lost customer greeted him, he found himself having to do a double-take. "AJ, what the fuck is this mess?" he scolded.

AJ could feel a blush creeping up his cheeks. Looking at himself in the mirror in front, he was more aware of his appearance than he had been in a long time. He laughed. Eventually, he said, "Just shut-up and do your magic. If you've still got it?"

An hour later, AJ felt a little like his old self. His hair was no longer wild and all over the place — it was cut shorter and slicked back. Jags was smiling at him. "Well, at least you look like a bit more of a polished bum. Come on, let's get down to the garage and see about getting you a car."

As they made their way to see Jags' friend, who owned a car garage, they were winding each other up as they did throughout their college years.

Jags was the only one who was able to take the piss out of AJ because he had never treated him any differently to his other friends.

"What's your budget?" he asked. Jags realised he hadn't checked whether he could actually afford one. AJ hadn't even thought of that. His dad had given him £1,500 to fall back on if needed, but he'd never had any justification to spend it. "No more than a thousand."

Jags instantly started scanning the car lot, recalling that he was restricted to those with automatic gearboxes. AJ managed to get an affordable silver Rover Montego and decided to celebrate his new purchase with a quick bite to eat at Jags' favourite curry house, the Sunrise Tandoori.

As soon as they ordered their usual parathas and Indian tea, they talked shop about AJ's new purchase. It felt oddly freeing now he was able to get around quicker and more independently. The chit chat brought them back to the subject of college and AJ's first car, the yellow Ford Escort Mark 2.

"That car was such a magnet for the ladies," he reminded Jags, with a smile.

"More like a glorified taxi service," he responded with a huge belly laugh and a wink.

"Well at least you had a car, eh."

"Mate, do you remember leaving a bunch of girls with holes in their clothes?" They both burst out laughing at the memory, startling some of the other diners around them. It had been such an accident that nobody noticed immediately. Part of the reason AJ had wanted a car so desperately back in college was to impress a girl he liked. He avoided remembering that particular reason for having a car. It was still painful to think about.

"Did you really think it would be a good idea to leave a car battery on the leather seat?" Jags asked him, shaking his head in hysterics.

"Oi, that wasn't me, it was you!"

They quibbled like an old married couple over whose fault it was until their food arrived, which temporarily halted them. "I mean at least 20 girls got a lift off me that day, surely one of them would have noticed a slight spillage on the seat when they sat down?" AJ smirked, "So if you think about it — it's really their fault."

Within minutes of sitting in the car, every girl affected had a six-inch hole appear in her skirt or trousers.

"Remember the next day? They were all having a go at us. No one really saw the funny side." AJ laughed uncontrollably for a short while and suddenly stopped.

He hadn't laughed so hard in years and it had a powerful medicinal effect on him, but then for no explainable reason, he felt an intense guilt. *Why am I laughing? I've got nothing to laugh about.* He felt his heart rate rise — his thoughts coming through louder and making him question his brief moment of happiness. The lights hadn't been dimmed but the restaurant started to feel dark. The atmosphere felt damp as if it was about to rain.

The day had been a good one, and it had been a while for AJ. Getting a haircut and a new car, even a second-hand one, was the most attention he had paid himself for ages. But now, he knew he needed to withdraw. Jags sensed something was wrong but decided not to push it.

As they continued chatting and ordering more parathas, they made plans to catch up later in the week. Jags was still mocking him about their college exploits,

"AJ, if you need to change the battery, chuck the old one away, yeah, don't leave it on the backseat. Don't want to hear of ladies complaining about their arses hanging out."

CHAPTER 14:

WORKING MAN

The weekend with Jags felt like a homage to their student days, especially with the new haircut and new car. He finally felt like he had it together and was ready for work when he woke up on Monday morning. It was a start, even if he knew his state of mind meant he just wanted to stay in his flat and not leave.

He was apprehensive about the volunteer role at this disability charity. As he made his way over, his trip to the day centre with his parents was running through his mind. What if this place was exactly the same? The training programme meant more income, so he could swallow his pride and just carry on for the extra cash, right?

AJ arrived and steeled himself for a "shit-smelling" day ahead. It was the first time in his life he had directly been associated with other disabled people. He was still a little annoyed with the woman at the job centre for her assumptions. With no other prospects for work, however, he wasn't in any bargaining position.

He entered and noticed a mix of people ranging from wheelchair users to those with visual impairment. He immediately found himself staring, stopping before it became too obvious. He felt disgusted with himself as someone who had to deal with similar reactions most of his life and hated it when that happened. "I should know better. I'm as bad as the rest of society," he whispered to himself.

Walking over to the receptionist, AJ informed her he'd been sent as part of a training programme. Within twenty minutes, he was enrolled as a 'Volunteer Information Officer', whatever that meant. As he was being shown around, he decided it seemed easy enough. *Beats sitting around the flat all day,* he thought.

The day was a standard induction into policies and procedures, as well as getting to know others in the team. He soon realised he wasn't the only unpaid member of staff, which injected a certain level of comfort. The role wasn't complex, but his anxiety in being around other disabled people manifested in strange ways.

He found himself talking louder the few times he engaged in conversation and consciously had to dial it down. People had done the same to him over the course of his life, because apparently being disabled also meant you were stupid. Talking louder and slower was a reflex that people had around him early in his life. He berated himself later for his own behaviour and prejudices.

As the day came to a close, he said his goodbyes to be polite. He didn't want to be too aloof, especially on his first day. Plus, it was easier to be polite where nobody knew him enough to question his unusually polite behaviour.

Then, as he was leaving, he decided not to come back. *How could they think I'm one of them? I'll just have to find something else. I don't belong here*, he thought to himself.

On his way towards the door, he was caught by the founder and CEO, Ron Shires.

Ron was severely disabled himself — a wheelchair user who had a lifetime of championing and demanding rights for disabled people. He had a twinkle in his eye, but his tone and manner indicated a sharp mind that didn't miss much. Ron motioned for AJ to follow him to his office.

"How did your first day go?" he asked. AJ was taken aback by his deep *Barry White* monotone.

"It... it was okay." AJ wasn't going to confess he wouldn't be back, and was in a rush to leave.

Ron smiled, "That bad eh?" AJ offered a weak smile at the rhetorical question. "I thought we should have a chat and a check-in. You have an energy about you, Amraj. I can sense some emotion, some anger, perhaps a fight inside you."

AJ didn't know how to respond. He knew he hadn't exactly put on a facade the way he did in front of his family and Jags, and to some extent even with Dr Khan. But he thought he'd done a decent job. Ron, however, was too perceptive for his liking and he edged forward in his chair to indicate he had to be on his way.

"You know, you're very lucky, Amraj."

Ron clarified what he meant after seeing the incredulous look on AJ's face. "You're mobile, you have a disability, yes, and your own struggles, but you have a unique perspective on life. I'm not for one second saying that you've had it easier than I have, not at all." Ron indicated his own chair and situation with his eyes. "But you have a fear inside you that's misplaced. You could turn it into something productive if you weren't so consumed by it. Use that to drive your hunger and passion forward. Just imagine using the experiences you've had in life, both good and bad, for the benefit of others." Ron knew he had hooked him into the conversation as AJ's face started to show signs of interest.

My experiences? My life? I have nothing to offer anyone except misery.

Within a few milliseconds, AJ's life flashed in front of his eyes in stills. Medical operations, bullying, college, singing, love, lost love, pain — both physical and mental. It was all there.

"You have lived in a world consumed by self-interest. This place can be your calling to help people out there." They both felt the need to look out of the office window, which backed straight onto the high street.

On that note, AJ, already feeling inadequate, felt even worse. Ron's words had hit a nerve and AJ's feelings of inadequacy grew all the more because Ron was calm and reassuring, smiling as he spoke.

"Think about what I said, Amraj — it was just an observation. I could be wrong." He nodded but indicated through his tone that he hadn't been wrong at all. "See you in the morning."

*

AJ was in a sombre mood when he arrived home. Ron's words were rattling around in his head, and he couldn't shake the feeling of unease as Ron had been so perceptive about him. *Well, that settles it then — I'm definitely not going back*, he thought.

As he entered his flat, he heard his phone ring. "Hello?" he answered a little sharply. He wasn't in the mood for chit chat.

"Amraj?" He heard his uncle's voice — it sounded off and his stomach dropped. "It's Baba, he's been taken to hospital."

After the call, AJ rushed back out of the house and headed straight to Derby hospital to visit his granddad. His uncle had not sounded hopeful — the heart attack had been a major one, and whilst AJ thought of his grandfather as a strong man, age had taken its toll.

When he arrived, he asked for the right ward and made his way there as swiftly as possible. He had been in and out of hospitals visiting consultants for most of his childhood and quickly found the ward where his grandfather was. His parents and uncle were already there. He went over to his grandmother and gave her a hug as a greeting, then he turned and saw a frail man he didn't recognise in the hospital bed. He walked over slowly and saw that his granddad was conscious.

"Amraj?" his granddad said in a strained voice.

"Yes Baba, I'm here." AJ took hold of his hand and was startled by how small it was in his grip. He held it loosely for fear of hurting him.

"You should come home, puth; you belong with your parents." AJ held back his reply. His granddad had always been against him moving out and living alone. His fragility and condition didn't alter the fact that he had his reasons for leaving.

"Shh Baba, you need to rest," he responded.

"Are you still singing or have you got a proper job now?"

AJ immediately felt guilty for wanting to quit the volunteer role. Between Ron and his grandfather, how could he tell them he despised the role as he was lumped in with other disabled people and he wasn't one of them. He responded with, "Yes Baba, I have a job now at a charity, I'm an Information Officer."

His granddad smiled before closing his eyes to sleep, muttering "Officer ban geya" as he was drifting off.

"Well, I guess I'm staying there then," AJ muttered under his breath and vowed to go back for day two even after deciding to the contrary earlier. Baba always had the knack of making him not want to disappoint him. This time was no different — he couldn't quit now.

His grandfather slept for the rest of the visit and AJ was encouraged to go home by his parents as he had work the next day. Little did they know he was only there part time and had his next session with Dr Khan in the morning.

CHAPTER 15:

CARS AND TEARS

"Hello AJ, how..." Dr Khan stopped short as she stared at him. Immediately, he was confused why she was looking at him. Then it dawned on him that since he last saw her, he'd had a haircut and smartened up for work, and he had even subconsciously made more of an effort today. Sonia was a little taken aback.

His appearance in the last few sessions had been very shabby, and she wondered whether he was making progress with her. Realising her stare, she shook her head slightly, motioning him into her office. It was the first time since meeting him that she had noticed how attractive he was; the small changes to his appearance made it all the more apparent.

AJ made his way into the now very familiar room and to his chair. It was almost comforting being there. As he sat down, his eyes landed on the photo of her with her husband and two children again and his interest in her life peaked.

"How has your week been, AJ?"

"It's been a mixed bag. I've been assigned a job, so I thought I'd just tidy up a little and get a new haircut. Is that why you were staring?" He couldn't help but smile as it was strange to be looked at for something other than his disability. He liked it. It was how people used to be around him when he had been on stage — he felt *seen*.

He had decided he wouldn't mention his grandfather being in hospital as he wasn't ready for that conversation yet. Besides, he was just two sessions away from getting the pills he needed and not having to come back.

"Yes, sorry, the new hair took me by surprise. It's a good step in getting better, looking after your physical appearance." She seemed pleased, though he wasn't going to tell her it was more an effect of Jags' bluntness than her sessions. "In our last session, you talked a lot about your popularity and being the designated driver. Are you still in touch with your friends from school?"

"Funny you should mention friends! I bumped into one of my closest friends this week, Jags. We sort of drifted apart after our studies. Once the gigs stopped, I distanced myself from everyone as it helped me deal with not being the person on stage that everyone knew. It knocks your confidence to go from being the centre of attention to having none at all." He paused with a smile on his face before continuing.

"Me and Jags were inseparable. He was one of those friends who could come round and just walk through the door and be part of the furniture. One particular morning, he let himself in and was quietly waiting for me in the living room. My mum was blasting prayers downstairs on the cassette player, so everyone was supposed to be quiet. I came bounding down the stairs singing some Bhangra track and my mum full-on smacked me for being disrespectful. She didn't realise Jags was there and I was so shocked at her that I just left with him quietly, then she shouted behind me telling me not to come back that night after being so disrespectful!"

AJ stopped speaking as the memory made him burst with laughter. He made a mental note to reminisce about this incident with Jags next time they met.

Dr Khan was smiling with him, "Well, we all know how much a Punjabi mum's smack hurts and it definitely doesn't detract from loud prayers on the cassette player, which no one listens to!"

"You're telling me," he responded, subconsciously rubbing his cheek as if the remnants of the smack were still lingering. "Jags was still pissing himself laughing when we made our way to college. As normal, we had a sneaky drink at college and found ourselves just sitting in my car."

"I think a mix of alcohol and Jags taking the mick out of me all day made me cry. I was replaying the slap and mum telling me not to come home and I got emotional over it. Jags saw me crying and for some bizarre reason, it set him off too. Because we were known and the car was so visible, within thirty minutes the whole car was surrounded by people asking why we were crying."

He was laughing at the memory as it sounded even more ridiculous now he was saying it out loud. AJ continued, "When our friends and other students came to the car to see what the commotion was, Jags would tell each person a different story. For some reason, it made us cry more and for some inexplicable reason, they cried too!"

Dr Khan composed herself. "It sounds like a fun friendship. Have you been able to speak to him about your situation today?"

AJ stopped smiling. For just one moment, he had forgotten about what his life was now; living in the past was somehow easier.

"No."

"I see, why is that?"

He hesitated. "He doesn't need to know. I don't want his pity."

"He's your friend, AJ, and it sounds like a long and happy friendship, so why would he pity you?"

"That's what people do, isn't it?" He sounded bitter. He'd been pitied his whole life because of a physical disability — people would not be any more sympathetic with a hidden one. "You're telling me nobody has ever pitied a part of your life that royally pissed you off?" he retorted angrily.

Dr Khan's eyes drifted to the photo of her family. AJ immediately felt bad for snapping at her as she looked incredibly sad.

"Dr Khan, I'm sorry," he said meekly.

"AJ, yes I have. My husband died eighteen months ago and there are always those who will pity your loss. The comments I've had about losing him so young have not been pleasant. But it won't stop me confiding in those I trust, even if it's just one person. It sounds like your friend Jags is that person for you."

AJ felt even worse — he had had no idea she was a widower.

"I believe that Jags has been good for you. He's someone you have grown up with and who knows you well. When talking about your past experiences with him, you sound very joyful. Be mindful not to live too much in the past though, AJ. It can stop you from moving forward and dealing with issues you have buried or are avoiding." AJ wasn't sure whether she was talking to him or discussing her own situation.

At the end of the session, Dr Khan wrapped up with, "We'll leave it there for today, AJ. We have one session left, but I think it would be good to continue once they are over. You've made great progress but we still have a long way to go."

He didn't like the sound of that. One more session and he was allowed his antidepressants. *What did she mean, a long way to go?* He wasn't going to make this a permanent fixture in his life.

CHAPTER 16:

TURNING POINT

AJ still had some time to kill before going back to the hospital to see his Baba. As usual, he nipped into the florist beside Dr Khan's clinic and picked up some flowers for his own home and the visit to the hospital.

When he arrived at the hospital for family visiting hours, his parents were there. They looked sombre and he had an uneasy feeling in his stomach that something was wrong. He walked into the room where his grandfather was, and noticed that he looked to be sleeping. He put the flowers he'd brought on the table, then turned to his dad to ask how Baba was doing now.

"He's in a coma. They don't think he will wake up," his dad replied. He sounded robotic, as if dealing with the emotional trauma of seeing his own father in hospital and on his deathbed was too much to bear.

AJ felt as if his legs had been taken from under him. How could his grandfather be in a coma? He was fine yesterday.

AJ decided to stay the night with his granddad, thinking of all the times he had spent with him and feeling guilty that there were fewer of them in the last couple of years.

He knew his grandfather had spent most of his life working every hour possible to enjoy time with his children. As AJ was his eldest grandchild, he had really wanted him to become something special, but AJ had been procrastinating and wasting his life, in Baba's mind. The singing was just a hobby and for fun, not something you could make a career out of; it wasn't a real job. This was the rhetoric AJ had heard for years and was one of the reasons why he stopped.

AJ felt more guilt creeping in — he should have made more of an effort in the last few months. Moving out of his family home had been his choice and not to visit was also his. He kept his distance as his parents and family had sacrificed enough for his disability; he couldn't keep disappointing them. He had to stay away; he was protecting them.

He felt a tap on his shoulder and snapped his head up; he had fallen asleep in the chair next to the hospital bed. He had been so busy reliving his childhood sitting with his Baba listening to his stories that he hadn't noticed himself drifting off.

"Let's get some food, puth," his mother suggested.

He stood and stretched and noticed just how fragile his Baba looked. He had been a strong figure throughout his whole life, but now he looked so tiny, wrapped in white bed sheets on the hospital bed.

"Please wake up Baba, I have to show you what I'm capable of," he whispered.

AJ wasn't an outwardly emotional man but the idea that his granddad might not wake up was hard for him to accept. As he turned to leave the room with his mum to get some food, he heard a loud noise from behind him. It sounded like a huge fart. The rest of his family were in the room and they all looked at each other. Had Baba just farted in his sleep? AJ burst out laughing. It was such a typical thing for him to do, even in a coma.

He got angry stares from his father and uncle, who were utterly grief-stricken. "What's wrong with you? Have you gone mad, why are you laughing?" The day had been long. AJ had allowed emotions to surface that hadn't seen daylight for a while.

He knew it was immature and highly inappropriate but the fart had made him laugh and with tears of laughter rolling down AJ's face, his Baba took his last breath and passed away.

*

The days after his grandfather's passing were a blur. There was a constant stream of people who came to pay their respects at his parent's house, where he stayed until the funeral—the first time he had been back since he moved out.

It was customary for everyone to descend on the home of the deceased before the procession. Frankly, it was starting to annoy AJ, especially when his mum's mafia gang were around. They made a big show of grieving and wailing to show their sadness. AJ was certain that most of them came for the gossip rather than to offer any condolences.

On one occasion, he was heading to the kitchen for some tea when he passed by the second living room, where more than ten women were sitting. He overheard his name and edged closer without wanting to be seen eavesdropping. He recognised the voice of the Devil's daughter — Kamala Aunty.

"Amraj should not have moved out," he heard her say, "Your father-in-law was never the same since he left. How can he fend for himself with his ..." there was a pause and she left her sentence unfinished.

He felt a rush of blood to his face, and was shaking with anger. He wasn't the only one. He heard his mum pipe up and say, "For your information, my son has a job as an Information Officer, and he will be just fine." Her tone was cold and there was no response from Kamala or any of the other women. It seemed that mum's little outburst had put them in their place.

When he finally got home, his mum's words rang in his head and the way she defended him stirred a sense of determination he hadn't felt in a while. Coupled with the image of his grandfather's smile when he heard that he'd got a job, he couldn't shake his feeling of guilt.

"I can't quit," he said out loud to himself, a little shocked to hear the resolve and determination in his own voice. He couldn't let go of the memory of his grandfather, especially as he had been so proud in one of his last moments of life.

CHAPTER 17:

MISSION ACCOMPLISHED

It was his last session with Dr Khan, and it had been a long six weeks. He just had to get through this last one for the sign-off that he could take back to Dr McKleish.

He was more determined to prove himself, especially when he went back to work, though he could still feel grief mixed in with anger bubbling beneath the surface after his grandfather's death.

The fact that things had been so busy and crowded leading up to the funeral meant he had managed to keep the anger at bay; he'd been too distracted helping organise things. But as he sat waiting to be called into the office, he could feel emotions rising like lava. He just had to get through one more hour and those pills would take it all away.

"AJ?" he heard Dr Khan's soft voice summoning him. His anger increased. He stood up and took a few deep breaths. Sonia sensed something wasn't quite right with him. He walked past her but refused to make eye contact. She had a bad feeling in the pit of her stomach.

Following him into her office, she noticed how he was pacing. He was staring at her fish tank, a recent addition believed to have a calming effect on patients, yet somehow it seemed to be agitating AJ as he picked up the pace.

"AJ, please sit down." He jerked as if in a trance and did as he was told.

"Are you okay?" she asked. It was technically their last session but she was keen to keep him as a patient. There was a lot left to uncover and she believed that with long-term help, she would be able to help him achieve so much.

"Am I okay? Well, where the fuck do I start?" His voice was calm and cold, and unlike him.

"My grandfather passed away last week, and some interfering bitch of a friend my mum has was bad-mouthing me and my disability. So let's start there shall we? How are people still continuing to write me off?"

Sonia was taken aback by his outburst. It wasn't uncommon for patients to display bouts of anger when triggered, but she hadn't expected this from him. To date, he had been quite docile.

"AJ, grief is a terrible thing to have to endure; it's okay to feel pain and anger. It's a natural part of the healing process. I'm sorry for your loss…"

He scoffed at her and turned to look at the fish again, "They're being judgemental," he said pointing to the tank. "There, that smug little shit keeps smiling and staring at me." With disbelief at the ridiculousness of his insinuation, Sonia looked between AJ and the fish tank. He was staring at one particular fish, which seemed to be going about its business.

"AJ, you're projecting your anger onto the fish. Talk to me please. This is a safe space. You can vent and be angry all you wish," Sonia said reasonably.

"You know what, Dr Khan, sure let me vent to you. I just need you to sign off so I can get some pills. I'm sick of talking about my problems and would rather take a pill to bury them. The constant pain in my leg is enough to torment anyone, but on top of that, I've had to deal with snide shitty remarks from birth and then again at my grandfather's funeral."

"The woman I loved had no choice but to leave me for another more suitable match because her family wouldn't give us their approval back in college. And yeah, you guessed it, because of my disability. I just want to be left the fuck alone now that one of the few people I truly loved has died and left me too."

He turned once again to the fish tank. "Your fish is also a judgemental shit and I need you to just sign whatever it is you need to sign so I can leave in the next fifteen minutes and get what I came for."

AJ was panting, and his voice had risen the more he spoke. He couldn't control the words as they left his mouth and as soon as they'd departed, he barely remembered what he'd said.

Then, as he got his breath back, the fight seemed to have left him and he slumped. He soon realised his stare-off with the goldfish was totally irrational. He looked over to the tank as if to apologise through some sort of telepathy.

Dr Khan was looking at him with concern written all over her face. "AJ," she said softly, "I can't begin to understand all you have been through, but I do understand the pain of grief and betrayal when you lose a loved one."

Her voice had caught in her throat and made him look at her. He was starting to feel embarrassed about his outburst. With tears in her eyes, she said, "AJ, my husband was in a terrible accident two years ago, which left him partially paralysed. The physical and emotional pain it caused him was too much to bear. You see, he was such a proud man and couldn't stand the idea of being looked after and being so reliant on me and others to get through the simplest of tasks. One day, I got a call at work to say he'd be rushed to hospital. He died there, AJ. He took his own life, overdosed on his painkillers."

Sonia's voice had cracked as she told her story and her eyes were on the picture of her husband the whole time. AJ wasn't sure what to say — he had underestimated her and often thought of her as a barrier to what he most wanted. Now he realised she was human. She was in pain too, trying to support him whilst wrestling with her own pain.

"Anger is normal — express it and feel it. Grief will come in waves. Everything you're feeling is valid. Bereavement is natural, and you spoke highly of your grandfather in our first session. The betrayal and hurt you feel at losing someone you love, even emotionally, such as this woman from your past, will manifest in the same way. As per your doctor's recommendation, I will sign off on your antidepressants, but I strongly urge you to continue sessions with me, AJ. Take my card, and let's organise more regular sessions."

AJ took the card and pocketed it, knowing full well he wouldn't be coming back. He wanted to give the impression that he was taking her seriously though. She wrote out her assessment to take to Dr McKleish. Finally, he was done. The purpose of these sessions had been fulfilled, and now the tablets could numb the pain of everyday life.

At the beginning of his sessions with Dr Khan, he had had one goal, but now he had the slip of paper in his hand, there was an unexpected feeling creeping over him. *Guilt, sadness, relief?* He couldn't pinpoint what it was but as he stood up to leave her office for the last time, the realisation that he wouldn't be seeing her again hit him. Despite everything, his reluctance to come to the clinic and share his feelings, he enjoyed her company.

The revelation of her deep pain, which she had hidden so well throughout his sessions, hit him hard. He knew what it was like to be on the verge of wanting to end it, especially due to physical pain and a disability he had never asked for. As he said his goodbye, his arm voluntarily moved forward as if to squeeze her shoulder, but he stopped himself in time. A flashback to an earlier session, where he was certain she was going to do the same thing, came back to him.

"Thank you, Dr Khan, for all your help. Goodbye," he said as he shut the door behind him. He was unsure whether he had imagined it, but he was sure he had heard a stifled sob as he moved away.

CHAPTER 18:

THE UNPROFESSIONAL PROFESSIONAL

When AJ left her office, Sonia tried to stifle her cries to not be heard by anyone. She hadn't expected to open up to him, but his anger at his life had compelled her. As she took stock of herself and the sobbing subsided, she had a feeling it might be the last time she would see him. A feeling of panic rose in her chest, and she stepped out from behind her desk and went to run after him.

She burst into the reception, searching left and right and eventually onto the street, but he was nowhere to be seen. As she made her way slowly back to her office, she hoped he wouldn't do anything rash. The passing of his grandfather might have been the straw that broke the camel's back.

"What do I do?" she muttered to herself. She was pacing her office, wondering whether she should have stopped him from leaving, whether she should make contact to ensure he was safe. As she sat back down, her eyes fell on his file and she saw his address on some correspondence. She knew it was unethical to go to his home but maybe she could just check in on him on her way home to make sure he was safe and didn't harm himself.

AJ had been her last client of the day, so she hastily got her things together and decided to head home early, detouring past his house. As she was getting into her car, she saw him coming out of the florist with some yellow flowers. She drove slowly to keep an eye on him. About ten minutes later, he was letting himself into his flat.

It was still early. "I'll just stay for a little while, make sure he's okay," she tried to convince herself out loud that it was okay. She stayed longer than she had intended, and it was getting late.

"Go home, Sonia," she muttered to herself. "He's okay. He's not Taj. AJ is stronger than you give him credit for. He'll be okay." Just as she was convincing herself not to get out, triple-check, and knock on his door, she noticed movement. He was leaving the flat. With a sigh of relief, Sonia ducked down in her car so he wouldn't see her and as he disappeared round the corner, her sense of dread lifted.

"Time to go home."

*

AJ left his flat as he had plans to meet Jags at the Sun Inn. The aftermath of his last session was still with him and so was his own guilt. He felt that he had abandoned Sonia, but it wasn't his responsibility to make sure she was okay. The sessions were a means to an end and they had ended; he had picked up the prescription on his way home and he would let the pills do their job.

He felt restless. When he got home, he had spent two hours cleaning and organising his already spotless flat. It was the only way to get rid of some of the anxiety and relief that flooded through him now he had what he needed.

As he made his way to meet Jags, he slowed down — there was a car he recognised but couldn't quite place and he was sure he saw movement behind the steering wheel. He shook his head and carried on. "No, it can't be," he thought. "It's dark — you're just seeing things."

Jags had already arrived at the Sun. AJ walked in and ordered a couple of beers.

"Cheers!" he said as he sat down. He needed a drink after the day he'd had. The events of the last few weeks had intensely affected his mental well-being. So much had happened and it was hitting home all at once.

They ordered food, chatted about current affairs, and generally had a laugh at each other's expense. Jags was one of few people he felt he could just be himself around. Even though Jags had no idea about the counselling or antidepressants, there was a comfort being in his company that made AJ forget what was happening in his life.

After a hellish day, his guilt about Dr Khan and her revelation about her husband was subsiding — the beers and company helped too. As he made his way home, his mind drifted to work.

He had decided to give the volunteering another shot; between the look of pride on his grandfather's face before he passed and the intuitive talk with Ron, he simply couldn't quit now. It was part-pride and part-determination to prove everyone wrong — all those who had ever said he would amount to nothing.

Whilst driving home and for the first time in many years, he felt a fire in his belly. A belief. An energy. He suddenly felt anxious but in a very different way. Almost excited. He looked at a crowd of men in their forties and mumbled to himself as if he was talking to everyone he had ever met, "I'm going to be something special. Just watch." He surprised himself with how resolute and determined he sounded.

CHAPTER 19:

PAIN IS YOUR DRIVER

AJ's new-found determination and the feeling of wanting to better himself carried through until the morning. As he made his way to work singing along to some Bhangra tune, he slowed down at traffic lights not far from work. He was drumming his hands on the steering wheel and in his own world when he saw a woman who looked familiar parked up ahead.

She was getting out of the car with a man who looked around the same age. He was very tall and good-looking, with an athletic build. He put his arm around her. He glanced up at the lights and saw that they were still red, urging them to turn green so he could shoot off but the lights seemed to be enjoying this situation. He kept his eyes straight ahead, not wanting to be noticed by the couple walking his way towards the shops down the road.

Just as they approached, in the corner of his eye, he saw her notice him. Before he could fully lock eyes with her, the lights changed and he didn't hesitate to leave. His hands were pale against the steering wheel from holding it so tight, and he was on autopilot the rest of the way. Once the shock wore off, he could feel a rising anger.

"Why now?" he asked himself. "Six weeks of therapy for her to just swan past randomly on the street, fuck!" He got to work and pulled into a spare bay, searching his pockets frantically for the pills. "Shit!" He'd left them at home.

"Calm down, she didn't see you," he told himself. He waited a few minutes before heading inside, as he was still shaking and needed to settle. He knew she had married not long after college, but he never knew anything concrete about her husband. This made it real.

Still angry and grief-stricken, he used that energy to drive him forward over the next few days. His job as an Information Officer was to answer calls and redirect queries where he couldn't provide the answers. It was a much-needed distraction, and the fact that he had a lot to learn kept him busy.

His lack of experience in office work was beginning to show. Small instances in his telephone manner were picked up on by a colleague who advised that he should be a little less blunt and a little more tactful. AJ was initially a bit naive in his approach to how other disabled people navigated their worlds. Despite everything, he had never thought of himself as disabled and from a young age had interacted very little with that particular community.

Now, he would watch and listen to everything that was going on around him. In the early days of the job, he kept himself to himself as he didn't want the anger and grief he was suppressing to spill over. In his new-found efforts to do well, he would start earlier and finish late. He spent his free time reading all he could on disability rights and observing everyone else around him. It was clear that he didn't quite meet their calibre of office etiquette and he disliked that intensely about himself.

The distraction of work was what kept him going though, after seeing *her* and her husband. If he had ever felt alone before, it was doubled after that chance encounter. Working and learning were the best antidote to going home to an empty flat.

CHAPTER 20:

ALL LIGHTS ON AJ

AJ woke up with a start. He had been dreaming and something had shocked him awake. He rubbed his hands over his face and squeezed his eyes shut but the dream was disappearing and all that was left was a lingering feeling. He felt unsettled. He kept his eyes tight shut for several minutes, willing his mind to remember what his subconscious had brought forward whilst he was sleeping. He gave up trying to recall what the dream was about and noticed that his alarm was about to ring.

As he became fully conscious, he straightened his arm and leg. He must have been more clenched than usual as it was stiffer than normal when he got out of bed. He wasn't paying attention as he took a glass from a kitchen cupboard and heard a rattle, then something fell onto the counter. It was a bottle of tablets. AJ picked them up and turned them over in his hands: his antidepressants. The seal was unbroken. The realisation that he hadn't taken any since being prescribed them a few months ago hit him with force.

"How did I forget about these?" he mumbled. His end goal was always these tablets to keep him from the dark thoughts that would creep up on him. Yet once he had them in his cabinet, he found excuse after excuse to avoid taking them. Something inside was telling him he could do it alone.

He arrived at the office an hour early, unsettled not only by the dream that he couldn't quite remember but by the knowledge he hadn't taken his tablets the whole time he'd had them. He pocketed them on his way out of the house, just in case.

His office etiquette had improved as he was at least attempting to not be blunt on the phone. He was beginning to get noticed for the knowledge he had acquired in such a short space of time. His hunger to be the best, a hunger he didn't know he had for the work he was doing, was powering him through life.

He was a little distracted and didn't hear the phone, the one he was meant to be answering, ringing for several seconds then disconnecting and ringing again. "Hello Disability Rights, how can I help?" he answered on autopilot, not noticing the call was internal.

"AJ, it's Ron. The board needs a favour. It's the Annual General Meeting today and our speaker has given his apologies at the eleventh hour. I need you to go in and cover what's been happening and share ideas on how we can move forward."

"What?" he said, not fully understanding. "Why me? I'm just a glorified receptionist." The words left him before he had a chance to think about what he was saying.

"AJ, go! The meeting starts in half an hour, so take that knowledge you've been absorbing over the last few months and smash it out the park." With that, Ron hung up.

"What the fuck?" AJ said in disbelief as he stared at the phone in his hand. "Surely this is a joke?" He walked across the office and down the corridor to Ron's office, but he'd already made his way to the conference room. In stealth mode, AJ decided to peer through the glass panel in the door. There were at least fifty VIPs seated in theatre style alongside someone with a heavy-looking gold chain around his neck.

"Shit, the Mayor is here and they want me to talk! I'm going to cock this up."

As he made his way back to his office and desk, he could feel all the confidence he had banked over the last few months drain away from his psyche. He sat down and looked around the office. There were two members of staff looking straight at him as if they were going to attack in a pincer move.

AJ came to the conclusion that they were not too happy he had been chosen by the boss ahead of them. The piercing looks were enough to validate his thought. *Well, fuck it, I'm not going to let them think I can't do anything.*

He sat for twenty minutes and scribbled his very first attempt at a speech. He tried to recall presentations and speeches at meetings he had been forced to go to since he started. He hated meetings. "They're an excuse to not do any work," he would often say to Jags. But now, he wished he'd paid more attention to the mannerisms and style of guest speakers instead of doodling on his notepad.

Introduce yourself

Your job role

The current picture — blow them away with some project stats

The need for local and central government to recognise user-led charities such as ours

Thank them

Any questions?

He calmed himself and was comfortable with the battle plan. However, the feeling didn't last long. The soft whistling sound of Ron's electric wheelchair coming up the corridor brought him back to reality.

"AJ, you're up." Ron almost smirked as if he could tell he had put AJ in a challenging situation.

As AJ stood up and began walking towards Ron, he gave his two colleagues a cock-sure smile, as he didn't need them to see he was actually bricking it. As he followed behind Ron to the conference room, he felt the need to run the basics of his speech by him.

"I thought I'd start with an intro…"

"No need to tell me, AJ. You have my confidence. Now get in there and show them that I made the right call."

AJ walked through the door. On his side of the glass, it seemed like there were hundreds of people waiting to hear him speak. In reality, there were over fifty, but they held concentrated gazes that were reading his every movement. The blood started draining from his legs, which felt ten times heavier than usual. His face turned warm and he gasped for breath.

In his mind, he heard "AJ! AJ! AJ!" What was he stressing himself out for? He recognised that familiar sudden surge of adrenaline and the comfortable feeling of being in front of an audience. He knew exactly how to handle this.

CHAPTER 21:

THE YOUNG PADAWAN

AJ headed straight for the podium with a new-found confidence
and swagger. He stared right back into the many eyes, which
were fixated on "the new kid". Recalling one of his old cheesy
tricks, he smiled and winked at one of the women in the front
row, then immediately regretted it. She smiled back out of
politeness rather than appreciation for his tactic. Nevertheless,
he was back and in control. Ron made a short but effective
introduction.

"I'm pleased to introduce you to one of the latest additions
to our new charity. Someone who in a short time has proven
himself vital in making us known to people hidden within our
communities. Someone who tells me what I need to hear rather
than what I want to hear, and someone with a bright future
ahead of him... Mr Amraj Rai."

There followed an appropriate round of applause, which almost
instantly disintegrated into silence. Ron had said more than he
needed to in his introduction but enough to massage AJ's ego.

AJ needed a microphone but there wasn't one in sight. On
stage, the microphone had always occupied his right hand,
which wasn't affected by his impairment. In tense situations,

his hand would often lock into a painful position. *Doesn't matter. I'm in the right place for a dodgy hand.* Almost making himself laugh out loud at the thought, he rearranged his face and started speaking.

"Ladies and gentlemen, thank you for having me here today. My name is Amraj Rai, but you guys can call me AJ. After today, I'm probably going to become a permanent fixture on future AGM agendas, if not to report on the great work we do but to charm you with my youthful good looks."

He looked across to the panel at the front, straight at Ron who looked back with a nervous smile, simultaneously giving a nod of approval as if to say, *"That's my boy."*

They laughed and seemed eager to hear more of his thoughts, concerns, and hopes for the future. For the next ten minutes, they were locked into his speech. After every serious project update, he followed up with a little joke or an amusing story linked to the project.

"I'd like to finish by thanking you all once again. I'm the new kid. I'm well aware I'm a little wet behind the ears and still an apprentice in the world of disability information services. But I'm happy to be here in such an organisation, which allows me to spread my wings and to express myself without judgment. I have a great guru," he looked across at Ron, "a man who, without realising it, talked me out of packing it in on the first day here." Ron seemed taken aback by the revelation. He hadn't thought about the conversation with AJ since that day and was very touched by it.

AJ continued, "Sometimes, an innocent conversation with a peer can have a profound effect on a person. That is what this organisation is about. To be there for people like me who need a role model, a virtual hug, a nudge in the right direction. Such support can only come from others who have already experienced it and been given that opportunity. I too will catch more people like AJ Rai and give them the confidence to be a pain in the neck to the society outside that window, which is too comfortable in labelling and pigeon-holing us."

Before he could continue, the conference room erupted into a frenzy of applause. AJ was on a roll and wanted to continue his Churchill-style speech but realised he'd said enough. Ron came across the room with the biggest grin.

"I can't say much more than that except that it looks like we're in for an interesting year," he said, looking directly at AJ. Again, the room gave a round of applause and everyone began to disperse and strategically settle into mingling positions. However, he noted three trustees coming in for a second round.

Robert, Paula, and Mark were founding members of the charity and hadn't said hello in the past due to their very busy roles working for the council. Robert was a large man with a big beard, a protruding belly, and a friendly face. Mark was quite the opposite but both shared confidence and conviction in their quest for equal rights for disabled people. Paula was visually impaired and had a guide dog although she was very aware of the environment around her.

Robert turned to Ron, "You kept this one hidden."

He replied with pride, "Padawan in training, he is." All three chuckled at the apt reference. AJ processed the joke a couple of seconds later but in just enough time to join in the laughter.

Mark finished the conversation as he grabbed his walking stick and pointed at AJ whilst addressing the other two, "He'll go far."

"He certainly will" Paula felt the need to add to Mark's prediction and smiled in AJ's direction. "Whatever you need, AJ, we'll be here for you."

AJ couldn't hide his smile. He had done it and proved that he was more than able, not only to himself but others around him. The feeling of being in front of people and the centre of attention was too high a buzz for him to just go back to answering phones. He could sense a shift happening and dare he say it to himself, it felt good.

As the delegates were winding down from the presentation, Ron and AJ made their way back to his office. Ron turned to give AJ a knowing smile. "Well, we can't have you being a glorified receptionist after that performance now, can we?"

CHAPTER 22:

ROUGH DIAMOND

AJ's euphoria from the day before was still with him when he swaggered into work the next day; he made his way to Ron's office and knocked.

"Come in," he said absentmindedly as he looked up and noticed AJ walking in, "Ah Amraj, I mean AJ, good. I'm still getting calls and emails about you. Now, I need you to take everything you've absorbed and help me. I need you to buckle down and learn all you can from me. I wish to leave here in the next few years and want to pass on the baton to someone worthy."

He knew he'd be moved away from just answering phones but hadn't expected this. He was sure his mouth was open in shock for a few minutes before composing himself.

Ron continued, "You have a knack for learning things quickly, which has been evidenced. But your inexperience working in an office is something we perhaps need to fine-tune. You'll shadow me and I'll show you the ropes, the ins and outs of what it takes. The quality and hunger I saw in you on your first day is there, AJ, but yesterday I saw something else: pride and purpose. You can't see it yet but there's a leader in you. We just need to work on bringing him out and polishing off everything else."

He has a point, thought AJ. *Maybe this is why my co-workers are frustrated with me?* He hadn't really paid too much attention to the way he fit in or his behaviour — he just wanted to know everything. The more he worked and read, the less time he had to think about his problems.

"Thanks, Ron, I won't let you down."

AJ spent the rest of the day with Ron, watching and learning how he ran the place, the queries he had to deal with, how he dealt with staff, and everything in between. The more time he spent shadowing him, the more he noticed that Ron's anger and frustrations became his. The way disabled people were treated in mainstream society, the way they were perceived, and what they had to endure day to day in a world not catering for them made AJ's blood boil. He knew these feelings were inherited as he'd spent most of his life not considering himself to be one of them.

The longer he spent speaking to those who needed the charity, the more he wanted to fight for them. Ron's direct guidance included regular reminders about the task he was bestowing on his apprentice.

"You have to become their voice and, to do that, you need to personally feel their pain and take it home with you each night. It's not going to be easy AJ. But highly rewarding. Remember: for the benefit of others."

Within three years, a once forsaken AJ rose three times in rank and eventually took on the role of Chief Executive Officer.

*

"Hello." He was so pleased not to be answering phones but it didn't stop a lot of queries coming his way. "AJ, the local Telegraph is on the phone and they want to ask something,"

"Sure put them through. Hello, AJ ... Amraj speaking."

"Hi Amraj, it's Dan from the Telegraph. We're running a story on some counterfeit blue disabled badges that have been discovered in a box. We wanted to know your thoughts on them being sold on the black market and what to do with them?"

"Well, I don't want them, and the charity doesn't have anything to do with them. But yes, we're aware that they are worth quite a bit. As well as better parking, they also allow people to discount congestion charges in London; hence they're worth more than you'd think!"

They spoke for a few more minutes, while AJ reiterated how unacceptable it was and emphasised that people should be more mindful of why these badges mattered. The journalist was all too pleased with AJ's answer and said he'd make sure he quoted him. AJ too had almost impressed himself by giving more perspective to the story. "Can we send a photographer over later to get a picture of you to go alongside the article?"

After agreeing to be photographed, he couldn't help feeling a little smug that he would be featured in the local paper. Not quite the same buzz as performing in front of others but it was a close second. When the photographer arrived, it didn't take too long to get set up and they went outside to get the photo taken. The premise was for him to hold up some of these blue badges that were counterfeit, then the article and his quote would work around it.

He had smartened himself up a little before the photographer arrived as it wasn't everyday he was in the paper. It was a big deal. He didn't have to wait long for the article to be published. He was getting ready for work one morning and as he made his way to work, he decided to stop off at his local newsagent and pick up a copy of the paper. It was something he was becoming interested in, the local news. He wanted to shout more about Disability Rights and the work they were doing but nobody knew him yet.

"Might change after today," he said to himself. He decided to read the paper at work and as he unfolded it at his desk, expecting to rifle through the pages to find the article, he gasped out loud. He wasn't hidden in between other stories — his face was plastered across the front page.

"What the fu…" He was too taken aback to finish his sentence. The article and quote itself were good, but he was more shocked at how he looked. How had nobody noticed? He hadn't shaved for a few days and the black and white grainy shot didn't do any justice to him. If anything it made him look older and haggard, and his tie didn't match his jacket or shirt.

"This is so embarrassing." He had told his parents and Jags about the upcoming piece and his first public appearance of sorts after becoming interim CEO. This is not the image that he had associated with other business leaders and now that he was being seen that way, he had to make some drastic changes.

Another makeover was needed. If he was going to be contacted by the local press, he had to be seen to look the part. "Get a shave and buy some suits this weekend," he said out loud to no one in particular.

"Time to look the part. I'm the fucking CEO."

CHAPTER 23:

WORK UNTIL YOU DROP

One of the many situations AJ found himself in as he became more passionate and obsessed with work was generating continuous streams of funding to keep the charity going. With little to no experience in bid-writing, he submitted applications to trusts, philanthropists, and any commissioning body that wanted to extend and improve its reach to disabled people.

At one stage, AJ became so knowledgeable in grant-making processes that he was selected by the National Lottery Charities Board to assist them in determining which charities in the region should be awarded funding.

He was also starting to annoy others in the charity sector at how ruthless he was becoming. Having overseen the charity's growth from three to fourteen staff with a 400% increase in income, he was treating the charity as if it was his own business. He would show delight in new income and complete and utter outrage at any expenditure. Staff would often hear screams of "*How much?*" from his office.

On the rare occasion that the charity did not win a tender, AJ took it personally and would lock himself away from the staff re-strategising for the next round. The board of trustees had every confidence in his approach and would celebrate or commiserate in tandem.

After accepting the role of CEO, he spent the next several years fine-tuning the charity to become self-sufficient. AJ became one of the first CEO's of a disability charity to directly charge for particular charity functions, previously delivered at zero charge. He could foresee that grants would become a luxury and the charity needed to survive at all costs.

"It's a no-brainer really," he would tell his staff who were a little resistant to the changes he was implementing. Obtaining funding from one source on one of the first bids and tenders that he submitted was a huge rush.

It gave him tunnel-vision when it came to getting huge funds from wherever he could. After one particularly heavy week working all hours and presenting at the AGM, AJ felt pretty pleased with himself. He was just sitting at his desk when a strange feeling washed over him. A sharp headache.

"Just a migraine," he muttered to himself. He took two aspirins and tried to carry on with his work. He couldn't shake the feeling though, and the next thing he knew, his PA was right in front of his face, shaking him slightly.

"AJ? AJ? Are you okay?" There was a tremor in her voice, as if she was terrified.

That's strange, thought AJ. *Why does she sound worried?*

"Call an ambulance!" he heard her shouting.

As he became aware of his surroundings, he realised he was slumped onto his desk with saliva dripping down the side of his mouth. The next thing he knew, he was lying in a hospital bed feeling disorientated.

CHAPTER 24:

TIA

AJ came to his senses and took in his surroundings. He noticed he was wrapped up tight in white linen, and there was beeping and whispered voices around him. He knew he was in hospital for sure from just the smell alone. Having spent a lot of time in and out of medical facilities throughout his childhood, he was no stranger to the aroma of the place.

He tried to move to make his consciousness known to a doctor or nurse and found he was unable to do so. He assumed it might just be due to being tightly wrapped up in bed, but he wasn't convinced. As he looked around to his left, he saw his parents in two hospital chairs by his bed. They hadn't yet realised he was awake.

Shit, it must be serious if mum and dad are here.

His mum saw movement from the corner of her eye. She looked over and noticed him staring at her.

"Amraj!" she shrieked; she looked teary. *This is not a good sign*, he thought.

Her voice must have carried as a nurse came through to check on him. "I'll get the doctor Mr Rai, then he can explain what's happened."

As she wandered off, his mum started fussing. He was struggling to respond or string cohesive words into a sentence, as his face and mouth felt strange and all that seemed to be coming out were gurgles. A tall, thin doctor who looked to be in his mid-forties arrived, followed by the nurse. His mum had been fussing over him, but out of an inbred old-school respect for the doctor's position, she moved to one side so AJ could be examined.

"Good to see you conscious, Mr Rai," he said with a small smile. AJ tried to respond but the gurgles were still present. The doctor must have seen the look of despair on his face as he tried to talk to him and couldn't.

"Don't worry Mr Rai, your speech will return in a few hours. Now that you are conscious, I should explain to you that you have had what we call a TIA or Transient Ischemic Attack." AJ must have looked a little bewildered. The doctor continued.

"A TIA can cause sudden symptoms similar to a stroke, such as speech disturbance, which I assure you will be temporary, and you may feel a weakness or a numbness in your face, arms, and legs."

Well that's nothing new, thought AJ sarcastically.

"Now, rest assured Mr Rai, a TIA isn't as severe as a stroke and the effects usually last a few hours and resolve themselves within a few days and weeks. However, I see here from your patient file that you have cerebral palsy so we'll be keeping a closer eye on you to make sure there are no further complications. I'll come check on you before my rounds are over."

He gave him a reassuring squeeze on the shoulder and left. The nurse stayed a few minutes to check his vitals and fiddled around with the machines.

Once the doctor had left, his mum still looked teary but seemed more relaxed. She had been soothed by the doctor's dulcet tones and trusted he would make sure AJ was home soon.

For what seemed like an hour but was actually only a few minutes, his mother recited all that was wrong with his approach to life and how he was still not settled and working too hard for people who didn't care about him. And of course, how this affected her own many, many ailments.

However, AJ felt more helpless than he had in his life. He was fully conscious but was unable to communicate and move. His mum was still muttering to him and all he could do to get some peace of mind was feign sleep. He closed his eyes and within a few minutes drifted off.

When AJ awoke, all was quiet. It seemed to be the middle of the night and he was thirsty. He tried to move and found he could. Slowly and gingerly, he was able to take a sip from a cup of water that had been placed by the side of his bed with a straw. He coughed and spluttered, and looked around now fully conscious.

"Fuck sake, still in hospital. Fucking hate these places."

Noticing the return to his speech, he immediately felt a rush of relief wash over him, which was instantly replaced by a cloud of despair. How did this happen? He was on top of his game at work and lived in upgraded accommodation. How then, just as life was looking up after all the years, did he end up back in hospital from a minor stroke? He felt a rising anger that he couldn't explain. It took him a few minutes to realise he wasn't angry with the situation — he was angry with himself.

"You did this to yourself," he told himself angrily. It was a feeling he knew deep down was right, rather than a statement he made out of self-pity.

He began to look down at his frame in the bed. He saw his stomach protruding through the sheets he was wrapped up in.

He was in shock as his appearance had improved over the years, especially now he was gainfully employed. He wore nice suits, crisp white shirts, and ties, looking less bedraggled than he had when he first volunteered all those years ago. His hands reached up out of his white linen sheet and onto his stomach, which he was rubbing without realising. This was new to him; whilst he wasn't a gym fanatic and didn't work out often, he had never had to watch his weight before. How had he not noticed how much weight he'd gained?

He cast his mind back over the last year — he had been so consumed by work. He had been able to stave off the darkness in his mind because he had kept himself so busy. He had been able to move out of his tiny flat and buy a decent house and car. Was that the reason: the fact that he did nothing these days but work? It was paying off, as the charity's balance sheet was in the black and he was pushing it forward to run like a well-oiled machine, but at what cost?

He was still holding his stomach, realising that maybe he had let himself go a little. There was a pizza shop right next door, and when he worked late, he didn't have the energy to cook when he got home so it was easy and served its purpose. He lay in his own despair, lamenting that no matter how much he was finally achieving, life had a way of kicking him back down to earth, or hospital in his case.

Something has to change AJ. If you continue as you are, you'll end up dead earlier than you think.

CHAPTER 25:

ANGRY WORDS

The next morning, a groggy AJ awoke to the sound of nurses and hospital noises seeping through his consciousness. He had had a fitful few hours' sleep with the despair he felt the night before coming back into consciousness. There was another feeling of unease. He could sense a darkness on the edges of his periphery. He closed his eyes tight and breathed in slowly for a count of ten. There was a feeling of rising panic.

"I need to calm down." He had been exhausted from the moment he woke up in hospital, and his mind was whirring with self-blame. On top of that, he was physically unable to move with a dead arm and leg. He wanted to just sleep, forever.

His eyes sprang open — it had been a long while since he had felt this internal battle with himself, the despair. There was a ward staff member bringing breakfast to the patients and he happily zoned out, watching her walk up and down the ward. It was oddly reassuring to focus on something else for a few minutes.

His parents wouldn't be back until the afternoon, and he wondered what the hell he was going to do all day. He was no longer accustomed to sitting around doing nothing, and wanted to jump out of bed and get back to work at the first opportunity. *Don't be a dick! That's what landed you here in the first place.* That soft but reasonable voice in his head was starting to annoy him.

"Mr Rai, how are you feeling this morning?" The same doctor from the day before was standing in front of him looking at his chart at the foot of his bed. AJ couldn't recollect his name, but that was nothing new. His capacity for remembering people's names was getting worse as he got older; it was either a severe short-term memory problem or he just didn't pay attention. It was a tossup between the two. "I'm okay," he managed, his voice sounding dry and a little coarse.

"Good to hear you speaking, just keep flexing the vocal cords. Nothing to worry about long term," he said with a slight smile.

He carried out the standard assessment of AJ's mobility and a general check-up, including AJ's least favourite: the Babinski reflex, where he scraped the bottom of his foot. As he came closer, he spotted his name on his badge, Dr Wilson.

"When can I leave, Dr Wilson?" AJ asked him. He was impatient and couldn't stand the idea of being stuck here longer than he needed to be. A TIA didn't seem too severe and he assumed he would be out of there by the end of the day.

"Ah, not so fast Mr Rai. You have lost strength and mobility in your arm and leg. I'll be referring you to a physio here in the hospital. You'll not be walking out of here anytime soon." He gave him a kind smile as he left. AJ couldn't help but display a look of horror.

AJ's parents arrived early in the afternoon, with his mum fussing as expected. She had brought him home-cooked food. "Hospital food no good," she proclaimed.

AJ was too preoccupied to really participate and pay attention to any small talk. He was worried he would be spending too long in hospital. The thought of being cooped up, governed by a regimental approach to his rehabilitation, began to eat away at him. The dark cloud that had persisted over the last couple of days was getting harder and harder to fight off.

Once his folks left, a porter arrived to take him to the physiotherapy clinic.

"Mr Rai? I've brought you some wheels. We're going for a ride down to Physio." AJ took a look at him and noted he could have been no more than twenty years old.

"You're going to have to help me into the chair for now," he asked with hesitation and a bruised ego. He also wanted to make it clear that just because he didn't look strong enough to support his weight now, it didn't mean he was unable to do it.

"No problem. I went to the gym this morning. Full of energy." The slim but deceptively strong porter helped him to his feet. This was the first time he had tried to stand since his TIA. He instantly realised he had limited control of muscle coordination with added weakness and fatigue. The porter was no stranger to seeing patients struggle this way and decided to speed up the transfer process.

"OK, let's sit you down on the chair." With a little force, he manoeuvred his patient into position with complete satisfaction; he had followed all his training in moving and handling.

AJ didn't feel the need to share the porter's joy. Instead, he fell into deep thought. His line of vision was restricted to one shared by his many friends and colleagues who used a wheelchair.

Was this his new world view now? He looked up at the ceiling of the corridor, which seemed to be whizzing by at speed, having an inward dialogue with the Almighty to express his displeasure at life.

You're unbelievable. Un-fucking believable! You gave me nothing but challenge after challenge and I had no choice but to accept and make the best of it. I've taken each disappointment on the chin. Haven't blamed you once. But now, what am I supposed to do now? What else have you got in your arsenal? I have a sense you're not quite finished with me yet?

Before he could finish his conversation with God, he arrived at the clinic and spent what felt like an eternity being subjected to tests and exercises. It was exhausting. By the end he was ready to scream, but the highly experienced team recognised when he had reached his limit.

An hour later, he lay in bed ready for round two with his maker when he noticed the hospital chaplain walk past; she made eye contact and redirected her path his way.

"Hello, I'm Sister Mary."

CHAPTER 26:

THE MESSENGER OF GOD

As she walked towards him, AJ noticed she was a short stout woman with what he felt was an unnecessarily cheery smile. He looked away, back towards the ceiling. He had just enough time to process the irony of what was happening.

"You're Mr Rai. I've seen you in the local papers."

Her voice was soft with a hint of a west country accent.

AJ was a little taken aback. It wasn't because she had recognised him, as Derby was a city with a small population; it was more her demeanour, as if she meant to seek him out to chat with him.

His agitation from the day subsided and he decided to converse. It was easier than pretending she wasn't there, plus not chatting seemed a bit rude. His mother wouldn't be impressed if he was rude to a man or woman of God. Besides, there was still always a showman inside him that enjoyed being recognised and known, a feeling that never left him, though this was a little different from performing a song or a speech.

They made small talk about his work, and she appeared to know a fair bit about his charity. This was an almost prescribed distraction for him. Work was his life and also the reason he was in hospital. If he couldn't physically be at the office, this was the next best thing. He knew how insane that sounded even to himself.

He found himself relaxing in Sister Mary's company. If anything, he did love talking about himself and his achievements to date. It was nice to offload, especially since she wasn't overly pushing the God agenda. He was opening up to her in a way he hadn't for a long time, and flashes of his sessions with Sonia flickered through his mind. He smiled to himself, remembering that room and particularly the fish tank.

"It's just so frustrating, that no matter how hard I try, your so-called God wants me back in hospital."

His tone was derisive when he mentioned God, but he had fluctuated between believing in a higher power and being convinced He didn't exist, particularly with the life he had had to date.

She smiled, and let him continue.

"Growing up Sikh and in the Asian community, having a disability makes you highly visible and incredibly invisible at the same time. People are finally noticing and respecting me through my day job though. People who didn't give a shi..." He stopped, horrified he was about to curse in front of the cloth. Sister Mary wasn't fussed about his language. Patients on the wards were understandably frustrated. AJ was no different.

"Then along comes a TIA. It feels like I'm taking several steps backwards."

He suddenly began to feel a sense of relief. His mind seemed a little lighter. Sister Mary had listened patiently and allowed him to vent. However, she now straightened herself in her seat and geared up to exert her own thoughts.

"Amraj, if I can call you that?"

"Call me AJ."

She smiled and continued, "AJ, you see your disability as a barrier to your life. You need to think of it more as an advantage that you have. You are mobile, so you have independence in a lot of ways others don't. That is a huge advantage."

She was mirroring Ron's words from several years earlier. A sense of déjà vu washed over him.

"You are feeling overwhelmed, helpless, and constantly suffering. But suffering is as important to the soul as being content. Suffering has a purpose."

He listened and nodded, but was more confused. His facial expression mirrored the moment in his childhood when he had only partially understood quadratic equations.

"I promise this will be my only quote from The Bible." She smiled, as she knew not to be overzealous and to be very particular in her words.

"And after you have suffered a little while, the God of all grace, who has called you to his eternal glory in Christ, will himself restore, confirm, strengthen, and establish you."

AJ was lost and ready to switch off but genuinely wanted to understand. "Translation please."

She looked at him and let out a little giggle. "The greatness of The Bible is that each piece of text can serve a purpose in numerous ways. Your disability...you use your perspective, your experiences in life for others to follow, yes?"

"Yes, I suppose so."

"Well, now you have an even greater perspective. The fire inside you should be ready to burn even more ferociously. This TIA had a purpose. It's not the end. It's the beginning of a new chapter."

Sister Mary was starting to make some sort of sense, but he'd be loath to share that thought out loud.

"A chapter where you have even more to do and a stronger character to do it with."

He looked towards his hand. It was weak. According to Sister Mary, that weakness had a purpose. What he did to reverse the weakness was going to make him even stronger? He was a little less confused but still enough to seek more clarification.

"You're telling me this is all part of God's plan? That I have more to do? I'm knackered, sorry, I'm tired. Exhausted. I've got no fight left in me. I'm the one needing help now. I can't help others. I'm just another disabled person. There's nothing special about me anymore."

The Chaplain wasn't having any of it. She had sat with him long enough to determine another plan to motivate him. As he lay counting the reasons for failure at the task in hand, she knew she had to translate it into a language he could understand. She looked at her watch, which showed she was running late for her meeting.

"Okay, AJ. Let's try this another way. You're disabled. The good Lord made you disabled with a destiny to improve the lives of your peers. Now if God has made you disabled, then go away and become the King of disabled people."

She had his attention and he wanted to converse more despite his fatigue. However, with her final statement, she stood, bade him farewell, and wished him a speedy recovery.

AJ looked around as if to ask for witnesses to the whole conversation. For a second, he thought he had dreamt the whole thing but was reassured by a final glimpse of her as she exited the ward.

Sister Mary's words stayed with him over the course of the next few days. It certainly helped steer away some of the darkness he had been feeling since he woke up there. He had a surprise visitor in the morning, his colleague, Sarah, who was sharp and feisty. She had popped by to see how he was doing. She had recently become his right hand at the charity and they both knew, although his ego would never admit it out loud, that he couldn't survive without her at work.

She also acted like a bodyguard from time to time, completely overprotective of AJ. That sort of loyalty meant a lot to him, even if it could be grating sometimes. He was a grown man after all. Sarah gave him a disapproving look when she saw him, but it was her way of showing commitment to the role. The moment she sat down, he asked about work. She scowled, not wanting to indulge him. She knew him too well and knew she had little choice but to answer as he would keep asking until he got his way.

"It's all under control. Don't stress about it. How long are you going to be here? How the fuck did you get into this mess? Everyone has told you you're becoming a fat git. Don't you look in the mirror? Yes, you're overweight, that's why you're ill. You better sort your shit out AJ. I mean it! Oh and I meant to ask, are you okay?"

AJ hadn't paid any attention to her rant whatsoever and didn't respond. He was miles away.

Sarah must have read his thoughts across his face. He wasn't as poker-faced as he assumed he was and was often easy to read, especially around those who knew him well. With a small sigh, Sarah decided to distract him with work talk and spent the remainder of visiting time updating him on the charity, the staff, and projects before heading off.

After an hour or so, during which he alternated between watching TV and napping, an orderly arrived to take him back down to the Physiotherapy Clinic. After initial assessments and some movement exercises, they got to work on rebuilding his strength to the point where he could walk unaided.

He found an inner determination unlike anything he'd felt before.

He was totally motivated to get back to normal and replayed the conversation with Sister Mary in his mind several times a day. He spent three full weeks in hospital and decided to devote every ounce of physical and mental energy to his recovery.

He was going to 'smash the shit' out of this treatment — he was still young, only thirty years old, and he refused to spend anymore of his adulthood in hospital. It had dominated his childhood already.

"No way I'm spending my best days here too."

CHAPTER 27:

EYE OF THE TIGER

The next few sessions were incredibly draining and tough. AJ felt like he was learning to walk all over again. He had to rebuild the strength that had been taken from him. Nevertheless, he was making progress, with a new determination to get out as soon as possible.

Apart from his own determination to leave, he was also driven by his hatred of hospitals. The smell, the food, the patients and their families, the odd distant moan from an end-of-life patient. He wanted to be back at his desk, his own version of heaven, to continue with a new-found purpose to add to what he had built.

He hadn't made his physio's life easy, even though the Chaplain's words had made an impact. The pace and regime they put him through made him angry. He often shouted out, "What are you playing at, don't you know what I've been through?"

The physios would be sympathetic but it wasn't unusual for patients to feel as though they were being put through the ringer.

"Yes, Mr Rai," they'd respond and continue with their session with him. The anger was from the pain, not the usual pain he had on the right side of his body; this was something else, a numbness he couldn't shift.

One particular evening, after an excruciating session, AJ sat at the side of his bed in tears. The pain and strain were increasingly unbearable and he began asking the Registrar on the ward for stronger pain relief.

Across the bay was an elderly man who hadn't said much to him except an occasional "morning" at the beginning of each day. He was tall and well-built with a white neatly-kept moustache. His name was John Beard. John could see AJ was distressed as he reached for his daily cocktail of painkillers. He walked over to AJ.

"No need to keep popping those things, old chap. They'll do you more harm in the long term."

AJ looked up. He was raised to respect the older generation for their wisdom. Whether they had endured struggles throughout the World War or the horrors of the partition of India, he had nothing but admiration for them.

"I know but I'd be in absolute agony without them. They help me sleep too."

John laughed out loud and sat down on the chair reserved for visitors. "There's only one medicine for pain. It's worked for me for decades. Laughter, old sport, laughter!"

AJ wasn't overly impressed with his advice. He had always associated laughter with people who were happy.

"I'm serious. I tell you what, put the pills down and come with me. We'll walk slowly over to the visitors waiting room. C'mon."

AJ's natural instinct to do as he was told by those older than him was the only reason he obeyed the summons. John instructed him to sit down as he inserted a VHS tape into the player and switched on the television set.

John sat down and within seconds he began reading the opening credits to *Laurel and Hardy, County Hospital*. He looked across at John who was smiling and whistling the Cuckoo Song, which immediately took him to his own memory as a child, sitting in the living room with his father and grandfather rolling on the floor and laughing at their antics.

Within a few minutes, AJ was laughing. Both patients laughed with each other and every one-liner by Stan Laurel and Oliver Hardy's reaction. Twenty-five minutes later, the episode finished. John stood up and turned to his new partner in laughter.

"Now then, do you still need those painkillers?"

AJ's laughter wound down to silence. His muscles were still stiff but the pain had subsided to the point that it no longer mattered.

"No. But I could do with a brandy!"

"Couldn't we all!"

For the next fortnight, both men made the same painful journey to the visitors room to watch at least one of the comedy duo movies. AJ reduced his daily need for painkillers to a few paracetamols.

*

One of the hospital's top neurologists, Dr Willis, became quite impressed with AJ's progress. During one of his physio sessions, both he and his patient noticed the change of gait during walking. Cerebral Palsy had meant he never walked a mainstream walk. Something felt wrong. He no longer had his usual stance and limp. Dr Willis was bemused, remarking on the possibility of the TIA reversing the stroke from his birth.

"Mr. Rai, what's happening to you is inexplicable. You are defying all my years of training and experience."

AJ was equally shocked but refused to rise to the same level of excitement. To walk in such a way required much effort. He was convinced he would revert to his old walk soon.

Dr Willis gathered student doctors and fellow consultants to try to understand this medical marvel. For two to three days, AJ was prodded and probed and visited on the ward by every doctor under the sun.

When his parents heard about the phenomenon that was their son, they could only believe it was a miracle and finally, after thirty years, their son was cured from his disability. It was short-lived, however, as his usual stance returned. In some strange way, AJ felt relief, much to the disappointment of the medical experts and his parents. His old walk was something that defined him. A cured AJ would be a different AJ, with quite possibly a different outlook on life.

CHAPTER 28:

NOT SO FAST

He left hospital a few weeks later, having regained his original walk. His determination not to leave in a wheelchair had paid off. He had a walking stick to help keep him stable but he could live with that, for now.

Arriving home, he felt relaxed for the first time in months. He was eager to get back to work but first he needed supplies as he stared at his empty refrigerator. The next day, he woke up earlier than usual — he was going to start his mornings doing what laps he could around his garden, with a new-found zest to keep fit.

It was a struggle as he was bigger than he had ever been, plus the after-effects of the TIA had taken a toll on him physically. He had to build his strength up, but his only obstacle now was impatience. His mind was working at full speed whilst his body had only hit the ignition. He felt like there was a switch inside his head that he couldn't turn off.

His personality wouldn't allow him to slow down. If he did, he would have to process feelings and his environment and that wasn't an option. He would tackle getting back into shape and looking after himself the way he would handle work—with gusto and sheer stubbornness and an impatience to get things done. Instead of berating his employees, he would now berate himself into shape.

He tried to get back to work the next day, but it seemed as though his family had anticipated this. His brother Toni and sister Shindy were at his house at 8 am just as he was getting ready. It wasn't usual behaviour on their part and he questioned the intervention.

They were close but kept enough distance to ensure they did not step over the line in each other's lives. However, AJ's health was the exception to the rule. They both had the natural respect shown to older brothers but today Shindy wasn't having any of it.

"You've only just left the hospital! It's not wise to be rushing back to the office so soon. I'm sure they're getting along fine without you."

He played along. They both stayed just over an hour but as soon as the coast was clear, AJ took to his car against the advice of the discharging doctor and drove to work.

He walked in slower than normal, making his way to his office. He noticed the staff staring at him as he walked past, as if he was a ghost. They certainly looked perplexed. He gave them a small nod as he continued and just as he got to his desk and sat down, Sarah barged in after him and exploded.

"What the heck are you doing here?" She had a face like thunder.

"Nice to see you too," he responded sarcastically.

"Well since none of you bothered to come visit me again, I thought I'd come back to work and get stuck in."

He could see his staff trying not to eavesdrop. They were craning their necks to hear the exchange. AJ was beginning to feel he wasn't welcome.

"The cheek! It's my bloody charity. I'll come and go as I please," he mumbled, but made sure Sarah couldn't hear him as he didn't have his full strength back yet.

He tried to catch up on what he'd missed and whilst he would never admit it out loud, it was tiring. He wasn't going to let his family or staff have the satisfaction of thinking they were right about him coming back to work too soon. Having arrived in the morning through the front door, he decided to slip out the back way directly through the car park to go home. He was exhausted and needed rest.

Three months after his initial attempt to return to the office, a fresh and fully recharged AJ was ready to reconnect with the rat race. Whilst dressing and admiring himself in the full-length mirror in the corner of his room, he couldn't help smiling a cocky smile. He buttoned up his crisp white shirt and reached for his suit jacket to finish off the look for today.

As he pulled into the car park at his offices, he debated whether to sneak in or go through the front door. "You didn't work this hard to look this good to not show it off," he said to himself with a smile.

With another quick glance at himself in the rear-view mirror, he got out of his car and made his way to the front entrance with his new-found swagger. As he entered, his staff froze, not because they had ever felt he was a tyrant, but in shock.

Three months ago, AJ was a plump man leaning heavily on a walking stick that looked like it might not be able to bear his weight. The AJ standing in front of them was walking unaided and confident and had never looked fitter or leaner. The transformation left them a little gobsmacked as he wove through the building, smiling and making a point of greeting everyone.

As he sat at his desk and closed the door behind him, he revelled in their reaction to the new and improved AJ. The wait had definitely been worth it.

Still smiling, he booted up his computer to get started on taking this charity forward. The last three months, working hard on getting fitter and looking after himself physically had cleared his mind. The words of the Chaplain were still at the forefront of his mind, *"Go and become the King of disabled people"* was the driving force for the last few months. He had too much to do and not much time to do it in.

As he put into action the ideas and thoughts he had accrued during his time off, he heard the word *frenzy* from Sarah and his board members. The need to get things done instantly was one they didn't quite share with him. His board of directors were happy to have him back but were also slightly concerned he might take this new-found enthusiasm too far and end up back in hospital.

CHAPTER 29:

TEARS OF A CEO

The phone buzzed in Sonia's office. It was Carole, her receptionist. "Mr Rai for you." There was a hint of breathlessness. Even though the appointment had been made a week earlier, she hadn't expected him to turn up. It had been several years since he left with what he wanted, not forgetting the emotional aftermath for Sonia. "On my way," she responded and put the phone down whilst composing herself.

AJ was one of the few clients she felt she had failed. He regularly crept back into her thoughts. However, she was both curious and surprised he had reached out for another session, and intrigued about the reason and sudden need to speak with her on a professional level. She knew he was doing fine. AJ Rai made regular local headline news with his work as CEO at Disability Rights. He certainly had made a name for himself over the years.

"Morning Carole." AJ greeted her with the confidence of a very different man from several years ago. "I'm here to see Sonia, I mean Dr Khan, how have you been?" Carole was a little bemused by the interaction. The last time he had been a patient with them, he had never uttered a single word outside of announcing he had arrived for his appointment.

Sonia was in reception and noticed him chatting to Carole, puzzled too by the interaction as she approached the front desk. His transformation was still shocking to see in person; even though she had kept track of him and seen his picture, the reality was something completely different. She cleared her throat to announce herself and said, "Mr Rai, good to see you, come on through."

He followed her through to the all-too-familiar office. AJ was pleased to see Sonia. She hadn't changed a bit since their last interaction, which was starting to make him feel self-conscious as he made his way down the corridor. The minute she closed the door behind him and made her way over to her chair, the confidence he had displayed when he first entered started ebbing away. They hadn't made small talk and as the silence lingered, it grew a little uncomfortable for him. He was getting pangs of regret for making this appointment, as their last conversation hung in the air between them. He was internally struggling with whether to mention it when she cleared her throat again and said, "Mr Rai, please take a seat."

She broke a little of the awkwardness by talking first. He went to his usual spot, and noticed that the office hadn't changed all too much. He noticed his favourite yellow flowers on a small table behind her and wondered if they were purposely there for him. As he sat, his eyes fell on the fish tank. Sonia noticed his gaze; he was staring intently. She had felt his indecision and the atmosphere felt awkward when she closed her door. She decided to clear some of the tension. "Don't worry, no judgemental fish today." AJ looked at her, but her face was serious. Slowly, a smile crept across it and they both burst out laughing.

"Well, enough of the formalities, Dr Khan, please go back to referring to me as AJ. Mr Rai is more like my dad," he said with a cheeky smile.

"Well in that case, call me Sonia. Now I'm sure you remember the drill. Truth be told, I was surprised to hear you had booked in to see me." Her voice was a little hesitant during the last sentence, not entirely sure whether it would bring up some painful memories of his time here.

"Me too. Much has happened since I was last here and yet it feels as if nothing has really changed." He seemed to be talking more to himself than her. Sonia started taking notes; he smiled slightly, the feeling of déjà vu washing over him. "Nothing really changes, does it?" There was a lingering anger in his statement.

"AJ, why are you here? What made you to feel you had to come back?" Sonia prompted him. She was aware that he loved to talk, but he just needed a prod.

He looked tense. Incredibly tense. His face displayed a battle of smiles and frustration before eventually the latter won.

"Well Sonia, since you ask, I feel shit. Pissed off. Vexed. Angry. I can't believe I'm fucking back here." His eyes darted round her office again as if he'd just realised he was there. The confidence he had when he walked into reception was replaced by what seemed like disgust. Sonia was swiftly reminded of his ability to curse with ease and almost felt comfortable being in a familiar dialogue. She let him speak.

AJ continued with a rush of words, as if he couldn't say what he needed to fast enough. "It was all going so well. I thought I'd moved on. I had made something of myself. I've been so focused. Nothing fazed me anymore." For a brief moment, he stopped to ensure he had her attention but before Sonia could interject, he continued more coherently.

"Do you know, I look after million-pound budgets now? I have 20 staff who I lead and mentor, with the power to make real change for those who need it, the most vulnerable in society. People are always ringing me wanting my advice. I have parents wanting me to talk to their children, to inspire them and help them make better life choices."

"AJ, look at me," Sonia implored. She was again reminded about his inability to talk to her, instead focusing on inanimate objects around the room or outside through the window. In this case, he had been talking to the flowers. "Those are some amazing achievements, what caused the setback?"

He looked into her eyes. Some of the guilt he felt was still there, even though she had made it easier by breaking the tension early on and not discussing their last encounter. He started to shake slightly as he spoke, telling her the reason he was there. "For the first time in a long time, I took time off. I wanted to travel and to treat mum and dad, you know. I took them to New York and California. Showed them places outside India for a change." They both smiled, as her own parents also habitually visited the motherland.

"Well, the break was exactly what I needed. I felt refreshed and full of beans. The force was strong in me." The Jedi reference was lost on Sonia as she just carried on scribbling her notes. He cleared his throat and continued, "We were hiring just before I left as one of my staff had moved on to pastures new and I trusted my management team to interview and hire someone, especially as I'd be away. When I got back to work the day after my holiday I was introduced to the new recruit." He stopped talking.

Sonia looked up confused as there was a look of bewilderment and pain across his face. "AJ?" she prompted and put her pen down to pay closer attention to him.

"I started to walk over to this woman, the one they had hired; she was in her thirties and from a distance, she looked familiar. I couldn't quite place her, my memory is shit at the best of times. I was wracking my brains over why she looked so familiar to me. Each step took me nearer to her and my memory cells began regenerating faster than lightning." He paused and he had a vacant, far-off look in his eyes. His mind was clearly elsewhere.

"AJ? Are you okay?" She was desperate to know who the mystery woman was but he needed to volunteer the details himself. If she pushed him too much, he was likely to withdraw. He looked directly at her and then back towards the vase. His face now looked like a lost schoolchild.

"Life has a strange way of resurfacing buried shit, you know, demons you thought you'd slain." Again, he stopped, only this time to pour a glass of water from a bottle placed in front of him. His mouth felt like sandpaper as he relived the encounter for Sonia. She was well aware that AJ was one of the few patients in her portfolio who had the fantastic ability to narrate past events with tension but at that precise moment, she wished he would arrive at the point of interest right now.

He took a sip and placed the beaker on the table, then continued.

"She brought it all back. I thought I was over it. Time's not a great healer after all. I just want to get on with my life."

Sonia was wondering if there was ever going to be an outcome to the story but kindly said, "Take your time AJ. Whatever it is that's brought you here will reveal itself when you're ready."

"She just sat there, looking at me, totally ignorant about what she had done all those years ago. I mean, how can people not remember that they've treated someone so badly, even in the past? Didn't she have a conscience? Didn't she know I worked there? For fuck sake, didn't she know I'm the boss?"

Sonia asked him directly; she could sense him slipping away and at this rate, she would never know the real cause for what brought him here after so many years.

"Who was it AJ? Who was sitting in your office?"

He turned to Sonia as if noticing her for the first time. Shaking his head to bring himself back to the present, he said, "It was the ringleader of those girls who destroyed my life at school. I think the Puppet Master upstairs was bored again. Probably thought it's time to pull AJ's strings some more. She had come to interview for the job in my absence and got it."

Sonia recalled the revelation he had made years earlier and began searching for the right thing to say. As she gathered her words, she spotted tears running down his cheeks. Her favourite ever patient was crying.

Sonia was no stranger to tears, and every counsellor had a box of tissues waiting to be used between themselves and their clients. They would often demolish a box a week, so she was well-stocked and reached over to hand one to AJ.

It wasn't that she felt any achievement in steering the individual to an outpouring of emotion; rather that over time, she could chart incidents in case files, which would help her understand the root cause of their need for her support.

"AJ, I'm stunned and so sorry you had to deal with that. When was this?"

"Oh, about ten minutes before I randomly found a crumpled-up card for Dr Sonia Khan and rang to make an appointment." He looked at her with a smile, the tears having dried up.

"You know the funny thing? As I realised it was her, I had to remind myself that she was now working for me. I was the CEO, how fucking ironic, and yet I felt like a twelve year old again. If it wasn't for the law, I'd probably have gotten physical and I'm not a violent person. She was on my turf for fuck sake." His anger was replacing the sadness that had overwhelmed him a few minutes ago. "You know what I did? I greeted her with a handshake and a fucking smile to make her feel *welcome!*"

Sonia smiled. "Well, that was very mature of you. Now that you know who she was, how did she react?"

"She didn't let on that she had recognised me. Can you believe it? It was actually one of my managers who told me a few days later that she had, as I hadn't really bumped into her again after she started. She'd told them she remembered and was too embarrassed to go anywhere near me, let alone apologise." He snorted his derision.

"What the fuck would her apology do for me anyway? The little girl who fucked up my life went on to have a great education, get a degree, and find herself a great job, with me!" He hadn't realised he was rising from his seat; his voice was definitely several octaves higher as he worked himself up.

"AJ, apologies and forgiveness can help more than we realise. How did you cope with her working for you?"

"Clearly not that well. I'm sitting here again talking to you, aren't I?" he replied sarcastically. Sonia felt her hackles rise, as the condescension was a little grating but she also had to sympathise and be professional as much as she wanted to reply with a comeback of her own. Sometimes, patients would test her patience. She let him continue whilst she let herself calm down.

"My right hand, Sarah, flipped her lid when I told her about our history. I had to calm her down, ironic I know. She promised me she would stay as professional as she could around her. I think I created a monster in her, but she's very loyal, so swings and roundabouts."

"Well, I'm happy to hear you calmed her down when you must have been raging yourself. Is this particular individual still with you? If so, how will you cope long term with her working for you?" Sonia probed.

"Want to know the funniest thing?" Sonia nodded with a weary smile. "She resigned. She said the job wasn't for her and left. What a load of bullshit!" AJ burst out laughing. "The irony being that, even though we had this history and she could never face me, she actually grew up to be a polite, well-rounded individual. From her interactions with my staff, she was fucking nice!" AJ was shaking his head in disbelief.

Sonia put her notepad and pen down. In all her years as a counsellor listening to people's woes and helping them recover from traumas, she had never heard of anything like this—incidents turning full circle.

She felt saddened that this had happened to him when he was clearly at the peak of his career. She knew her craft well enough to know that it would take him a long time to recover from this. AJ's tendencies fluctuated between a confident swagger, arrogance, and vulnerability. But there was no more going through the motions for a bottle of pills — they would do this her way. She would be in control of ensuring that he dealt with his traumas.

"AJ, I'm pleased you felt the need to reach back out. There will be no prescription for antidepressants this time. You came here voluntarily so we do this my way. Let me help you heal." She sounded firm, and it was a tone AJ hadn't heard from her before.

"OK doc, didn't know you had it in you, but yes, as you wish."

CHAPTER 30:

A REALLY GOOD FEELING

As Sonia left her office, she hummed to herself. AJ's session with her had led to a mixture of emotions, from anticipation of his arrival to embarrassing awkwardness as they both skirted around their last encounter until she finally took control and set the rules for how she could help him.

It had been a much more productive session than either of them had imagined and she felt she could finally shed the sense of failure she had been carrying around since their last interaction. It had never left her and was part of the reason why she had kept tabs on him and his rise to success. Back when they first met, her sense of doom around him had a lot to do with her own grief at losing her husband, but the more he talked, the more she knew she couldn't fail him. It had felt so ingrained, not just as a professional but on a personal level.

Her sense of relief at seeing him now had been palpable and left her feeling a little giddy and lightheaded. She was in a good mood and actually left the office on time. AJ might have changed but Sonia still buried herself in her work. As she drove home, she wondered whether her boys were still there. They had a myriad of activities after school these days as young teenagers; she wanted to share an evening with them and hoped they were in.

Life wasn't much easier with teenage boys, and as she worked so much, they often resented her neglect of them. The sweet young boys who had lost their father at such a young age were drifting further and further away. She had a sneaky suspicion her mother-in-law had something to do with it. Poisoning their young ears about how it was their mother's fault their father had left them.

She had been somewhat ostracized from her own community. Even now, being a widow was a source of shame to those she knew and thought she could depend on to get her through the hardest part of her life. As a young, newly widowed mother, she had been abandoned. It wasn't long before she herself stopped attending the mosque and doing her daily prayers. She had turned her back on it all.

She walked in and shouted, "I'm home." There was no response; she checked their activities calendar as she walked into the kitchen and saw they would be at football practice until later. She decided to make a homemade lasagne and some cookies for when they got back, as they'd like that. She got to work in the kitchen, still revelling in her successful day and finally getting some closure on one of the few clients she felt she had failed.

CHAPTER 31:

TWENTY WHITE SHIRTS

It had been a week since his reconnection with Sonia and strangely, he was looking forward to his session today. He had experienced a little trepidation when they first saw each other after so long but found it relatively easy to fall back into the rhythm. He hadn't realised how much of an impact recent events could have had on him. *At least you're not in hospital.*

AJ was still a little worried that they hadn't addressed the elephant in the room: their last encounter. It was just beneath the surface of their interactions, meaning they might never quite be comfortable around each other. He wondered what the etiquette was in asking her out for coffee so they could at least put it to bed and move forward. "Look at me therapising myself. Sonia would be so proud," he chuckled.

As he lay in bed, he contemplated having the day off and reached for his phone, dialling the same number irrespective of the time, day or night. Sarah answered instantly. He smiled. *So loyal*, he thought. "Sarah, I don't have any meetings today so I'm taking the day off." He reeled off a list of things for Sarah to do, which he repeated numerous times to her before hanging up. He could almost feel her rolling her eyes as he did so.

"OK, no worries. Are you doing anything special today?"

"Nothing special, hoping to invite a friend for coffee and a catch up. See you tomorrow." He had made his mind up to ask Sonia for a coffee between patients to clear the air once and for all.

AJ sat on the edge of his bed and completed his five-minute stretch of both Achilles tendons, his usual morning routine. He would often grunt in pain with a simultaneous curse at Steve, his physiotherapist, who insisted on a basic set of stretches.

He looked around his minimalistic room. A chest of drawers stood to his left with his usual items: his wallet, some loose cash, and his watch and keys laid sporadically on top. To the right of his bed was a line of clean, white fitted wardrobes containing twenty suits with an equal amount of white shirts and three rows of ties of every colour and pattern imaginable. He now employed the services of a domestic cleaner, Steffi, who would often joke about his clothing addiction and the fact that he loved a suit and white shirt. The bedraggled AJ of the past was long gone.

"Mr Rai, you have more clothes than a Hollywood star," Steffi teased him every few days. She came round every morning at 9 am, regular as clockwork. Alongside his parents, she was the only one with keys to his four-bedroom detached house, a source of pride for him. It was almost a visual reminder of how far he had come and how much he had achieved.

"You need a wife. She will put a stop to this," Steffi would tease and had a sharp tongue; she was comfortable enough to say what she felt. They both knew how much he relied on her. "You have an unhealthy fixation for white shirts! I've never seen it before. It's pointless, nobody needs that many!"

"Who needs a wife when I have you Steffi, moaning about my mess and how many clothes I have?" he would respond with laughter. She would shake her head and ignore him.

AJ would chuckle every time he reached for one of his shirts, Steffi's voice ringing in his ear. "No woman can come between me and my white shirts," he said out loud with a laugh.

He grabbed one and a fresh pair of jeans, placed them carefully at the end of his bed, then hopped in the shower. He had assumed Steffi had left, but could hear movement downstairs, and frowned thinking, "She's a bit quiet today. Hopefully she'll be gone by the time I'm done." Not that he didn't enjoy her company but he wanted to ask Sonia for a coffee sooner rather than later.

An hour later, he was sitting on his bed. It was wet around him and he was on the phone.

"Emergency services. Do you want Fire, Police, or Ambulance?" the voice on the other end said.

"Police please," AJ trembled down the phone as he gave his address. He found his right side stiffening as he was naked and cold, with a towel barely wrapped around him. His eyes slowly scanned the hallway and staircase outside his open bedroom door. There were red stains on the cream carpet and a few on the top steps. He scanned his own body and then still on the phone, "Ambulance as well please, I've been stabbed. There's blood running down my leg."

CHAPTER 32:

ALI G IN DA HOUSE

His mobile was next to him and ringing but he was being wheeled to a hospital bed and couldn't answer. He had rung his parents on the way, though he hadn't told them what happened. It was a little embarrassing now that the shock had worn off but it didn't stop him shaking once his adrenalin levels returned to normal.

It didn't take his parents long to get to the hospital and find him.

Thankfully, the knife had only managed to make a superficial cut but there was enough damage to draw a fair amount of blood. The wound was cleaned, sterilised, stitched, and bandaged.

The police took his statement and description of the felon with interest; AJ could tell they were trying to control their laughter at his story and was suitably unimpressed. After four to five hours of medical intervention and police questioning, he was discharged. It wasn't just AJ that was relieved — his parents were too.

He rang Sonia's office later after he had slept, as the shock of what had happened tired him out. "So much for a relaxing day off," he said sarcastically to himself. A few seconds later, he heard a woman's voice, "AJ?"

"Hi Sonia, I wondered if you wished to meet me for a coffee tomorrow?" He felt slightly embarrassed asking her for a casual catch-up, as their relationship had always been patient and client; this was exploring something new. He sensed her hesitation. "Don't worry, it's nothing romantic, just as a friend," he laughed.

He thought he heard her let out a breath of air in relief. *Rude,* he thought.

"Sure, I'll meet you at 12.30 outside the coffee shop near my office."

*

AJ arrived a few minutes before Sonia and ordered them both drinks; he took a guess and assumed she would be a latte drinker. It seemed to be all the rage at the moment. He saw her heading towards him; he sat facing the window so she could see him immediately. There was a newspaper in her hand and a look of worry and concern on his face.

"AJ," she said, putting the paper down in front of him, "What the heck happened?" she exclaimed as she sat down opposite him. He took the paper and opened it up. There was an article on his recent altercation inside.

"How the fuck did they find out?" He scanned the article for the name of the reporter. A vague memory of seeing him at the hospital the day before came back to him.

The reporter had overheard his parents at the hospital talking about what happened. He saw the headline — *Man stabbed in an attempted burglary.*

"Must have been a slow news day," he mumbled to himself as he folded the paper and looked up to see Sonia sitting angrily with her arms crossed waiting for an explanation. AJ responded with his usual reaction when in trouble — he began to scratch his head.

"Oh, yes sorry. Papers, hey? So, yes, I was, er, yes... I was stabbed. There was some burglar who looked like Ali G who decided to break into my house whilst I was having a shower," he said calmly. "I got you a latte." He pushed the drink towards her.

Sonia ignored the drink. "Wait, he stabbed you in the shower?"

AJ shook his head, "No, no nothing like that. I had come out of the shower, with a towel around me, and spotted him in my bedroom stealing my cash and wallet. When he saw me, he asked if I had any gold at home. I was a bit shocked, as you can imagine, plus you know... So, I was trying to convince this fucking dickhead that I didn't have any gold. Anyway, he didn't believe me and decided to lunge at me with a knife. We, er, we wrestled and fell to the floor. My towel unravelled and..." He stopped mid-sentence and looked up at Sonia. She let out a burst of laughter at his story, particularly the latter part.

She noticed him staring and tried to compose herself.

"Sorry, AJ, I don't mean to laugh, but, but..." She broke down again. He started laughing with her and after a few minutes, their laughter subsided. They became aware that the other coffee drinkers were staring in their direction.

"Anyway, I tried to fight him off but I think wrestling a half-naked disabled man might have made him question the meaning of life. He subsequently ran off." Sonia resumed her hysterics.

"When I got up, I was shaking and sat on my bed, and that's when I noticed the blood running down my leg." He decided to finish his story quickly, sensing that Sonia was on the verge of falling to the floor.

"AJ, I'm so sorry for laughing. It's been a long time since I've belly-laughed this much and I'm honestly very happy that you weren't hurt."

It was strange seeing her laugh and be so open; he was a little confused by it but also a little pleased that he could make her laugh so much.

"I had actually intended to invite you for a coffee, you know before the stabbing, I thought it would be good to, er, chat." His sombre tone calmed Sonia down.

"Well I don't have to be back for a while for my next client so let's catch up now, shall we? You can fill me in more on your naked wrestling moves. But first I'm going to get some tea. I don't do lattes."

CHAPTER 33:

DISSATISFYING SATISFACTION

AJ went to work the next day with a feeling in his stomach that could only be described as dread. Now that the story of what happened to him had made the papers, his phone had been ringing off the hook from worried friends, family, and board members. No one from the office had rung to see what happened though, so he naively thought that perhaps they hadn't seen the story and he could get away without having to relive the embarrassing tale again.

"AJ," Sarah greeted him as he sat down at his desk. "So good to have you back! Did you enjoy your time off and your little fracas with Ali G?"

AJ wasn't surprised that she used the Ali G reference; the sketch artist had created an image that was too similar to the famous TV character based on the description he gave of his attacker. "You're so funny, Sarah. Now can we get back to work?" He responded with a note of steely resolve to indicate that he didn't want to discuss this again.

Ignoring the jibe, Sarah asked, "I suppose you want me to make you coffee today as you will probably spill most of it on your way back from the kitchen?" Sarah was the only member of staff who could get away with speaking to him like that without fear of being disciplined. The other staff wouldn't dare, plus she acted as the conduit between him and them. She knew how to word conversations and grievances, quite diplomatically, to ensure that AJ didn't hit the roof.

"If you insist, Americano, one sugar."

"You'll get a normal coffee and you'll love it too!" She stormed off towards the kitchen muttering, "Americano? Ha!"

AJ's eyes wandered around his office, his sanctuary. He would often sit alone without any disturbances for hours, just the way he liked it. As he was looking absently towards the carpet, he noted a crack in the sideboard. His office nemesis, Japanese knotweed, was sprouting through the walls. "For fuck sake," he said out loud, indicating the knotweed as Sarah walked back in.

"Yes, it's back with a vengeance!" Sarah exclaimed as she made her way back to his office with his coffee. "Your office, the ladies toilets…it's everywhere."

"What's on the menu today?" AJ asked her. He had a habit of changing the subject sporadically, something she was used to but could be irritating to those who didn't know him well.

"The knotweed…" She stopped mid-sentence and realised his eyes had glazed over and were focusing on his coffee. His attention span had diminished of late, and she knew he would be thinking of a hundred different things for the charity to do, while ideas were constantly vying for attention in his mind. Sarah had asked him on multiple occasions for someone, anyone, to come to the office to destroy the menacing weed popping up everywhere.

"We have an interview at 11 am for a new Direct Payments Officer. Plus a Telegraph reporter wants to talk to you about inspiring leaders of tomorrow." To keep up with his thought process, she changed tack in the conversation to refocus his attention. "No idea why they thought of you," she added.

This got his attention as the jab irked him slightly and she continued with, "Oh and there's a message on the answerphone from Jim Staines at the Council, who would like to speak to you as soon as possible." Now *that* fully grasped his attention. He looked at the door indicating for her to leave so he could phone Jim back. She left without question. AJ reached for the phone and dialled as if his life depended on it. "Jim, AJ here. How are you?"

Fifteen minutes later, AJ emerged into the main office in a cool, composed manner. The staff all had their backs to him but he knew they knew he was there. The atmosphere always changed, very subtly, when he walked out of his office. His trustee Paula, would always comment that people knew when AJ had entered a room. He had a presence — an almost perceptible aura that people could feel. "And I'm blind!" she would exclaim, knowing every time he was in the room. AJ never understood this but loved and accepted her superhuman senses.

He nodded to Sarah. "Grab your things, we're going for a drive." Making his way to his car, Sarah could sense something big was about to happen and made haste. She picked up her coat and handbag and followed without question, with a curious gleam in her eye.

She got into his car, recognising a look of quiet contemplation on his face but knew better than to ask too many questions. He would reveal all in his own time. He had a tendency to go off-topic when asked a direct question. Working with him was often like unpicking a riddle. With AJ, the information was inside his head. Retrieving it was often as painful as trying to do a 1000-piece puzzle.

AJ felt quite calm. He knew that Sarah was waiting for an explanation about their sudden office outing but he wasn't in the mood for talking. He switched on the radio to fill the deafening silence in the car. He cranked the volume loud, and as his car filled with Motorhead's *Sweet Revenge*, AJ smiled to himself and thought, *how fitting.*

Ten minutes later, they pulled up outside a nondescript three-story building. AJ didn't seem to be in much of a rush to leave as they sat silently with the engine humming, his eyes taking in their surroundings.

As they made their way to the entrance, three staff were occupied with their cigarettes whilst discussing something that appeared controversial enough to lower their volume as Sarah and her boss walked by.

Sarah, needing an explanation now they were inside, looked to AJ. She was taken aback by how pale he looked.

"Are you okay? What's this about? Are we going to be working with these folks?"

She stopped talking as AJ glanced at her. So busy in his own thoughts and memories, he had almost forgotten she was there. They had arrived at the Ryegate Centre, the very institution his parents had brought him to at the age of twenty-four at the suggestion of the infamous Kamala Aunty. He remembered his vow all those years ago to himself and to the condescending manager Riz that he'd make something of himself. *Well, I certainly fulfilled my promise,* he thought to himself with a wry smile.

Sarah noticed him smiling to himself. AJ decided now was the time to take her into his confidence.

"Before I started volunteering at Disability Rights, I had a short visit to this very centre. The manager then was a condescending man with a backward view of the capability of disabled people. He suggested I join 'the club' here and assessed me as only being capable of doing basket-weaving in this place. I was so annoyed. He thought I was only good for vegetative activities."

AJ knew she would be vexed. As he finished talking, he saw her face change from being inquisitive to angry and then bewildered as the very man he described, albeit a bit older, walked through the double doors behind him. AJ saw her staring and turned round.

"You mean him?" she said in a loud whisper. AJ nodded and stared at an older Riz; he couldn't believe he was still here.

As he approached them, he introduced himself, "I'm Riz, the Centre Manager here. You must be Mr Rai and I apologise, I don't know this young lady's name?"

"Sarah Morton, Services Manager," she replied. AJ noted her voice was a little icy. Riz didn't notice and continued.

"Delighted to meet you both, thank you for coming down so quickly. So I hear you will be taking over the centre in the coming months? Jim Staines rang me last night to explain the process. I must say the staff here are quite excited about the new change and becoming part of the Disability Rights family."

AJ didn't want to disappoint Riz and alert him to the fact that his staff outside didn't seem to be as excited as he made out.

"Would you care for a tour?" Riz asked them.

"Yes, that'll be fun," AJ responded with the slightest hint of sarcasm. He was a mixed bag of emotion on the inside but was impressed with how calm he was coming across. They followed Riz through an almost identical tour from when AJ came for the first time as a much younger man. He noticed Riz staring at his walk and held his gaze to make him feel uncomfortable and embarrassed, which worked. He knew too well that people who stare don't like being seen staring. AJ felt a little smug in making him feel that way.

As the double doors opened, he spotted Sarah's face scrunched up against the smell. With another loud whisper, she felt it was her duty to comment, "Smells like shit!"

AJ chuckled at her. The smell was bringing back his own memories, but he interrupted her and asked her to find out a few important details. The Council had asked him to take over, not realising the irony of the request. AJ needed her to ask the all-important questions about the number of staff and running costs. She could comment on the smell later. He still had to think like a CEO, not a twenty-four year old seeking revenge. He had a business to run and despite the temptation, he was not prepared to sign on the dotted line unless the numbers worked.

"Come into my office," Riz said and motioned. "I can give you all the information you need." He was in a good mood. He knew too well that this deal was going to be very important for them.

It hadn't gone unnoticed by AJ that Riz had no recollection of ever having met him all those years ago and his attitude towards him back then.

As they sat down opposite Riz, he asked if they wanted any refreshments. Sarah answered for them both and was still discreetly holding her nose. AJ had noticed her spray her hand with some perfume from her bag, which thankfully lingered for their remaining time at the centre.

They spoke in detail about finances, the charging structures, and visitor needs. After about twenty minutes, AJ stood and declared his interest, subject to approval from his board of trustees. Despite his history with the place, he knew it made good business sense to take this on. As he stood to leave, he said as much to Riz, who looked even more pleased than when they came in.

"You don't remember me, do you?" he said, unable to hold it in any longer.

Riz was taken aback and looked cautiously at AJ. He didn't want to offend the man who would be helping them. He shook his head. "No, apologies. Have we met before? I know you from the paper but I don't recall meeting you in person."

AJ straightened himself and walked towards the window to make his dramatic revelation. He looked into the car park at the staff who still seemed to be on a very extended cigarette break. He mapped their destiny at that very moment. *They're fucking sacked, for starters.*

"Many years ago, you thought I would benefit from being a service user, that all I would ever be capable of doing was building bird tables and weaving baskets to sell in charity shops." AJ could feel his anger rising. He had stopped himself from saying anything when they first met as his parents had quietened him, but this was his moment.

"You had decided there and then that I was a no-hoper and had little to no chance of leading a successful life."

Riz looked dumbstruck and there was a blush creeping up his cheeks, almost turning his white beard red in embarrassment. His eyes darted between AJ and Sarah, hoping the latter would help, but she kept quiet with a smile plastered across her face.

"He's going to be your boss," she exclaimed as they left his office, leaving Riz looking stunned in their wake.

CHAPTER 34:

INTERVIEW WITH RANI

Sarah had decided to keep quiet on the journey back. AJ was too wrapped up in his own thoughts to engage with her and she needed him to be on top form for their interview later with a new member of staff. He was terrible at the best of times during interviews and after their eventful morning, she needed him to be focused. Sarah advised the staff to leave him be for the day and direct all lines of enquiry to her as AJ holed himself up in his office.

AJ disappeared into his own thoughts, thinking about how ironic his life was turning out to be. Without him realising it, past encounters had shaped his behaviour and his destiny, and seemed to be returning for whatever reason. What was next? He wasn't sure he could take any more surprises.

There was a knock on his door, which broke him out of his reverie. It was Paula, who walked in with her trusty guide dog, Jill.

"Oh hi, Paula, sorry I didn't see you when I got back." He stood as she made her way into his office.

"Something on your mind, AJ?" She asked.

"No. No I'm fine."

"That's bullshit, AJ. I may be blind but I can tell when you're not firing on all cylinders. What's on your mind?" Paula always shot straight from the hip and AJ admired her for it. She was one of the few who knew when he had added a little too much seasoning to his updates for the board of trustees and would happily ask for explanations.

"C'mon, don't beat around the bush."

AJ couldn't help but smile and recognised it was time to submit.

"Oh you know, just questioning whether I'm making a difference. Is this place an illusion or is it actually making people's lives better?" Before he could continue, doubting himself out loud with all his old insecurities at the forefront of his mind, Paula raised her hand. She wasn't having any of it.

"AJ, now is not the time to doubt yourself. Look at how far you have come. Sarah filled me in on your outing this morning. That man who has managed to get under your skin again is from a different era, one where people like you make people like him uncomfortable because you go against whatever medieval views they have on how disabled people should live."

Her words were like a double espresso shot of caffeine, but only enough of a hit for him to sit straight and focus on her words. He knew it would bother him for longer than he was going to admit to anyone. He gave Paula a small smile.

"Those who come through this door for our support only do so because you are sitting where you are. Their parents are looking at you as a beacon of hope — you're a role model for them."

AJ let her continue uninterrupted; his ego was being stroked and he was okay with it too.

"This is just the beginning of your journey. The centre has come under your wing because you can make things happen and make real change that makes a *real* difference. The staff out there are incredibly loyal and would jump in front of a bus for you because you inspire them. When they find out about today's achievement, that loyalty will double. Now I've been informed by Sarah you're needed in the meeting room for an interview. Go on, do your job."

AJ stood to do as he was told. He knew too well that both Sarah and Paula had conspired against him in a pre-meet. Nevertheless, it was the kick up the arse he needed.

"Good man, I'll see you next week," she said, and with that, Paula left his office with her faithful assistant, knowing that her job was done for the day.

AJ met Sarah in the meeting room. He hoped it wouldn't last too long as he was meeting Sonia at lunch and would rather have sat in his office and snuck out without anyone noticing. He found interviewing for new staff incredibly tedious, often zoning out and letting his team do the heavy lifting. But he also knew he had to be here as they were interviewing for an important post that had come up.

The charity had been awarded a contract to support disabled people in the recruitment of care staff within their homes. It was a complete game-changer for the organisation as it officially gave them the right to use the strap line: "A Centre for Independent Living". It was all coming together.

The first candidate arrived — a smartly dressed man in his late twenties carrying a briefcase. Sarah leaned over to AJ at the sight of it and whispered, "I bet it only contains half a sandwich and different coloured pens."

He snorted and as the candidate walked over to sit down, AJ pulled himself together to go over the introductions. The interview lasted twenty minutes with AJ drifting in and out, not really paying much attention to the answers given. At the end, the candidate was asked if he had any questions about the role, and the response made AJ shake his head in disbelief.

"Er, yes. Can you tell me what Direct Payments are?"

AJ and Sarah both looked horrified at the question and locked eyes before responding with a mutual telepathic *"What the fuck?"* passing between them. All three knew that the last twenty minutes had been a waste of time. In total embarrassment, the candidate left in a hurry.

"How did he get through the interview sounding so competent?" They were both amused as they looked through his application. It was now pretty obvious from his answers that he had just copied and pasted the requirements for the role and answered in a way that made him sound competent.

"The next guy better not be a waste of time, I have a meeting to get to." He was anxious to leave and see Sonia. He knew it wasn't a session but he was so used to talking to her about what had been bothering him he needed to vent today.

"Well, for starters, AJ, it's a *she*."

AJ was a little disappointed. He was outnumbered at work and another male colleague would have helped increase the testosterone levels in the building. The women who worked for him revelled, on an almost daily basis, in the fact that the ratio was in their favour.

"Rani Kaur," AJ said out loud as he read her application. He spent a few minutes trying to digest what was written but it felt like there was a darkness creeping into the edges of his vision. He tried to shake it off but to no avail, so he gave up reading what was in front of him and trusted Sarah to take the lead, again.

Rani was a young woman in her late twenties, smartly dressed and luckily not carrying a briefcase. Sarah started the first round of questions. Rani seemed pretty eager from the get-go and went off on a bit of a tirade when Sarah asked her to tell them a bit about herself.

"Well, I'm married, I have two young boys, and I used to work for Punjab TV looking after Bhangra artists." She paused to look at AJ with a nod of acknowledgement. In her research, she had come across his profile and his brief stint as a singer; she hoped the not-so-subtle nod in her answer would make him warm to her. AJ had zoned out the moment she started talking.

The darkness blurring his vision from earlier was still there. He couldn't shake the feeling that an all-consuming panic attack was on the verge of making an appearance. He could feel his hand tightening and his body was wracked with tension. He was in and out of hearing what was going on around him as he tried to ignore the feeling of impending doom. He suspected that recent events were causing him to relapse, though he would probably get a better psychological explanation from Sonia.

Fifteen minutes had passed with little or no interaction from AJ, who just gave the odd approving nod at Rani's answers.

Sarah occasionally glanced across and could tell he was agitated. She finally felt the need to speed up the candidate's textbook recital of Direct Payments.

"Gosh, you have certainly done your homework, Rani." Sarah almost gave the impression that the job was about to be offered on a plate but AJ mustered enough composure to bring the interview to an end.

"Thanks ever so much Rani for an enjoyable interview. We're hoping to make a decision by the end of the day and will get back to you by the weekend."

Rani was happy it was over but equally confused about how it came to a swift end. She grabbed her belongings and walked out of the room with a strange look at AJ. He had been quiet the whole time until that moment.

AJ stood up, pretty eager to get out of the room too. He needed some fresh air and to get out of there as fast as possible.

"Give her the job. She's good. Trust me. I can tell she is the perfect fit. The other one was an embarrassment."

"But you never even..." Sarah interjected with a sigh. She realised the question was rhetorical.

"Yes, okay. I'll call her tomorrow."

"Good I'll leave it in your capable hands. Please cancel my meetings this afternoon. I'm going home. I have a headache," he said and without looking at her, he left the room as fast as he could.

CHAPTER 35:

SYNTAX ERROR

AJ decided against going straight home, as he knew he would just end up in a pool of self-pity and he was doing his best to ignore the symptoms of the impending panic attack for as long as possible. He popped into his favourite café and ordered himself a decaf green tea; he needed to sit and people-watch to clear his mind a little before heading home. He was still looking after his health but not in the manic way he did after his TIA. With his heightened sense of anxiety looming, caffeine didn't seem like such a good idea right now.

He noticed that a couple of Asian men sitting at a table were fixated on his walk. He paid them no heed as he didn't have the mental capacity to challenge anyone at that moment. He sat down facing them and even with his poor lip-reading skills, he deduced that the older of the two gentlemen was submissive to the younger. They glanced at him and he sensed that they were talking about him, which only added to his heightened sense of anxiety.

After a few minutes, he noticed them getting up to leave and felt a sense of relief. He could relax and lose himself in his thoughts of despair before Sonia arrived. He was taken aback when the younger one returned and asked to sit with him.

"Mr Rai?" he said.

"Er, yes hello? Have we met, I can't quite place you?" He had expected the man to have a strong South Asian accent, which wasn't the case at all.

The other gentleman laughed. "No, apologies. I recognised you from the paper and wanted to introduce myself, I'm Yusef Amin. May I join you?"

AJ indicated that he could. He still had his guard up but didn't want to appear rude. Being recognised by this man had massaged his bruised ego and this chance meeting might be just the distraction he needed.

"Yes, of course. I've got someone joining me in a short while so you'll have to excuse me then but, yes, please sit for now."

Yusef made himself comfortable before introducing himself again.

"I'm Yusef Amin, a student of Islam, I'm hoping to become an Imam one day. Insha'Allah," he said looking up.

"Nice to meet you Yusef. How can I be of assistance?'

"I'm a bit of a fan of yours. Such a remarkable rise to get to your position. I always wanted to be my own boss, a CEO, but a greater purpose called."

AJ glanced up and saw Yusef staring at him with a beaming smile. AJ felt a little unnerved but kept his cool and decided to break the growing awkwardness by taking control of the conversation.

"I hope I don't come across as nosey but the conversation you were having with the elderly chap earlier...I sensed I was the subject of that conversation." AJ remained calm in his demeanour.

"Yes," Yusef told him, "I was watching him as you walked to your table. He seemed to focus strongly and in my opinion, unnecessarily on your walk."

AJ felt relieved that he had not imagined it regardless of how insignificant it was. Yusef continued, "Maybe it was wrong of me to ask him his reason for doing so, as I do feel a little bad about confronting him." He shrugged his shoulders as if to indicate that he did what he felt was right.

AJ was a little taken aback that a stranger would confront someone on his behalf. It was quite touching yet very rare.

"Don't worry," AJ said, "I'm used to it. It really doesn't bother me anymore. The Asian community will always be quite fixated with disability, viewing it as a source of shame or feeling that if they get too near, it could be contagious. It's more of an issue with the older generation."

"I only asked him why he felt it so important to stare at you. I said that perhaps, if he was intrigued by your walk, he should ask you. It's rude. You have shown his generation that disability can be overcome. That society needs to change. You aren't the problem. You see, I have a disabled younger sister. She needs to know that people like you, people like her, are able to not only live in society but in fact to lead it. So, in all honesty, my discussion with him was also for my sister." Yusef looked directly at AJ as if to apologise.

Yusef's outpouring of support and the motive behind it took AJ by surprise. It was music to his ears that a member of the public was quoting the Social Model of Disability, a definition that was his mantra in all of his speeches, particularly those about the barriers faced by disabled people in society. Yusef had pleased him no end.

"Mr Amin, with such an outlook on disability, you will make a great Imam. Our communities need dragging out of the dark ages! In fact, I hope you don't mind if I share a little personal story with you?" He felt a connection with Yusef. Ordinarily, he wasn't one to trust others and certainly not a random person in a coffee shop, but Yusef had an aura about him that invited confidence.

Yusef nodded his head — he looked honoured that AJ was sharing with him.

"I don't know if you're a follower of the beautiful game: football?" Yusef nodded his response, not sure where AJ was going with this.

"I don't know if you remember a few years ago, there was an incident with the England Manager having to resign?" AJ wasn't a big football fan either, being honest, but the particular incident he was describing was a little too close to home for him, so it had always stuck in his mind. "Well, the manager at the time had made certain comments, implying that disabled people were being punished for deeds from a previous life."

Yusef's face indicated that he also remembered the incident in question. After all, it was big news at the time.

"Yes, I do recall. Obviously as a Muslim, I don't entertain the notion of reincarnation as a principle, but I remember thinking that his view was outdated and will upset many people." Yusef was very diplomatic with his response to a subject outside his own beliefs.

"Yes. Well I was sitting in a room with around seven or eight elderly women when the story came out. One of them had clearly heard the news the night before with her children and as she began to share her anecdote and thoughts with the rest of the group, she admitted to agreeing with him. The other ladies nodded along with her, each reciting their own version of karma and how it follows you into every life, with disability being the proof that you did it wrong last time round."

AJ could feel his voice rising and that he was showing a little too much passion in front of Yusef, who held a much calmer disposition.

"That's what I've had to struggle with my whole life. It's bad enough trying to cope with day-to-day struggles. The very people who are meant to collectively lift the next generation to greater heights still single out those of us with disabilities. In a nutshell, they're saying, 'It's your own doing and you should have behaved better 150 years ago if you didn't want to suffer.' How can you educate people who had such a backwards view injected into their DNA?"

AJ was breathing hard. Trying to calm down hadn't worked and he was unknowingly getting himself wound up. The morning with Riz was still at the forefront of his mind and Riz was one of those people with a backward view.

Yusef nodded in agreement and was enjoying the stimulating conversation. He had seen AJ in the papers and once on TV and had always hoped to meet him in person. When he finally met him, the chat was one of hope. He listened attentively to

AJ's every word, yet was equally anxious to go home and tell his sister about his encounter.

"And another thing…!" AJ was on a roll and he felt good having an audience.

Yusef, however, interrupted him before he got back into the flow of things. AJ was slightly abashed, realising he'd taken up too much of this stranger's time.

"Mr Rai, you think I am the kind of person to work with the next generation. I say that you are of equal importance. Disabled people being visible in everyday life and doing things that support the wider community is the way we are going to make the change you so desire. I can spread the word from my end but shining examples like you are what is needed."

He continued, "You mustn't wrap yourself up in the stigma created by fading generations. Over time, their views will disappear with them. In their day, back in the motherland, people like you and my sister were either sitting in the corner away from the family or begging in the streets. It's not really their fault. When a person from their era looks at you, they're not staring at you. Look closely. Within their brains, if they were computers, you would read: *SYNTAX ERROR*. They simply don't know how to process what they see when people like you are high-flying in mainstream society."

"You are something special," AJ said, "I'd like to stay in contact — let's exchange numbers." In usual AJ-style, he made it sound more like an order than a request. Yusef obliged and got up to leave with a shake of the hand and a promise to keep in touch.

As he said his goodbyes and made his way back to his car, he felt his phone buzzing. Wondering if it was Yusef already wanting to engage further, he noticed that it was Sonia.

"Oh fuck." He remembered that the reason he had gone to the café in the first place was to meet her. He hadn't meant to stand her up and really did want to clear the elephant in the room, but decided that could wait until he saw her next time. He let it go to voicemail. *I'm sure she'll be fine.*

CHAPTER 36:

HIS NEMESIS

AJ's meeting with Yusef had left him feeling energised. He was known in the area for driving around blasting his music and singing along at insanely high volumes, but he didn't touch the radio on his drive to his parents. His mind replayed the interaction in the coffee shop.

As he pulled up to a set of traffic lights not far from where his parents lived, he watched as two young adolescents enjoyed a water-balloon fight. They were both running on and off the pavement into the road directly in front of AJ, oblivious to the traffic. They were happy, having fun, and it reminded him of a younger AJ and Jags getting up to all sorts.

One water balloon landed and splashed across his windscreen, rolling onto the floor. It wasn't enough to put a halt to any laughter, which seemed to go up an octave, but it was enough for him to start disembarking from his car to have words. Before he could exit the car, the traffic behind began intermittently honking as the lights had turned green.

"Little shits, good job too, otherwise you'd have got an earful." With that, AJ closed his half-opened door and set off, giving them a deathly stare as he drove past. They paid little to no attention to him as they carried on.

He pulled up to his parents' drive a few minutes later. He had taken out a second mortgage to move them closer to him a few years earlier and always made a visit at the end of each work day before disappearing to his own house.

Oh, how the tables have turned. He smiled as he turned off his engine, remembering when they would periodically turn up to his little ground floor flat many moons ago.

As he made his way towards the front door, he spotted one of his least favourite people sitting on the sofa by the bay window, Kamala Aunty. He was about to turn around and head home when she locked eyes with him and waved.

"Fuck," he muttered. "Can't go back now." He didn't have the energy for her bullshit today. He let himself in slowly and spotted his dad in the hallway pretending to look through his coat, busying himself and most likely delaying the inevitable of going back into the living room. He looked up as AJ made his way inside and gave him a smile as if to say, *"Go, leave, save yourself,"* but they both knew it was too late.

AJ begrudgingly made his way inside as he did want to greet his mum. As he entered, he looked to the left; Aunty had made eye contact and stood up to greet him.

"Amraj, puth, how are you?" She walked over to embrace him as he made his way into the living room. She cupped his face and ran her hands across his hair, leaving biscuit crumbs in their wake.

AJ knew it was false. He was just another piece of gossip for her to take back to her tribe. Every second he'd ever spent in her company was an opportunity to judge him for any visible and (more often than not) invisible flaws. He hated her with a vengeance. *Maybe it's my fault because I mentioned her earlier*, he thought. He'd literally just described this woman to Yusef and here she was sitting at his parents, leisurely sipping tea and gossiping. He still remembered her whisper to his mum, when he was younger and thought he hadn't heard, *"No one will give him their daughter."* When it came to the question of him ever settling down, she always had an opinion under the guise of being friendly.

"Hello Aunty, how are you? How's Uncle?" He had been raised to be polite to his elders, a trait he often hated, especially in situations like this. She would give a stock response before she got into the swing of listing all their combined ailments, or she might need help with some benefit form. He excused himself as politely as possible and headed to the kitchen.

There were pots and pans everywhere and the room was filled with aroma. He looked in each one, still hot, to see what his mum had been experimenting with. He grabbed a fork and tried what looked like a strange version of Fusilli pasta.

"Good God, she's made curried pasta," he exclaimed, trying to muffle his disappointment. He often had a running disagreement with his mother that it wasn't necessary to add onion, ginger, turmeric, and chillies to every celebrated food from other parts of the world. She never listened, arguing that she could make any food from anywhere in the world taste heavenly by adding those simple ingredients.

He stayed in the kitchen for a good fifteen minutes, steeling himself to head back in the living room. When he did, he walked smack into the middle of Kamala Aunty's news bulletin for that week.

"Oh yes, he's very successful! He's an accountant and singer you know." She looked at AJ from the corner of her eye, with a sickening grin on her face as if she had waited for him to come back in before bragging about some relative of hers.

"Who's an accountant, Aunty?" he asked, scolding himself for letting curiosity take over.

"Oh my nephew, he's very big in the Bhangra industry," she continued with a proud look on her face.

AJ needed a moment to work out which nephew. He could feel a laugh erupting from him, one he had had no control over when he realised who she meant. His mother was giving him a death stare as she knew her son well enough to recognise an impending sarcastic comment and cautioned him against it with her expression. AJ ignored her.

"You mean Harry?"

Kamala Aunty must have sensed she was about to be shot down as she started to speak very fast, "Yes, he's a good boy and has a fantastic voice."

"He's not an accountant you know. He works as an admin assistant *in* an accountancy firm. Did he tell you he was an accountant?" He laughed. AJ knew Harry and that he wouldn't exaggerate what he did for a living. This was clearly a case of Kamala wanting to brag without knowing the facts. This was often the way with her generation, making their sons and daughters sound more important than they were. Her face dropped, though she recovered quickly as she wasn't going to allow him the satisfaction of getting to her. AJ sat back feeling rather smug.

"He has a record on sale you know." She was trying to recover from her embarrassment." The smile returned to her face. "And a new video."

AJ stopped smiling. He had no comeback for that. It was always a huge regret of his that he had no video doing the rounds on Asian music channels from his own musical adventures. They were just memories he and those who saw him live had.

He had moved on — he was a successful charitable entrepreneur and couldn't do both. It was still an unfulfilled wish, deep down, that he often didn't think about. He had made his choices and whilst he didn't regret his life path, the smug look on Kamala's face brought it all home to him. Before he could respond, he heard his mum speak up.

"Amraj is a very good son. He bought his dad this new house. He's always in the newspaper and news on TV. He comes here every day after work. We are very proud. No need to sing anymore. Done it. He is the manager now." She had never quite got the hang of telling others that he was in fact a CEO, simply because she couldn't pronounce it. The word 'manager' was one that all her generation knew, and it was simply the highest position in any company.

AJ felt a hot flush. His mum very rarely spoke up on behalf of her kids in front of them, especially when confronting one of her friends. AJ felt a sense of warmth spread through him at her interjection.

Kamala Aunty's face betrayed her shock. There was an awkwardness that lingered in the air. His dad had also wandered back into the living room, and Kamala Aunty felt that was her cue to leave. As she gathered her things to leave, she clearly felt the need to have the last word.

"It's not in your kismet to be a singer. You be a manager, good good." Kamala muttered, as she started to collect her belongings to leave. The awkwardness could be felt in the air. "Chal, I need to get going, bye."

AJ looked across to his parents after her departure. His dad was just as shocked as his son at the exchange.

"Ignore her! She's just a gossip who has nothing else to do but upset people wherever she goes." His dad had a point and though AJ knew his dad was trying to make him feel better, he was angry and rattled by her insensitivity.

"It's okay, dad. I'm fine." AJ didn't want to upset his dad further. His dad had recently been diagnosed with Parkinson's disease and he didn't want to create any further anxiety for him. He decided that no matter what was going on in his own life, his parents would only know about the positive things.

For the next twenty minutes, they talked, caught up as if the exchange had never happened, and fell into comfortable subjects. The rest of the family, his siblings, forthcoming weddings, birthdays, and of course the price of vegetables. AJ was doing his best to keep up appearances until he left, but a feeling of inadequacy was creeping in due to Kamala Aunty.

"Mum, dad, I've got to get going, see you tomorrow," he said eventually.

"Take some pasta," his mum said as he made his way out. They both knew he wouldn't as he only ever took home daal, but he grunted his confirmation as he left. His dad caught up with him at the front door and with a reassuring tap on the shoulder, he temporarily defused AJ's inner developing rage.

"Ignore her, you're a good son and a good singer."

CHAPTER 37:

SING FOR YOUR COFFEE

AJ smiled as he sat in his car; he hadn't driven off straightaway. He was deep in thought watching a young man across the road trying to fix something under the bonnet of his hatchback. He heard him singing along to a song that was playing, without a care in the world that the whole street could hear him. It was a modern tune he couldn't quite place. It had been fifteen years since he had turned his back on a life he could have had in the music industry.

Up until an hour earlier, he had been happily disconnected from his past musical exploits, but he could literally hear his stomach churning and felt like someone had it in an iron grip.

AJ switched on the engine and looked at the multimedia player in his car for a good few seconds. He decided to tune in to the BBC Asian Network. Driving home, he started to sing along softly to a song he recognised. An old Bollywood classic by his idol, the late Mohammed Rafi. Within a minute he began to sing louder, building up to a crescendo with twists and curves, spitting notes, stretching his vocal chords up and down the scales in a manner that he knew too well only a handful of singers could execute. His frustration and anger was still bubbling inside but in that moment, there was only one thought in his mind. He calmly pulled out his phone, dialling a number he hadn't rung for many years, slightly apprehensive that the person on the other end wouldn't answer.

"Sanj, how's it going?" he said, quite relieved the call had connected.

"AJ, my man! Long time no speak, how the devil are you?" Sanj was a music producer he knew from days gone by.

"Good, good, look I've been thinking and I might want to get back in the studio and you're the man to produce my track. Remember *Akh Largayee*, let's get it done."

They chatted for a few more minutes, with Sanj very excited at the prospect of working with AJ again. They reminisced about some of their adventures and arranged the recording session for the next day.

*

Arriving at the pre-set rendezvous, AJ was excited and gleeful for the first time in a long time. He had spent three days in the studio recording one of his favourite tracks and had required little rehearsal due to his daily singing routine while getting ready for work. He had kept his vocals in check, even when his musical aspirations had been buried. Not that he had ever admitted it to Sonia, but after her suggestion that singing was good for healing, he had continued to do so and it had helped the way she intended it to. Singing was his first love, something he had sacrificed to blend in with a society only interested in those with a job and a mortgage.

Belting out the song in the studio and working with Sanj again had been a major success and a complete rush. He wasn't sure how far he wanted it to go. For now, his goal was to destroy the arrogance of the likes of Kamala Aunty. His only focus was to play a well-produced song in front of her to put a stop to her bragging about her own useless kids.

He sipped his espresso and glanced up to see Sonia entering the shop and looking for him. He had rung her to ask if she was free for a chat, as he wanted to share details of his song with her. He couldn't read her full expression but she didn't look overly pleased when she spotted him and walked over. "Hi, I got you a tea."

Sonia sat down. She didn't acknowledge the drink and seemed a little frosty towards him. He shrugged it off assuming she'd had a bad day. "I've got some news..."

"AJ." Sonia's voice was cold and harsh, he'd never heard her speak in that tone before. She was sitting upright and rigid in the chair opposite him. It took some of the wind out of him and his exciting news.

"AJ, you asked me for a coffee and didn't show up. I had been hoping we could talk and speak about the elephant in the room. The last session you had with me all those years ago broke me." Her eyes looked unfocused as she reminded him of how he had behaved towards her when she confided in him about how her husband had taken his life. He still had trouble admitting how much he wished he could undo his behaviour at the time.

"This was your idea AJ, not mine. To end our sessions and the doctor/patient relationship we had. I blame myself because it was against my better judgement. I shouldn't have agreed to meet you but part of me thought by doing so I could still help you."

"I have been haunted for years by my own breakdown in front of you. I should never have allowed your case to affect me specifically, but the similarities to my husband in the traits you were displaying broke me. It was uncalled for and unprofessional. The reason I agreed to coffee was that I still wanted to help but didn't think I could with you as my patient. Being friends sounded like a good plan, AJ. But you are rude and disrespectful. Have you once asked me how I am whenever you've arranged for us to meet? Last week, you abruptly left and now you go straight into talking about your life."

AJ sat and listened, not allowing his face to betray his feelings of guilt. He had hoped by not talking about what happened just before she gave him antidepressants that they could move on and it would be fine. Clearly not. He was sipping away at his espresso whilst she spoke and, in true AJ style, couldn't make eye contact with her. He therefore decided to multitask by listening and watching two pigeons eat the remains of a half-eaten donut near a bin outside the window.

Sonia was still speaking, "This is only going to work if I ask about you and you ask about me. There's no financial transaction so it's no longer a one-sided listening exercise. It's a conversation between two adults who have been through a lot of trauma. You have other friends, is this how you are with them? What about Jags?" There was a long pause, which made AJ look at her. "Have you heard a word I've said?"

"Yes, yes. I heard you. Definitely, every word. Look, in all honesty, since I last left you, this is what I'm like, with everyone. I mean everyone, ask my friends, family, and especially colleagues." Sonia wasn't overly impressed. She had poured her heart out to someone who was not very good at the rudimentary task of listening.

"Look, Sonia, I am sorry. I tend to get wrapped up in my own thoughts, as per usual. You're not the first to comment on me being a little self-obsessed. I'll work on it. I do want to do right by you. That's why I asked you for coffee. Away from the performance of therapy, I just wanted to talk to you and get to know you better as a friend. I do have a tendency to just start conversations as if we're just picking up where we last left off."

She still gave him her hard stare before softening and looking at the tea in front of her, then she picked it up and said, "Well at least you remembered what I like to drink, so that's a start."

CHAPTER 38:

HE'S SICK

When making his way back to the car, AJ felt something in his pocket. It was the CD recording of his song that he'd intended to give her, but it felt inappropriate and meaningless after such a dressing down. They had talked for a good hour, or at least Sonia did as he couldn't quite bring himself to discuss the topic of music.

She had admitted to a new love interest in her life, Khalid, and from the sounds of it, all was going well. They were talking of marriage, and it would mean that she would be moving to London and whatever new-found friendship they had discovered was going to be short-lived. He wasn't the best at keeping in touch with those nearest to him, let alone further afield.

She seemed happy and he was glad for her. From what she had told him, her two boys were now teenagers; her eldest had anger issues mainly directed at his mother. She had a sneaky suspicion that her mother-in-law had been influencing her eldest son with her views on why their father committed suicide and had a tendency to blame her for not supporting him the way a wife was supposed to.

He looked at the CD on which he had scribbled the words *'Told you I could sing!'* and tossed it onto the passenger seat. It no longer mattered. She had suggested meeting again, but he knew he would make an excuse to get out of it and was already aware that this was the last time he would be seeing her.

Depressing the ignition in his car, he decided the journey home would be without music. Driving for ten or so minutes, he hadn't noticed the light patter of rain across the windshield. The wipers were activated automatically, leaving him to drive uninterrupted with brief mental visits to a world where he was married to the love of his life. Sonia's announcement had triggered his own thoughts about the woman who had luckily escaped a life of pain with him. *I hope she's happy. I'm sure she's happy.*

AJ knew too well, every visit to his dreamworld would leave him feeling worse but he also found the pain addictive, almost symbiotic, but now so familiar he felt comfortable with it. He knew it would pass, every time he heard of a new relationship, engagement, or marriage, which as he was a Punjabi happened almost monthly. There was that niggle in the back of his mind, *"Why not me?"* A question which his subconscious would answer ruthlessly, *"Because no one will want to give me their daughter."*

By the time he had arrived home, he was quite aware that he could not recall any aspect of the journey and instantly became concerned at his lack of attention to the road. Wallowing in his stupidity, he saw his phone vibrating on the centre console. It was Sanj.

"AJ, dude, I've been calling all morning, where the hell have you been? I can't bloody contain myself and you're never going to believe what's happened!" He was clearly excited, as his voice was reverberating inside AJ's car.

"Hey Sanj, now isn't a good time." AJ just wanted to get inside and crack on with work and have a brandy to distract himself.

Sanj either hadn't heard him or chose to ignore him. "Listen, mate. I've got some news that's going to blow your socks off."

AJ stayed quiet. He showed no enthusiasm as he didn't have it in him after his morning with Sonia; he began watching one of his elderly neighbours struggling with some overflowing bins. His silence prompted Sanj to ask, "Dude, are you there?"

"Yeah, Yeah, I'm here. Go on, it must be important if you've been ringing all morning. What's up mate?"

"Well, don't get mad but after our session, I sent your song to Hitesh at HIP Records." He was clearly pausing for dramatic effect, but AJ sat up a little straighter, Sanj had certainly got his attention now. "Mate, he loves it! He fucking loves it. In fact he wants it on a compilation album he's working on ... and guess what? As the title track! He says if you're happy with him, he wants you to back it up with a video. We're shooting next weekend." Sanj's excitement was palpable.

The news was a little overwhelming. He had recorded the song for himself, for his own collection and not for public consumption. He had made a few copies of CDs from Sanj to be given to family and friends but that was it. No plans for release. After his morning with Sonia, feeling deflated that he was achieving so much yet still alone in life, this news didn't really sink in. The whole song was for the benefit of the naysayers and to prove that he still had it in him. Clearly he did but maybe now it had been a mistake to get back in the studio.

"Sanj, I'll call you back, an album, a video. I need some time to process this." AJ was just about to hang up when Sanj again interjected.

"Sure mate, I'm in the studio until after five; any time after that let me know. Also Hitesh might be calling you to discuss finances for the track." With that, he left AJ knowing that he'd saved the last exciting piece of news until the end of their conversation.

He only had an hour to contemplate what was happening when his phone rang and it was the owner of HIP Records, Hitesh Kumar. He was of Indian origin and spoke with a strong Scottish accent, which threw AJ a little and he tried to hide his confusion when they spoke.

"AJ, what can I say? That track is sick, I'm telling you it's sick."

In an already confused state of mind, AJ honed in on the use of the term *sick*, which he assumed was a good thing. "Yeah, er, sick, definitely sick." He sounded like an old man saying it out loud and it must have sounded that way as Hitesh paused before he continued.

"Yeah well, it's a great track AJ and I want to put it on a compilation album I'm working on, with a lot of fresh new talent. It's that good! I want it as the header, the lead track," he clarified. AJ could sense he was toning his music-producer's voice down so AJ could readily understand him.

"Oh, OK, sounds good but..."

"No buts AJ, you have a great voice, let's get it out there for people to hear and make you famous hey, what d'ya think?"

AJ was intentionally looking at the mirror in his bedroom whilst in conversation with Hitesh; he noted his own facial expression, which resembled a child being given a box of sweets. He needed to take control of the conversation, which

208

was about to enter a delicate phase and thus he composed himself.

"Yes, sounds good, I'm glad you like it and think it's *sick*. What are your terms and conditions of release? Are you signing me for more or just interested in the one track?" His tone of voice shifted to AJ the CEO, no-nonsense straight-to-business, firm but monotone. He didn't want the excited child he could see in the mirror reflected in his voice.

"Whatever suits you. You got any more like this? If so, I'll take them; if not, I'll have this one and we'll work on more tracks after this release. It's up to you." Hitesh wasn't beating about the bush and AJ sensed a tonal shift and respect for AJ's abruptness. "I'll give you a grand for the track as it is. I'll have sole rights over it after that. I'll get it re-mastered to match the EQ of the rest of the album."

AJ was stunned — he was getting paid to have his song on an album! When he was younger and in the band, he would have killed for this opportunity. Here he was on the phone to a man who wanted to pay him for a song he had just recorded for himself; he had never envisaged it receiving this sort of attention.

"Yes, that's fine. I suppose you have a contract. Email it over to me and I'll take a look at the T's & C's and we'll make it official." He was wondering if he should have negotiated more but was noticeably looking forward to celebrating; he could feel himself smiling broadly.

They finalised the details and arranged a time for the official video shoot the following weekend. Minutes later, AJ was inserting the CD that was originally planned for Sonia into his home music system. For an hour, he danced around his living room to the track on a loop, singing along to the tune that was going to mark his re-entrance into an industry he had long forgotten.

After exhausting himself, he sank into his sofa with a brandy in hand and looked directly at a photograph of himself from his earlier days on stage featuring long mullet hair and a beige double-breasted suit. He took a sip and sighed.

"I'm back."

CHAPTER 39:

THE RAW TRUTH

After a whole day shooting for a two-minute music video, AJ had enough excitement left within him to formally announce his return to the music scene to his family. Having asked his siblings to meet at their parents' house that evening, he walked into the house with sweets and chocolates and a huge bottle of champagne. He could hear commotion in the lounge as he walked in — it sounded like more than just his immediate family. He smiled, *The more the merrier, the bigger the announcement.*

As he quietly walked through the door, he was mentally going over how he would break the news to his father. Rai Snr, like his grandfather, had never entirely been comfortable with his interest in music, let alone taking it on as a career. He was incredibly proud when AJ had become CEO. He was proud he had a job enabling him to hold his head high within a community which wanted to pigeon-hole his son. He was even more proud knowing his son's role was servicing and helping others less fortunate. Yet, there had always been an underlying fear that AJ would catch the music bug again and leave all that he had built up for an uncertain life on the road. He just had to reassure his dad that his job was paramount. He knew what to say — that singing was just a hobby and a little stress release, nothing else.

Unfortunately, no such conversation was to take place. AJ had walked into devastating news. Both siblings looked directly at him and rushed him straight back out of the room. AJ caught a glimpse of his father who was in tears. His sister explained that a couple of hours earlier, the family had received a call from India. Rai Senior's elder brother had died suddenly of a heart attack.

AJ had been to India with his parents on a number of occasions over the last decade and had enjoyed his uncle's company whenever he visited. He had the exact same strong but silent characteristics of his father and they bonded instantly. His uncle would often sit next to him with a bottle of whiskey and recite stories about their ancestors and his childhood for hours. It was through him that AJ learned of a theory about his ancestry; his family were direct descendants of a 17th Century Maharaja of Himachal Pradesh. It was only years later that AJ researched his own family tree to confirm the theory.

AJ stood in the hallway and discarded his champagne bottle and sweets on a side table. *Dad needs me.* He took a deep breath and re-entered the room, making a beeline for his father who was so distressed he couldn't acknowledge him. Instead, AJ decided to sit down and pay his respects appropriately. Looking around the room, he noted that all Rai Senior's other siblings and their respective partners were present, all equally distressed by the news. The deceased brother was the eldest and only sixty-four years old; he hadn't made the original journey to the UK decades earlier at the order of AJ's grandfather, who insisted that someone needed to stay behind to look after the land.

The room was silent for a few minutes but for the sound of tears and sniffles. The youngest of the brothers decided that they should all catch the first flight to the Punjab in time for the funeral. AJ had decided there and then he would be joining them.

Their tickets and visas were arranged within two days. It was the first time AJ had been pumped and full of adrenaline that had little to do with work. He knew too well the experience ahead would be incredibly heart-breaking, yet nothing could prepare him for what the next three days would bring.

*

After a 13-hour journey, they arrived at their home to crowds of people inside wailing in pain and disbelief over the grief of his uncle. His fathers and siblings, already jetlagged and in desperate need of a shower and some food, were plunged into the heart of the hysteria. AJ felt emotionless; he had been experiencing a frenzy of internal emotions since the news was broken to him but was yet to shed a single tear. He had as per normal internalised his pain and grief and he knew he would pay for it later.

The extended family had made allowances: it was customary to arrange funerals on the day of the death or within a couple of days, but they had waited for their British relatives to arrive. The funeral was arranged for the next day.

AJ's father, cousins, and uncle were to carry out the rituals, starting with preparing and washing the body, a ritual thousands of years old. They were to lay the body out for the five hundred or so mourners to pay their last respects and view his uncle before the cremation. AJ managed to find his way to the front of the funeral procession and past the crowd to join his immediate family. They were taking his uncle's body through to a designated area on the outskirts of their ancestral home to be cremated in full view of only the male mourners.

His eldest male cousin performed the final duties of preparing wood for the fire. The priest said a prayer, lumps of butter were smeared around the mouth of the deceased, and the pyre was lit. There was not a sound to be heard as everyone fell silent. This was not a welcome development at all for AJ. Back in the UK, AJ had attended countless cremation-based funerals but was now reminded that curtains were usually drawn around the coffin to protect all from what he was about to experience.

"Shit, I'm not prepared for this," AJ muttered to himself, feeling a slight panic settling over him.

He decided he needed to move out of sight but needed to signal his father who was standing close to the pyre. He couldn't move without his father's consent as it would seem disrespectful to his cousins. As he was about to shuffle away, hopefully unnoticed, an elderly man sensing his intention grabbed hold of his wrist firmly and gave him a stern look full of disapproval. The man holding him was his grandfather's sole surviving younger brother. That was it — he was now locked into position and any move would be disastrous on his part.

AJ looked down at the floor and then straight at the slowly developing fire ahead of him. His uncle's body was totally covered in logs, branches, and twigs. So far, all that was visible was a small fire at one end and smoke, lots of smoke. AJ's heart began to race a little. It was still silent. Everyone knew what was going on except the anxious foreigner.

AJ was flying back two days later and started to think about everything except what was going on in front of him, hoping it would help. To his relief, after ten agonising minutes, everyone started walking away. AJ followed and almost immediately felt back in control of himself. For an hour, he sat at the temple where passages from the holy book were recited and the family were consoled by all who had attended the procession. AJ was well-known by literally every person who had attended and started to feel overwhelmed by having to repeat his level of grief to relative after extended relative. It was all becoming too much for him again when his cousin suggested he accompany him to carry out an important task. AJ couldn't leave the temple fast enough.

They walked for a few minutes when AJ realised they were heading back to the funeral pyre. AJ wished he had stayed at the temple. They conversed in Punjabi on their way.

"Where are we going?" His legs were starting to feel heavy and he could feel his heart racing, hoping he was mistaken on their final destination.

"We agreed to take shifts to go back and add more wood to keep the fire burning," his cousin, many years younger than AJ, replied; his tone was very matter of fact and showed no emotion.

AJ was desperately trying to think of a reason to avoid this. He needed to find an excuse but then noted a small tear rolling down his cousin's face. He hadn't really played a part in the rituals so far and his cousin needed him; he'd just lost his father and AJ couldn't back out now. As they reached the funeral pyre, AJ noticed his uncle's clothes had been left in front of the entrance.

"Why are Thaiya Ji's clothes there?"

"The poorer villagers from the surrounding area will make use of them." His cousin was now visibly crying.

The pace of change for the grieving family was too much for AJ. This was another example of how things were done with a little more respect back in the UK. Having previously been to the subcontinent a number of times, he had learnt quite fast not to question tradition. What seemed absurd to him was the norm in India. Being overly inquisitive often led to showing disrespect. AJ was however more concerned about how he could console his cousin. This situation was totally alien and he could not think straight enough to be of any help apart from doing as he was asked.

They turned the corner past the bundle of clothes and went straight to the burning remains. AJ coughed and gasped for air. The smell was completely unfamiliar but soon became of secondary concern as his eyes locked onto what was left of his uncle. He could not help but stare at the flames, not noticing his cousin crouching on the floor crying uncontrollably.

"Brother. Look what they've done to Papa Ji. Look what they've done."

He looked across, searching his vocabulary for some words of comfort and couldn't for the life of him think of anything to say. He had nothing to offer and felt useless. The only thing to do was to go over and hug the younger man. With an embrace, he felt he was of some use. His own eyes began to fill too. Emotions were about to be released with some relief as he feared he didn't fit into the traditional way of handling death. AJ was ready to let it out when he saw an image that would haunt him forever.

Whilst the cousin was crying on his shoulder, AJ had a full view of the fire. Amidst the flames, a gap appeared. For a second, he thought additional wood needed to be added around that particular area but as he looked closer, he saw his uncle's shoulder and the top of his rib-cage being burnt right there in front of him. Despite the intense heat, AJ felt cold. His eyes had dried. His body had almost locked into an ice-cold position. He couldn't help but mutter out loud knowing his cousin wasn't going to understand a word of English. "This place is raw. Too fucking raw."

Fortunately, two elders had also made their way and attended to the pyre. The cousin who by now had taken control of his emotions had to pull a shocked AJ away from a scene he did not want to visit again. He went back to the house and decided to lock himself away from everyone, finding an empty room in one of his late grandfather's many properties. There was commotion everywhere outside but this room was, in some strange way, comforting. It was where his father slept as a child.

Two hours later, he emerged to a family who understandably hadn't missed him in the slightest. His father wanted to head to the villa he had built a few years earlier, hoping to hand it down to his own children one day. It had all the comforts of a western house and was within easy reach of shops and takeaways. Whilst feeling a little guilty at leaving the wake, AJ couldn't get into the car fast enough. On the way back, his younger uncle recited a similar experience quietly in his ear, having gone back to witness his brother's burning remains.

CHAPTER 40:

A PERIOD OF REFLECTION

The next day, AJ packed his few belongings earlier than necessary. He was keen to fly back and began to check his watch intermittently. He was still emotionally very numb. His father had learnt of his grim experience and decided another visit to the village was necessary. Not able to refuse, he agreed to go as long as he could spend the day at the family farmhouse away from everyone.

The farmhouse was actually a row of houses built by his grandfather on a plot of land which included a watering well, a lock-up for the tractor and several troughs for at least eight water buffalo. On arrival, AJ found his great uncle, who yesterday had insisted he take the front row at the cremation, taking a siesta on a *Manja* next to the livestock. The scene was almost picturesque and inviting for AJ, who was desperate to return to the UK with another memory to counteract his experience the day before.

"Come, sit here next to me." The old man was always pleased to see his brother's grandson. However, despite his beaming, welcoming smile, his eyes were fixed on one of the buffalo only a few feet away.

"She gave birth yesterday to a male calf." His voice could not hide his disappointment.

"Isn't that a good thing?" AJ looked to his far left and noted a frail but beautiful little beast. Confused, he felt the need to ask why his elder was not so impressed.

"What good is a male to me? The females produce milk. I can sell milk. That thing is just a burden on me." His tone now appeared to venture into anger.

AJ shook his head and tried his best to hide his disbelief. In English, knowing he could air his frustrations, he said, "This country! Desperate for women to have sons and cows to have daughters! God help them."

Having made up his mind to move the conversation on, the respected elder called out to whoever was in the kitchen for a round of tea for AJ and himself. Minutes later, one of AJ's many sisters-in-laws came out with tea, biscuits, and pakoras which were obviously left over from the day before.

The two sat and discussed many topics. and despite AJ's utmost efforts to avoid any conversation about the cremation, the old man recalled every step of the ritual at the expense of AJ's fears. Images of burning flesh kept appearing in his mind. AJ was sure he could even smell a hint of smoke. It was out of his control. Great Uncle Rai was in full flow for what seemed eons but then stopped mid-sentence, distracted by the buffalo.

Relieved by whatever had ended the conversation, AJ began to slurp at his tea, savouring the taste of cardamom and fennel. Great Uncle Rai, however, despite being over eighty years old, galloped over to the row of dairy producers to clean up after the one who had given birth. She had delivered what looked like a placenta accompanied by more blood than AJ wanted to see.

He was advised by a voice behind him to move out of the way, one of the millions of Rai nephews who was approximately ten years old.

"I'm telling you, move out of the way. You're in the line of fire of that cow's tail." The child displayed a cheeky grin as AJ turned around again.

He turned towards the cow which looked like it was still recovering from labour. She rapidly and continually swayed her tail from left to right and reverse.

"I'm a good 40-50 feet away. I'll be fine."

"Don't say I didn't warn you." He pulled up a chair at a safe distance. The British Uncle wasn't going to listen, therefore he might as well grab a pakora and enjoy the show.

AJ continued watching the old man clear what under normal circumstances he would consider a stomach-churning mess. Sipping at his full flavoured tea, watching man and beast on his family farm was a memory he realised there and then needed to be appreciated. He reached for a biscuit, realising he hated Indian biscuits but nevertheless fancied a dunk. The plate was being circled by flies who arrogantly had first dibs on all food across the continent.

"Move out of the way!" The youngster shouted at AJ who was now overly invested in the plate of biscuits and wasn't paying him any attention. AJ looked back towards the very concerned child who turned a look of horror into shock which, after scanning the plate and AJ's face and shirt, soon turned into laughter.

AJ couldn't believe it. Looking down at his once crisp white shirt, now covered in a lumpy red substance, he froze, realising things were about to get worse. His face felt warm. Very warm. Something began to drip and make its way down the centre of his forehead and along the right side of his nose, resting across the whole of his top lip.

The child was no longer laughing and ran inside at lightning speed to return with a towel. His foreigner uncle was still frozen in the same position. The old man by now had left his chores to run to AJ's aide, grabbed the towel, and went straight for the face without any decorum, smudging if not spreading what seemed like a litre of menstruating cow residue.

"I don't believe this. First the mother of all funerals and then this! Fucking animal period on my face."

CHAPTER 41:

BITTER GOURD CURRY

After arriving back in the UK, AJ's first desire was to shut himself away from everyone but he was well aware he had taken time off already and needed to focus on work. Both parents had decided to stay behind in India to support the family in whatever way was necessary. AJ continued his tradition of going to work the very next day after a life-altering event and hoping to defeat any physical drain due to jetlag.

With no desire to explain his sudden need for leave, he headed straight for his office and put up a makeshift sign on his door: 'Do not Disturb'. For at least half an hour, the corridor outside was almost silent. However, the staff were desperate to either pick his brains or update him on the successes and concerns of each project.

One by one they came in with a minute spent on condolences and a further fifteen about their own lives with a final five minutes about what they actually came in for. Under normal circumstances, AJ would have interrupted their flow and made it quite clear he had no interest in their personal lives but they had him in a weakened state with his thoughts drifting to the incident he was very much trying to forget.

After a few hours, he left the building for the day without informing the staff. During the drive home, the temptation to reach out to Sonia was strong, although not strong enough for him to dial. He needed to leave her be; she had moved on and was looking forward to a future with her new man. He didn't need to bring her back to his mess and it was time for him to deal with his own life and issues on his own, with no help.

As the days and weeks went by, AJ was acting like the CEO of a huge charity by name only. Around him, the rat race continued and day by day, guilt consumed him. However, the competitors were making the most of his silence. During one meeting, he sat and watched as funding was being ring-fenced for charities without any expression of interest in his own.

"AJ, there is £20k on the table for us, say something," Sarah was nudging and whispering into his ear. Her frustration had actually brought him back to the present day, away from repeated images of burning flesh and blood.

"Not much we can do with £20k, let someone else have it." He sounded emotionless and robotic with no hint of the AJ who would normally be fired up and snapping off hands for funding. He knew logically how absurd it was to pass it up but he found himself collecting his belongings and walking towards his car. His angry side-kick followed him and was in no mood to hide her disappointment.

"What the fuck is wrong with you?" she hissed at him, too angry to shout. "Even on a bad day, you would have eaten them alive and taken the whole pot for us. They'll be having a field day and laughing at us with your attitude."

AJ continued walking to his car and ignoring her. It didn't do anything to deter her rant.

"The man who cries at the ever-growing price of paper-clips has just turned his nose up at £20,000 for our charity. I can't believe you. What's wrong with you? Talk to me!"

Sarah was gasping after her outrage at him, shocked at what she was witnessing in her boss. She was used to him zoning out and not paying attention but this was a man who was switched off completely. She wasn't sure any of what she'd said had filtered through.

He hadn't responded to her question and he wasn't going to answer her about what was wrong with him. He knew if he spoke, he wouldn't stop; there was so much inside his head that needed to come out. He had often asked himself the same question — *What's wrong with you?* — and it was not a question that was satisfactorily answered. From now on, he would only respond to questions on his mental wellbeing if they asked what was upsetting him. That seemed reasonable.

He could sense in his peripheral vision that Sarah was staring at him, and it registered in his brain that she had stopped talking and asking him questions. He was ready to go home and make a fresh curry.

"AJ." Sarah was speaking a little more softly now. "Please snap out of it. You know we all care about you but you have to talk to us. You've not been right since you came back from …"

"Have you ever eaten bitter gourd?"

"What? Are you for real? I'm talking about what just happened at the meeting and you're thinking about food?" Her voice was incredulous, and she no longer recognised the man standing in front of her.

"It's an acquired taste, but it mixes well with dry chicken." He had drifted off again. "Think I'll stop by a shop to pick up some ingredients on the way home."

"Oh for God's sake, shut up." Sarah had reached her limit and was gearing up for another angry rant. "The second part of the meeting is tomorrow morning, so you had better cook yourself silly tonight because I want the full kick-arse, take-no-shit bastard I work for back in there on top form tomorrow."

Feeling good about her pep talk and hoping her point had registered, Sarah stormed off.

CHAPTER 42:

RETURN OF THE BASTARD

He awoke the next morning smiling at the memory of Sarah's comment the day before.

"Bastard, I love it," he said to himself."

Steffi was in earlier than usual and was walking up the stairs humming out of tune, irritating AJ no end. He remembered his one and only girlfriend all those years ago trying to sing in front of him, missing all the notes and very much out of key. He could still recall her saying, "*It's not about the tune. It's about the feeling behind the tune.*" He instantly forgave Steffi's attempt and smiled at her effort.

"Mr Rai, are you decent?"

"Yes, come in Steffi."

"I've got three white shirts here but I can't for the life of me remove the stains from this one. I've washed it too many times." She came in to catch AJ in the middle of his routine of creams and facial lotions.

"Stop putting your make-up on and tell me what you want to do about this."

He glanced in the mirror and recognised the very shirt which had fallen victim to the menstruating buffalo.

"You tried your best, just bin it" He always felt very uncomfortable with letting go of his shirts but realised there was nothing more he could do to save this one.

"Well, it's not like you're going to have to buy some more." Steffi couldn't hide her sarcasm, once again reminding him of his unhealthy addiction to white shirts. AJ gave her no response. His love of white shirts was not a matter for discussion and instead he made a mental note to order another one.

She began to hang the remaining two, looking across at AJ who had finished his morning regime, left the room, and headed down the stairs.

"See you tomorrow. Oh, I made a really good curry last night. It's in the fridge, take some home for your husband. He'll love it."

"Don't worry about my husband Mr Rai; he can have fish fingers whilst I keep the curry to myself." Steffi gave him an evil smile and left.

As AJ made his way to the office, he was well aware that Sarah was probably still frustrated at his lack of concern yesterday. Deep down inside, he agreed that his limited fight for the funding a day before had not only cost the charity financially but reputationally too. Despite the jovial exchange with Steffi earlier, his mojo was still nowhere to be seen.

"C'mon you *bastard*. Get your shit together."

As he pulled into the car park, Sarah was by the back door finishing off a cigarette. She headed straight for the car, not giving her CEO any chance to disembark.

"We're getting there early. Let's go." If AJ didn't mean business, Sarah certainly did.

"Yes. Yes. I'll fix it today. Don't worry." AJ sounded more confident than he actually was, just to placate her. He wasn't looking forward to a second round with someone who had admitted he was a force to be reckoned with when it came to third-sector business.

"Enjoy your curry last night?" she asked sarcastically.

He looked across at her in the passenger seat and could tell she had no interest in his gastronomic experiments in the kitchen. The question was delivered with complete and utter sarcasm.

"Yes, quite ni —"

"What's the plan? If you're not feeling up for it, tell me now and I'll explain on our behalf." Straight for the jugular, she was clearly done with his bullshit.

"Patience, young Padawan. Patience." AJ immediately regretted the Star Wars reference.

"I'm going to stay quiet but if you don't fight for our corner, I'm stepping in. Don't complain afterwards." Her voice was icy and they both knew too well she had no intention of undermining her boss in front of peer agencies but hoped the threat would be enough to keep him focused.

As they walked into the meeting, they immediately noted that no one was paying attention to their entrance. This was not a good sign, as AJ always had an unexplainable ability to turn heads when he entered a room but not today, which just further exacerbated Sarah's irritation at him.

"See! No one gives a shit. They're usually all over you," she hissed. AJ kept his calm and was busying himself with unwrapping a menthol cough sweet, in the total absence of any cough or sore throat. He turned his eyes towards the table at the back which had rows of beverages.

"I'll have an Americano."

Sarah seemed to relax a little. There was an air about AJ which began to reassure her; he had something up his sleeve. She was used to busting his balls and started to feel that her efforts were paying off. However, she regularly looked at his facial expressions for any assurance and, just as the day before, he wasn't really in the room — although this time she could see his mind was busy. He was calculating. Now comfortable in knowing that a game plan was about to go into play, she also knew too well that he wasn't going to tell her anything and that a menthol sweet and a coffee were enough to sharpen his thoughts.

"You'll have a plain white coffee and you'll enjoy it." She walked off a little less anxious and with the hint of a small smile. Returning with his drink, she found him sitting at the corner of four rows of tables all laid out to make a square, giving the attendees an easy vision of others.

The meeting started a few minutes later with all the seats taken. Sarah counted twenty people. The Chair opened with the usual reciting of house rules followed by more time than necessary recounting discussions from the day before. He was an older man in his late sixties, shabbily dressed with an out-of-control beard desperately in need of conditioning.

"OK. To the main point which needs a decision today. There's £20,000 in the pot for a number of organisations to improve signposting and referral protocols for disabled people and their carers across the city."

Sarah was busy scanning the body language of people who had declared their interest the day before. At least seven agencies had thrown their hats into the ring. AJ on the other hand had his eyes fixed on the Chair, whilst slurping his coffee and couldn't help but think, *"He looks like he should be delivering a lecture on botany rather than handing out funding."*

The conversation around the room started and a further four agencies declared an interest in the funding. AJ noted the local MS Society, Parkinson's Self-Help Group, Carers Alliance, and other small voluntary organisations, all operating with volunteers.

"Right. I think we have a bit of a consortium. At the end of the meeting, I would ask the eleven agencies to stay back to work on funding agreements and expected outcomes." The Chair was in full swing and satisfied he was about to solve a £20,000 headache.

Sarah was ready to explode and in her usual way, whispering loud enough to grab the attention of the reception staff in the lobby.

"Are you going to…"

AJ silenced her question with a look and raised his hand at the correct moment to not only alert the Chair but to lower Sarah's blood pressure.

"Chair. AJ Rai here from the Disability Rights Service." His voice was confident if not smooth.

"Ah yes, AJ. Glad to have some input from you. I was getting a little worried by the silence from your corner!"

"Don't worry, I've still got my voice. I was just keen to hear the thoughts and ideas from my colleagues around the room before I gave you the view of the city's pan-disability organisation."

Sarah's eyes lit up just as others in the room began to look a little agitated by what was about to be said. She knew her boss well and had a sense of what was coming from him. She felt more relaxed and relieved that he was finally talking.

"Yesterday, on the way home from the meeting, I realised I fancied a bitter gourd curry. Yet I also wanted a chicken mince curry with my usual added capsicums, thick chunky onions, sweetcorn, etc."

Sarah was observing the expressions of people around the table who were openly confused and glancing at each other. It was not what they had expected when AJ raised his hand to speak. Sarah smiled; they didn't know him like she did and his random tangents almost always had a point.

"Quite a few ingredients, I'm sure you'll agree?" AJ continued to talk directly to the Chair, who took a sip of water as he wasn't sure where this was going and felt the need to do something with his hands.

"Ahem," he cleared his throat and said, a little distracted, "Yes. That sounds delicious but can we get back to…"

"Yes, it was Chair," AJ continued, ignoring the obvious discomfort that everyone around the table was experiencing. "Because you see, what I did was not make two or three dishes but one. I mixed them all together and I must say I came out with a masterpiece of a dish. Now you're all probably wondering, as are my colleagues, where I'm going with this?"

The question was rhetorical and the room remained silent.

"Let's be realistic, Chair. You've only got £20k to give out and between eleven organisations too. That's less than £2k each and, on top of that, you'll have eleven funding agreements with eleven sets of monitoring reports. That's a lot of admin for such a small pot."

The Chair began to smile and agreed. Too many agreements and monitoring forms was the bane of any commissioning body. AJ had a point.

"However, I think I have a solution which will be a win-win for all."

The Chair cleared his throat again, still trying to digest how the statement about AJ's dinner last night was relevant. "Yes. All suggestions are welcome. Nothing has been set in stone."

"How about you have an agreement with one over-arching pan-disability organisation which can distribute funding to organisations within the partnership of eleven, based on the number of actual referrals made rather than a blanket split? This will ensure one point of contact for the funder and one accountable body for the funding."

The Chair had caught on, "And I presume your charity, Disability Rights Centre, would be that organisation?"

"Well yes. Unless anyone else here has the capacity to take the lead. I would be more than happy to work under the expertise of any other organisation which works with all impairment groups."

Sarah was smiling like a Cheshire cat. "You sly bugger," she muttered just enough for AJ to hear.

AJ was scanning the room and it was obvious to all that there was only one organisation in the city which was not limited to one client group. AJ had pulled a fast one and was not only back in the race but in pole position too. However, AJ wasn't finished yet.

"If my organisation gains the confidence of all around the table today, I will commit a further £5,000 towards the overall pot in match-funding so a total of £25,000 will be available for the project."

The comeback kid, as he had been referred to in recent years, had placed the Chair in checkmate. The proposal was full of logic and merit. A few sighs and mumbles later, all reluctantly voted in favour followed by the traditional cliques gathering to moan about what had just happened.

AJ wasn't overly concerned with cliques in the sector. He had decided many years earlier that they resembled insecure and very silent bullies and the only way to defeat them was to outsmart them rather than directly challenge them.

Sarah was struggling to contain her delight after having witnessed AJ's masterstroke and had completely forgotten his shortcomings the day before. The Chair walked over to them both along with two younger men and an older woman. His facial expression was congratulatory, if not relieved.

"AJ, that was something quite special. A little cheeky but special. However, you may have upset some of your friends in the sector."

"Yes. I know but I'm not too fussed about that. I've watched them divvy up pots like this in the past with little to no return on investment. I'm past the need to work with them. My proposal is fair. This way, if they want their £2k, they will have to work for it."

One of the younger men accompanying him felt the need to join in. "Well, we certainly cannot turn our nose up at an additional £5,000. Your organisation is quite a force AJ. I'm new to the sector and was genuinely refreshed by what I just witnessed today. I was told you took no prisoners and I must say, a little curious about whether you or the charity will experience any backlash from those here today?"

AJ looked across at him. He hadn't noticed him earlier despite him sitting at the side of the Chair throughout the whole meeting. He was in his late twenties, perhaps early thirties, dressed quite sharply in a navy suit, tie, and crisp white shirt, which of course had now caught his attention. This was how he expected the next generation of voluntary sector staff to dress. AJ smiled.

"Sorry, I didn't catch your name?"

"Pete, Peter Norton. I'm from the newly created Housing Advice Centre."

AJ wasn't really interested in where he was from and wasn't fully convinced, he had just been paid a compliment and thus felt the need to end the discussion.

"The truth is Peter, the ultimate aim of any charity like the Disability Resource Centre is to no longer be needed by society or groups like this lot. Until then, they'll have to deal with pains in the neck like me."

CHAPTER 43:

BHANGRA CALLING

As they walked back to the car, Sarah felt a couple of inches taller. AJ knew she wanted a breakdown but he could feel a headache coming on.

"Yes, I know I doubted you. There was obviously a game plan in play, but you should have at least told me what you had in mind. Fancy keeping me in the dark overnight."

AJ smiled as they drove back to the office. He didn't want to admit the lack of a game plan. The truth being that he had to muster every ounce of concentration from his inner core. So much that his head was pounding. He needed to lie down, away from everyone. The need to live up to his reputation and to preserve the charity's honour had drained him. On a normal day, he would have celebrated today's achievement but his emotions were still too high.

As they arrived at the office his phone rang. Sarah got out of the car, leaving AJ to take the call. On the screen, the name displayed was 'Hitesh - HIP Records'. He audibly sighed, "Shit. I'm not in the mood for this." He accepted the call. A loud excited Glaswegian voice greeted him.

"AJ! How's it going? You're a busy man. Been trying to get a hold of you since last night."

He looked at his phone and noted the small icon in the corner indicating missed calls and decided the phone must have been on silent while he was cooking.

"All good thanks. Just came back from Ind…"

"Excellent. Excellent. Anyway, the track is on the album *Pure Desi Volume 2* as promised and it was released yesterday and guess what? Smashed it, AJ. You smashed it!"

For the next few minutes, the excited Scotsman explained how the track was being played across the country on all Asian TV and Radio stations, including taking the number two position in the BBC Asian Network charts. The number of clicks on YouTube was climbing at a record rate too. AJ listened in silent shock.

"Phenomenal man. Sick. Phenomenal. Sick. I need more tracks. Sick tracks like that!"

AJ was reminded how he just didn't understand the use of the word '*sick*' in this manner. *Why can't people stick to plain English?'* He instantly realised he sounded like an old fart and decided that successful singers should be more in tune with how youngsters spoke.

"Yeah. Man. Sick." He actually felt a little vomit make its way up the oesophagus, taking it as a sign the word was not for him.

"Anyway, I've got a string of interviews lined up for you and a few guest appearances at student gigs. People want to meet the man behind the voice. Gonna make you famous, sir!"

AJ felt overwhelmed. He'd forgotten about the endless interviews which went with each album. *Jeez, I'm forty-*

one years old. I haven't got the energy for this. This thought shocked him; he had been sure he wanted to record one track, but the aftermath was not part of that plan.

"Your first one is on one of the satellite TV channels tomorrow evening. I'll send you the address by text message. I think it's in Manchester. Keep it up! We're gonna make you famous Mr Rai!"

"But I have…" He was cut off. Hitesh had other calls to make.

AJ went into his office and switched on his computer. He needed to check his diary to make sure the TV interview didn't clash with any pre-arranged evening meetings.

"Shit. I've got meetings almost every evening." He could hear staff banter in the main office and heard echoes of Sarah's rant fresh in his mind. He slumped in his chair and let his mind race through a number of scenarios.

"Can I make this work? Singing, meetings, radio interviews, funding bids, TV interviews, staff problems, charities, businesses. After all these years, they want me to sing again. They like my voice. And fuck me, I haven't got the time or the energy to do it. I love my job. This place. I can't turn my back on these guys. I've built a little empire. Do I gamble my career for a few months of fame?"

AJ sat in quite despair after his monologue to himself, unable to commit to a firm decision either way about his job or his music.

His staff began to come into his office over the next few hours to air their own thoughts and woes about work. It kept him distracted from the inner debate and before he had time to gather his own thoughts, it was time to go home, still with a heavy weight on his mind.

Arriving at his house, he noted leaflets, half-posted through his letterbox. AJ hated junk mail, particularly if it was left hanging in his hallway, unless it included any special offers for pizzas. He immediately recognised them as electioneering pamphlets. It was coming up to that time of year where they started knocking on his front door making every promise under the sun about what they'll do for a better city.

As CEO of a local charity, he had to remain politically neutral despite not being overly impressed with any of the three local power-hungry promise-breakers. Before he sat down to read each one, he poured himself a Cognac with a splash of lemonade and almost enjoyed the distraction of local politics as it allowed him to procrastinate and avoid thinking about his dilemma and a potential trip to Manchester the following evening.

CHAPTER 44:

CLARITY

AJ arrived at the office the next morning an hour earlier than usual, mainly due to wanting to dodge any encounter with Steffi. Over time, she had become comfortable about making him aware of her disapproval of his drinking. Despite being an industry leader and feared out of respect for his leadership qualities, he was quite self-aware of his inability to argue his point of view to a handful of women who included Steffi and his mum.

The office was cold, dark, and quiet, which he considered the best conditions in which to make his impending decision. He had tossed and turned all night in doubt and was still confused when he woke and drove to work this morning. He began by sipping a piping hot coffee and squinting his eyes whilst scanning a row of box files at the other end of the office, which he hadn't noticed before. He had walked past them hundreds of times with no need to look inside. Filing was not one of his skill sets. He stood up and walked across to one particular file labelled *History*.

He sat back down and opened the box to learn it contained all press cuttings and photographs of staff from the early days of the charity. Reminiscing about simpler days made him smile and almost warm inside, only to be disturbed by his mobile phone which pinged to notify receipt of a text message. It was from Hitesh at HIP Records.

Quick! Tune in 2 BBC Asian Network.

AJ clicked a few icons on his PC and logged into the popular national radio station, instantly recognising the song. His song. His heart started to race. It had been fifteen years since any radio station had played a song featuring AJ Rai. He felt the urge to text everyone he knew to ask them to tune in too but instead decided to calm down, continue his coffee and enjoy the moment.

A minute later the song faded and the DJ boosted him further by saying how *sick* the song was.

"Who is AJ Rai? Great song, great voice with a modern twist on the classic 'Akh Largai'. AJ, if you're listening, get in touch!" The song continued to play in the background.

That was it. He could no longer contain himself and began to dance around the office to the ending of his own song like a giddy teenager. He was in the zone and flicked between the song and the memory he so often recalled of a crowd chanting "AJ, AJ, AJ". As the music began to fade, he sat down and picked up his phone intending to answer the DJ's call. With a huge grin and butterflies, he said to himself, "They want me again. I'm definitely back."

He found the number in Google and punched the digits into his phone. It rang and a man on the line answered.

"Hello. BBC Asian Network."

"Hi. I'm…" Before he could finish the sentence, he noticed that hanging partially outside the box file was a picture taken by the local paper of an elderly disabled woman on an electric three-wheel scooter next to AJ and another man. In a split second, he remembered the story.

The woman lived on the street where he was born all those years ago and had reported her scooter stolen a few days earlier. AJ made a couple of phone calls to a local retailer of mobility related equipment and persuaded him to donate a scooter. The paper loved the story of how a local charity had turned a sad situation into a message of hope.

AJ could no longer proceed with the call. Seeing the news cutting at that precise moment was a sobering thought, partially eliminating the joy experienced in the last few minutes.

Historical echoes from his grandfather and Ron, his former mentor, joined in with present day visions of his staff, trustees, and the many hundreds of service users who benefitted from projects which AJ had initiated.

His inner voice was going through so many emotions in those few seconds after he'd picked up the phone. His thoughts whirled through past conversations about how he should act in society.

"Music doesn't pay the bills. You've had your fun. Now it's time to settle down. Use the pain you've experienced, AJ, for the benefit of others. Turn your anger into something more productive."

He looked at the phone in the palm of his hand and could faintly hear the person on the other end, "Hello, Hello." He slowly reached for the red icon to disconnect, pausing for a microsecond, then cutting him off.

A decision which required dedicated reasoning and rationale seemed to have made itself, as the reality of his true calling in life was too strong for him to ignore. His eyes filled up and a tear made its way down the right side of his face.

AJ shut down the radio and began to tidy the desk. The staff would be drifting in one by one. He needed to compose himself. They shouldn't see him in any other way than the strong bastard they all loved and respected.

Within a few minutes, those clocking in at 8.30 am arrived and were surprised to see him there so early as he had a habit of making his semi-glamorous entrance around 9.30 am. Nevertheless, two of them headed straight for his office. They were actually two student placements from the University of Derby, of Indian and Pakistani origin.

They were speaking over each other and he could just make out bits of what they were saying in their excitement.

"AJ we're sure we heard your name and a song by you on the radio?"

"It was you, wasn't it?"

"When did you record it?"

"You never told us!"

"This is awesome."

"We heard you used to be a singer."

"It sounded like you, was it you?"

AJ was shocked at their behaviour as they traditionally put their heads down whenever he walked in the main office. Staff had told him his position probably intimidated them, which was enough for him to keep his distance. He fell silent as they waited with hope that he was going to answer them to confirm their suspicion.

"Well. Yes. Yes, it was me but…"

"I knew it! I told you so!" one said to the other, whilst the other began to text message vigorously. AJ deduced it must be to friends and family to announce her new discovery.

"It's just a one-off. Seems to be doing well, I'll see how it goes but I'll probably leave it at that."

Neither seemed interested in his reply. As far as they were concerned, they were working for someone semi-famous. That was enough for them to add a juicy post to their Facebook timeline.

As the girls walked out of his office, he felt relieved to some extent, having made his decision known albeit to two girls not so bothered about his inner turmoil. Nevertheless, he was now committed and comfortable in turning his back on the dream, once and for all.

He walked into the main office after feeling the need to scribble something onto his notepad in big letters:

THE NEEDS OF THE MANY.

CHAPTER 45:

THE NEEDS OF AJ

Over the next six years, the decision to put his charity before any success he may have had in the music industry was blocked from his mind. It was the only way he could deal with not progressing his miniscule venture into fulfilling his lifelong dream.

He picked a new dream, one where he could make a real impact on real lives. He swapped out signing record deals for grant and tender application submissions, which at one stage made the Disability Rights Centre the biggest disability support service in the country, employing just under 100 staff.

He now had five senior managers in place who directly took over the day-to-day running of projects, often finding himself at a loose end, which led to an even greater interest in the wider community. The sector, which was previously at odds with his aggressive entrepreneurial approach, was now knocking at his door asking for the formula to charitable success. A more tranquil AJ would often advise charities across the country how to generate finance, parting with his once very guarded business acumen.

However, it was still not enough to keep the demons at bay. Bar a bi-monthly catch-up with Jags, he was quite comfortable sitting in a dark room without any desire to improve his social circumstance.

Jags would often comment, "You need to get out and get married instead of sitting at home admiring your receding grey hairs and fat belly."

He was right too. AJ had aged and spent more time in takeaways than the gym but secretly knew he needed to keep busy. He slowly found himself drifting towards an arena he previously avoided like the plague — politics. The very leaflets that would historically find their way into the bin as soon as they were posted through his letterbox were now scrutinised thoroughly.

Increasingly, he was becoming vocal about the lack of focus on the needs of disabled people or carers in every local party manifesto, mainly sounding off to his trusted inner circle of support: his managers and trustees.

"If you feel that strongly about it, stop whinging and do something yourself!" His managers would all give him the same advice, which he would laugh at as it was the very advice he gave them on their own work projects. They were getting increasingly frustrated with him. As the charity was running so well due to his leadership and delegating, he would harp on about the same issues just for something to do say and do.

After advice from two of his trustees who doubled as local councillors, he decided to join the Labour Party and subsequently stand for election. He had a small team of supporters who helped him pound the streets asking for support in the local elections. He was learning quite fast that the game of politics was alien to his operating style. A good portion of the electorate had heard of AJ Rai and were impressed with his venture into the political arena with many stating their concern that he may struggle with the direct attacks that were about to come his way due to his physical impairment. They would exploit any weakness they could find.

Such concerns were validated by AJ being stalked on social media by supporters of the opposition candidate early on. He would receive regular emails quizzing his interest in politics, which he deemed a valid question. However, the supplementary follow-up emails would relegate him to just a man who should concentrate on his day job. They often implied that he was a one-trick pony with a mediocre understanding of disability issues and knew nothing about community affairs.

Despite AJ's resolve and determination over the years to become an elected official, the first time he only lost by a small margin. There was still hope, and he seemed to have garnered support from the disabled community.

The concept of rejection was something he had not experienced for many years and was enough to focus every ounce of his physical and emotional energy on winning the following year.

He would become a politician even if it meant the end of him.

CHAPTER 46:

POLITICAL MADNESS

"Mr Rai, would you elaborate on your interest in politics? Why the sudden desire to enter the local political arena?"

AJ had agreed to be interviewed by a student from De Montfort University who wanted to capture his thoughts about disabled people in leadership roles. He had agreed to discuss his career to date rather than delve into his journey into the world of politics. She had clearly done her homework.

AJ got on with all party leaders at a local level and was on first-name terms with local Members of Parliament too. It was the nature of his job. A voice for those without one.

"I wouldn't say it was sudden." It had never occurred to him to run for counsel but after giving up on the music once and for all five years earlier, the step made much more sense to AJ. It was still relatively new and he wasn't going to let some student catch him off guard.

He continued, "I've always been very aware of who was in power and particularly their policies on disability or social care. In all honesty, none of them have a perfect record on supporting disabled people but that was why I chose to see if I can make a difference. I work for a service managed and delivered by the people it wishes to serve. To simplify things, lived experience makes all the difference. I became a councillor because I truly believe decisions are made by people who have no first-hand experience in the matters which they are debating. If I can give them a disabled person's perspective, that can only be a good thing? "

"And what difference would you like to make?"

"I'm aware of the limitations of one voice amongst so many. However, if that one voice shows substance, sincerity, experience and passion in its delivery, sooner or later someone will listen."

"You weren't successful in your first attempt at getting elected. What do you think went wrong?"

AJ certainly wasn't expecting such a question but was impressed by her level of research. He did his best not to react to the statement; he couldn't let her feel she had the upper hand, especially as they were deviating from the original point of this interview: being a leader, not a politician.

"We will be getting back to the original subject about disabled people as leaders?" He sounded commanding but he needed a little reassurance before proceeding having thought for a second that perhaps she might be a journalist in disguise or had even been sent by the opposition party. During the run-up to the first election and since winning his seat, he had experienced dirty tricks by supporters of the defeated party.

"Yes. Sorry. Just one more question about politics. Considering your day job, why choose the Labour Party as your vehicle to be elected?" She seemed hesitant in asking but with just enough determination to provoke an answer.

"I've always got on with every party until recently. As CEO of a disability charity, they all kept links with me. Two councillors from the opposition sit on the board of trustees here. I have to give credit to them; they've kept the relationship almost enjoyable. However, a few of the minority parties went into attack mode. Strange really, I'm not used to this type of behaviour but I'm not going to say I wasn't warned. Many did tell me it brings the nasty, dirty side of people to the surface. I won't rise to the bait."

He hoped the tone indicated an end to the political party talk so they could move on and speak about the charity, the reason she was here after all.

She took the hint and reverted to her real reason for the meeting. He had agreed to be interviewed after her third email; he was the last of the four CEOs and she needed to bag this interview sooner rather than later. AJ's truthful answer was enough for the inquisitive student to draw a line under his political ambitions and she swiftly moved on to his favourite subject.

"OK. Tell me, what enthuses you enough to stay in the same company for more than twenty years?"

AJ sat up straight and displayed the cheesiest of smiles. "Now you're talking,"

The interview continued for another hour as AJ gave detailed examples of his desire for social change at a local level and the different leadership styles he adopted, depending upon the task in hand.

Sarah walked in at the end of the interview and advised him the trustees were gathering in the boardroom. AJ bid a polite farewell to his inquisitor and gathered a few papers prior to heading towards a partially filled meeting room to join a queue for a buffet lunch.

AJ was experienced in board meetings and worked with trustees from many walks of life. However, he was particularly proud of having retained at least five who had been associated with the charity from the very beginning. This gave him confidence in knowing there was expertise on the board to step in should he ever be 'hit by a bus', a phrase they would use to ensure there was always a 'Plan B' in place. His relationship with the board was envied by his peers across the sector as he often cited the fact that the board gave him flexibility to get on with the job with little interference in day-to-day operations being one of the reasons for the success of the charity. In return, AJ would not make any major decisions without consulting them, most of whom were the founding members.

"Right, shall we start? We have a rather long agenda." The Chairperson, Sam, was religiously on time and efficient too. All of them settled and quietened except for the shuffling of papers.

"Welcome, everyone. I hope you all enjoyed the buffet lunch. Let's crack on. Our CEO is now a Councillor and Cabinet member and is probably in a rush to get to his next meeting, of many more!" The room filled with laughter as there was a running joke about AJ, who was on record as saying meetings were an excuse to avoid doing any actual work.

AJ smiled as the Chair was right. Council meetings were plentiful, particularly since his taking on the role within the Cabinet, but necessary to keep the wheels of local government turning. However, AJ's favourite part about being a politician was getting things done rather than spouting political rhetoric. He even added the hashtag *#ActionNotJustWords* to all his social media posts and leaflets.

"No apologies, Chair."

"OK, let's go straight to the minutes of the last meeting."

CHAPTER 47:

CLLR AJ RAI

AJ arrived at the Council House with increased pains in his back and hips. Three years of canvassing for votes across a ward had taken a toll on his health, causing irreversible corrosion in his lumbar discs and both hips. Nevertheless, opioid-based painkillers were always on hand and clever at masking the pain, though also addictive.

As a Cabinet Member for Leisure Culture and Tourism, he was fortunate to have his own office and a shared PA. His office was dull and he had made no attempt to personalise it with paintings and photos. He was well aware that the balance of power could shift between parties at short notice due to yearly elections and defections in between.

The world of local government was not that much different from charitable support services. AJ often commented that both were full of people trying to deliver vital services with reduced finances and with little to no gratitude. However, his one disappointment was being witness to silly games played by a handful of politicians which were more about self-interest ahead of public need. He decided very early on to keep a safe distance from it all.

In his third year of office, AJ had made a marked difference to many in the wider community. Since taking office, he received countless phone calls from disabled people and carers across the city asking him to take up their particular issue. On most occasions, he would have to refer them to their own councillors, which wasn't a bad thing as it often meant that they would happily pick his brains on disability matters for the benefit of the resident.

Fellow councillors from all parties could see through the glass door and AJ often waved or invited them in regardless of which denomination they favoured. All in all, he was content. The day job was as rewarding as always and now he had the added satisfaction of helping non-disabled citizens with improving streets, neighbourhoods, and traffic flow across the city.

AJ had a series of meetings booked with senior officers from a number of departments within his portfolio. This was to be followed by a full council meeting in the chamber with a packed agenda and traditional pomp to give the whole theatre the gravitas expected by the public.

Each meeting was chaired by the Mayor, supported by a stream of legal advisors and constitutional experts who kept the councillors in check. AJ joined at a time when party politics was at its worst and this did nothing to encourage anyone wanting to contribute to conversations about the city. He hated such meetings, much preferring face-to-face conversations with residents within the ward. However, he accepted that they were a necessary part of council bureaucracy and played his part in each theatrical show.

As always, AJ received a text message bang-on five minutes before the start from his political sidekick, Salman.

Good luck mate and SMILE for the camera! Remember. Out & about tomorrow 5 p.m.

He looked up towards the balcony and easily singled out the man who had literally knocked on every single door alongside him during the run up to his election win. Salman was fifteen years his junior and keen to learn AJ's technique in engaging and winning the trust of residents. Always smartly dressed and clean shaven, regardless of whether he was out in the community or at work as a licensed cab driver, he would be available at the drop of a hat if needed. He was transparent in declaring his desire to stand for election himself in the future but for now was content in his dedication to the cause.

AJ gave his traditional salute and sat down ready for at least three hours of political mayhem. The Mayor, preceded by the gold mace, walked in and the whole chamber stood out of respect.

Once settled, councillors from all parties would debate on existing and planned projects and services which were to improve all aspects of city and suburban life. Naturally, every opportunity was taken to enhance dialogue with wit, sarcasm, and even sometimes personal attacks which were often dealt with swiftly by the Mayor. AJ would keep his head down, answer any questions from the public or fellow councillors and go home. Having two opposition Councillors as trustees of his charity made it much easier to get on with others on the opposition bench and they would walk over to each other for a friendly chat during breaks.

He hoped it wouldn't take too long today as he had a full-on day tomorrow for the charity. Each year they would host an exhibition with over 100 service and product providers, raising awareness of how they could enhance the quality of life for disabled people. The event was AJ's brainchild and even though his trusty sidekick Sarah did all the hard work in organising it, he would still share the excitement along with his ever-present companions: high levels of anxiety and stress.

After the meeting, AJ walked out towards the car and met up with Salman who had waited for him to confirm tomorrow's arrangements for the neighbourhood walkabout.

"These meetings don't get any better, do they? Glad it's you on the receiving end rather than me." Salman chuckled behind a serious point. If he ever became a councillor himself, it was not anything he was necessarily looking forward to. As a member of the public observing from the gallery, he often felt sad having to witness unnecessary jibes from each party.

"Scoundrels, the lot of you. Dirty rotten scoundrels." Salman chuckled. "Don't forget 5 pm, usual place."

CHAPTER 48:

KARMA IS A BITCH

It was late and AJ had not eaten all day. During the drive home, he decided on a stop off at the local chip shop to treat himself to a greasy fish supper. Outside, he could see a number of younger teenagers pulling impressive but menacing stunts on their bikes. He manoeuvred his way through them and made his way inside. The reassuring nostalgic smells of salt and vinegar on hot chips hit him instantly. The queue was short, thankfully, with only an elderly woman in front; his turn for a dose of gluttony soon came.

Not able to resist, he ordered enough for a family of four, knowing too well it meant he would be eating the same thing for at least three meals. With his meal steaming inside a plastic carrier bag, he headed towards his car, noting the young bike riders taunting the old woman who had exited the shop a few moments earlier.

The scenario caused a change in his planned direction and instead he headed towards them. As he came closer, he realised their chosen reason to pick on her was due to her walking stick having made contact with one of the spokes in their bikes.

AJ picked up his pace and made his presence known. The little crowd was by now circling the woman in an intimidating manner. "What's the problem here?" AJ raised his voice enough to attract their attention.

There was no reply as they all stopped and turned around, including the victim. He directed his question at the woman who seemed vaguely familiar.

"Is there a problem here?'

"These silly, rude, and disrespectful children have no manners. I just want to get to my car." AJ's sole focus was now on the woman whose voice was so familiar to him and was desperately trying to search his memory banks for a clue. She looked and sounded as if he knew her but as usual, he couldn't quite place her.

"The old bag was walking too slow in front. We were just trying to get past her and she hit my bike." The leader of the pack spoke in a soft voice but with enough self-justification.

"I did no such thing, you silly, insolent, little man." AJ was more confused than ever, concerned with her identity rather than the matter in hand.

"Perhaps you should walk faster instead of hogging the pavement you old bat!" They burst into laughter and rode off as the leader raised his middle finger at AJ.

The old woman looked at AJ and made a comment which reignited his memory cells. "No respect. Poor parenting, nothing else, just poor parenting. If I could walk any faster, I would!"

AJ stood as if hit by a stun gun. His head and in particular his face could not stop mimicking a confused little puppy as he watched the angry woman seat herself slowly into her car. His concentration was interrupted by a call from another direction.

"AJ! Everything ok?" It was his trusted partner in politics, Salman, who had stopped off with the same idea for chips after a council meeting. "Do you know her?" Salman was looking at both his friend and the woman intermittently.

AJ smiled at him followed by a laugh which quickly turned to a look of sadness. He continued to watch the woman drive off into the distance.

"Humans are the most intelligent creatures. Yet they can't think beyond the present. They're obsessed that they are always going to be strong, powerful beings, not at all worried that their arrogance will one day be destroyed by karma."

Salman was completely bewildered as he watched his friend holding a hot steamy bag looking into the darkness. "AJ. Have you been at the sauce again?" He chuckled knowing too well AJ would only pour himself a drink once safely home.

"No. No. No. It's just that woman." AJ appeared to re-enter the present day.

"That woman, around forty years ago, made me stand at the front of the class at school and told me off for walking too slowly to each lesson. I just saw karma playing out as some rowdy teenagers said pretty much the same thing to her, right in front of me. She didn't even recognise me, let alone recall what she had said to me. Yet, deep down, I feel sorry for her."

"You know, Salman, my grandfather once told me a tale and I think I've just seen it play out." AJ recited the short tale for his friend.

"A very frail, elderly man lived with his son, daughter-in-law, and grandchildren. The son spent most of the day labouring in the family-owned farm and came home each day to his wife's rants and complaints about the growing care needs of the old man. 'I have to cook for him, clean after him, and listen to his stupid and out-of-date opinions about how I should raise the kids,' she often wailed. Once, after a particularly hard long, hot day, his wife continued giving him the same grief. Tired and at his wit's end, the son decided he could not cope anymore and would take action the next day. The following morning, he grabbed hold of his weak, old father and slung him over his shoulder. After walking for miles, he came across a watering-well. With his eyes full, he turned to his father and cried, "I'm so sorry father, we can no longer cope with your care needs and I must therefore throw you down this watering-well." The old man cried, falling to his knees and said, "Please son, I beg you, don't do this." The son replied, "I have no choice, you must understand that we need to devote our energy to the children."

After a lot of pleading, the old man accepted his fate but said, "I understand but please, I beg you, please, not this watering-well—any other but not this one!" Very confused, the son asked, "Why?" The old man looked down to the floor and said, "This is where I threw my father."

"So you see, she got her comeuppance and I witnessed it. We should always be careful how we treat others, particularly those who need a little extra TLC."

Salman replied, "Wow, that's deep, AJ; you know I don't have to tell you that disability will happen to everyone. That is your proof." He joined AJ looking at the fading vision of an angry woman driving off. "Now, go home. Enjoy your chips!"

CHAPTER 49:

DIRTY ROTTEN SCOUNDRELS

"For Pete's sake! Can't she vacuum when I've left?"

AJ was awakened by the ever-approaching sound of the vacuum cleaner. Steffi showed no mercy. She had a job to do and had a few other house-calls to make. AJ was the only client who would often be asleep during the allocated time.

"Wake-up, lazy man! Time to go and push some papers around." She laughed with sarcasm as she burst into his room.

"What the fuck?" he muttered; he was not a happy chap after waking. "I could have been naked! Don't you think you should knock before going into a grown man's room, Steffi?"

"Mr Rai, you haven't got anything different from any other man. Now shut up, go shower, and choose which white shirt you're going to wear." She chuckled as she switched off the cordless vacuum and stood with her all too familiar stance, which gave credence to the point being made, her right hand placed firmly on her hip.

"But..." AJ looked up and noted the battle position displayed by his trusted employee. He sighed, knowing he had been defeated. "Yes OK. I was getting up anyway. Not because of you but because I have an important day ahead." She smiled and shuffled off; it made him feel better to at least reaffirm how important his day was going, whether she accepted it or not.

He sat on the bed wearing only his boxer shorts and doing his stretches. Steffi continued with her vacuuming; the floor was already clean but that would not distract her from her routine. She continued with one disapproving eye focused on her mostly naked boss, who after a few uncomfortable seconds of eye contact headed for the en-suite bathroom.

A few minutes later, AJ emerged to see that Steffi had left a note on his bedside table stating there was no milk and that she had finished the last bit of coffee. "Cheeky shit!" AJ hurriedly got dressed to stop at the coffee shop for his morning fix instead.

The cafe was busier than usual although his usual table was vacant and so he felt it wouldn't do any harm to head to the Exhibition Arena a little late as his staff really only wanted him there once it was ready.

The waiter brought over an almost bubbling Americano which wasn't going to deter AJ from immediately taking a sip as he sat gazing into the distance, thinking about the day ahead. However, his concentration was disturbed by a louder than necessary conversation between four women of Asian origin who appeared to be in their mid-thirties.

"Favourite Bollywood Film, it has to be DDLJ."

"Yes. Definitely DDLJ"

"One of the best." Three of the four agreed it was one of their favourites and they went on to talk more about the specifics of the movie.

AJ wasn't one for eavesdropping but he didn't seem to be alone. Most of the customers in the vicinity were forced to play their part in a makeshift audience. Trying his utmost to not look too interested, he took another sip of lava which had now definitely burnt the insides of his mouth. *I'm going to regret that later!* he thought.

"I don't know, I prefer the old classic Sholay." The fourth one declared; she had been silent up until now.

Sholay was AJ's favourite too. A timeless film from the 70s which pretty much every person of Indian and Pakistani descent had seen at least once. AJ was such a fan of the film, he could recite dialogues from most of the film on demand.

"You know what I really like about that film? The contrast between the two lead characters Jai and Veeru." The fourth one took control of the conversation once again. "One can't shut up and the other rarely says a word."

"Yes. Strong but silent. That's a quality I look for in a man."

"Yes, me too."

"There's something very masculine about a man who says little." They all giggled and agreed.

AJ couldn't hide his disapproval of such an outdated expectation and characteristic. His face displayed his readiness to put the women straight. His concern about the concept of a strong but silent type was something he had argued about on countless occasions with many women. His concern was that if such a type of man were the preference of women, it could lead to generations of men who would not talk about their feelings, leading to more repressed emotions and depression.

He put his coffee down whilst considering whether he should interject a comment but was disturbed by the notification sound of a text message. This was timely but quite inconvenient as AJ was fired up and ready to fight against what he considered an outdated view. However, as the CEO and also a politician, he was always glued to his phone and could not resist.

It was from one of his trustees who was also a Councillor from the Conservative party.

Hi AJ.

See attached screenshot of a post on Facebook from last night. This seems personal and in my opinion they have crossed the line but I'll leave that to you.

Jack.

AJ was intrigued. Attacks on social media against him were not uncommon. He was the only Labour Councillor in a mainly Lib Dem ward and for three years had endured unprofessional behaviour not only from his fellow opposition councillors but from some of their supporters too.

The attachment opened and AJ slumped back in his seat. He suddenly felt beads of sweat run down the left side of his face. As he read it, he felt chills running across his body; shock and disbelief found its way to his heart and it began to race.

Get rid of Labour in our ward. This one uses his disability.

His mouth was dry and he needed to drink something and hot coffee was the only instantly available beverage. He burnt the insides of his mouth. It didn't matter. His mind was in conversation with itself.

What do they mean, 'I use my disability'? Who the fuck would say this? Have they lost the plot?

It was a simple statement but too distressing for him to process. All his life he had heard judgmental comments about his ability as well as his impairment and had taken them begrudgingly in his stride. However, this was not the same. It was not an ignorant passing remark made by an Aunty Ji. This was deliberate and calculating.

He sat there with a million questions circling his mind, *How do I handle this? Should it be ignored just the same way as any other political nonsense?"* Doubt was creeping into his mind, *"Have I ever used my impairment to my advantage?* He knew logically he hadn't, but the doubt was creeping in; was this what people really thought of him?

He looked down at his right leg with full-on confusion; it was now beginning to stiffen due to the stress. This was a normal reaction for someone with his condition, as muscles tense during mental agitation. He stretched it out in front of him, which caught the attention of one of the women who were all still busy debating preferential characteristics in men. After making uncomfortable eye contact with each other, they both returned to their individual concerns.

I'm sure no one has seen the post. If nothing else, it just highlights their desperation to unseat me at the next election. Yes, just ignore it AJ; it's only social media.

With a final long sip of coffee, he stood up and headed out of the cafe towards his car. Along the way, he felt the urge to make some sort of statement to the women on the next table but as he approached them, he realised his confidence and ego was already ahead of him, sitting comfortably in the car. He quickly reversed direction, feeling embarrassed by his pointless zigzagging.

The ten yard journey to the car seemed strangely endless. Something wasn't right. His legs felt heavy. His heart was beating fast and he could feel his shirt was once again drenched. His right foot was definitely struggling to bear his weight. For a split second, he recalled the last appointment with his Orthopaedic Consultant where he was strongly advised to consider the use of a walking stick to aid his balance, which he declined. Opening the driver's door required more concentration than necessary too.

Shit, I'm having a fucking panic attack.

With great effort he managed to sit himself in position with the door left open by just a few inches. He unbuttoned a few shirt buttons to breathe better and what little breeze there was found its way through the gap and was enough to cool him down, although he really only kept it open to avoid claustrophobia.

AJ checked the time. It was 8.47 am. There was plenty of time before the exhibition started although he knew too well he needed at least twenty minutes to be safe enough to drive. Looking towards his back seat, he noted his spare white shirt, clipped in a seated position but ready for action.

As he sat in his car taking shallow breaths, he recalled many years earlier, when elders from the South Asian community across the whole country, including his parents, practised a set of breathing techniques as disciples of *Swami RamDev* of

India. With his left-hand fingers and thumb placed strategically across his face and nostrils, he closed his eyes and began imitating the breathing exercises which after a few minutes brought his anxiety levels down to an acceptable norm. However, they soon shot up again once he realised two of the women from earlier were both standing outside his car looking in and laughing uncontrollably at his actions.

"My grandmother does that and it just makes her fart," one said to the other.

AJ was embarrassed. He had refrained from interrupting their conversation earlier to give them a piece of his mind but they showed no mercy in laughing at his coping mechanism and now he needed to rectify his earlier regret. He pressed down the window switch and gave them both a set of words to take home.

"Ladies, before passing judgement, perhaps you should think why someone would need to do such breathing exercises in broad daylight. It might be the only option for reducing anxiety in the absence of medicine."

The giggling stopped instantly but AJ wasn't done. "People like you just add to the anxiety levels of those who already have enough worries. If the only issue of concern in your lives is to gauge what each other's favourite Bollywood film is, then consider yourselves lucky. Out here in the real world, others are happy just to make it to the end of the day without feeling the need to harm themselves."

A look of shock spread across both faces accompanied by a clear desire to move out of view and earshot of a very agitated AJ who was just warming up. However, both women looked straight at each other and as if through telepathy, decided to walk off leaving him fully charged with anger but no outlet.

AJ took a deep breath and sighed. He was beginning to overthink again and wonder if he had reacted too harshly. *Sort your shit out, AJ. It's time to put on your mask again. You have a job to do.*

He fastened his seatbelt, started the car and noticed his mobile phone buzzing. It was Mark, one of his trusted managers, wondering where he was.

"Yes I'm on my way. Just grabbed myself a coffee."

"Have you seen what the Libs have said about you?" Mark sounded agitated. "It's bang out of order, AJ. This kind of comment will deter others from becoming involved in public life! How the fuck could they do this?" He was getting himself worked up. AJ felt strangely calm after reading what he had earlier.

"Yes, Jack sent me a screenshot a few minutes ago."

AJ instantly adopted an almost dismissive tone. He didn't want anyone to think the social media post had affected him. However, the matter had clearly caught the attention of his staff and trustees who were just as incensed. Nevertheless, there was no more time to process the chaos in his mind and deal with their feelings. He had to be somewhere and fast.

CHAPTER 50:

AJ THE SHOWMAN

Having changed in the back seat of his car, AJ walked towards the entrance of Derby Arena, a new indoor-cycling track, which boasted training sessions by Olympic and world champion cyclists. Ironically, the venue formed part of his portfolio as Cabinet Member for Leisure, Culture, and Tourism.

At the front of the building, he saw Sarah talking frantically to two of the staff. As he approached her, he noted the traditional clipboard and headset demonstrating her role as the go-to person on the day. Despite continually cursing her boss for asking her to put on the annual event and being quite stressed on the day, she thoroughly enjoyed the sense of achievement with over 1000 disabled people visiting over 100 stalls. AJ could sense her stress levels from over 100 feet away and after making eye contact was able to lip read the words, "I hate you."

"No you don't. You love me and you love doing this!" AJ projected a strong voice and smiled directly at Sarah who in turn produced a grunt as if agreeing with his statement.

"Shut up. Go inside and do that thing you do where you take the credit for all my hard work." Her tone was jovial but the statement was quite factual and received no deflection from

AJ, who smiled and headed inside through the doors and past the security gates.

The hall was already full with exhibitors lined up row after row showcasing products and services which were the answer to the daily struggles of local disabled people. Multiple conversations between visitors and exhibitors created a cacophony of noise, and brought some sense of relief to him and his troubled mind. AJ had come up with the concept years earlier and each time would say it would be the last one if poorly attended, but it just got bigger each year.

Most exhibitors knew AJ as a founder member of staff, and it was therefore appropriate to stop for a few minutes at each stand and engage in polite conversation. After the third stand, he realised something wasn't quite right. He seemed to be listening rather than talking and missing chunks of each conversation. His mind began to float elsewhere, in particular to the text received from Jack. Additionally, he began to feel an air of paranoia creep in during each conversation. Whilst acknowledging points raised in each conversation, he could not help but wonder whether they too had seen or heard about the remarks made about him, and thus started to look unnecessarily for any glitch in facial expressions.

I bet they have seen it. They must think I use my disability to my advantage.

After a further ten minutes, he found his legs beginning to give way. On one of the most important days in his calendar, he was not on form. He felt hot, weak, and useless. He had passed a cafe at the entrance and decided that was where needed to go.

The cafe was busy but he joined the queue with one eye on where he could sit out of sight from anyone who wished to make small talk. With no empty tables, he looked across the whole seating area and noted Rani, who was interviewed years ago was now one of his trusted managers. She was waving frantically at him and pointing towards an empty seat next to her and two other staff. AJ acknowledged her with a nod suggesting he would join them once he'd got a drink.

Having drunk his daily coffee earlier, he asked the man behind the counter for an energy drink as he was feeling quite drained and headed for the table. Rani had been with the charity a while and had worked her way up to a Service Manager position.

"It's busy isn't it? Thought we would get a drink before it becomes too hectic. She studied him closer, "You OK, AJ? You seem a little flustered."

"No, I'm fine. Just the day you know, great turnout."

"So hot today too, oh well. I'm sure it'll be…" Rani continued making endless small talk but AJ wasn't going to get a word in. Even whilst heading over to her table, he knew it would pretty much be a one-sided conversation as he was in no state for any real interaction. He couldn't concentrate. A few minutes with Rani could be just the tonic, as he was hoping for a little light-hearted distraction despite not fully separating himself from his main anxiety.

 AJ often joked with her that he simply could not keep up with her rapid conversations. However, right now, AJ was more than happy to listen to a monologue for a few minutes.

He sipped away at the bottled drink and soon realised his heartbeat had elevated. He had forgotten he did not react well to high energy drinks with boosted levels of caffeine. Looking down at the bottle, he noted it was still two thirds full and knew he needed to try and relax, so he decided to occupy his thoughts by reconnecting with Rani partway through her conversation.

"...and I said that's not a song, it's just music. Of course she disagreed."

AJ looked directly at her in total confusion, how much of the conversation had he missed, why was she talking about songs? Rani continued, oblivious to his confusion.

"Anyway, I just agreed to keep the peace. Sometimes, it's just easier, you know what I mean? AJ nodded in agreement, not having a clue what he had agreed with.

"Oh and by the way AJ, what are you going to do about that Facebook post?"

AJ was startled by the comment. He was now very interested in the conversation and not at all surprised Rani had mentioned the subject after getting all the unimportant matters off her chest.

"It's nothing. Just the Lib Dems highlighting how low they will sink to try to discredit me." He once again displayed a level of calmness in order to downplay the seriousness and his own panic. Internally, a multitude of emotions were slowly destroying his ability to deal with the matter.

"Nothing? Are you serious? It's not nothing AJ, it's everything!" Her indignation was growing. "Everyone who knows you expects you to fight for some kind of justice. If you don't, then future generations of disabled people will think twice before taking up leadership positions." Rani could tell he was listening but equally felt the fight had drained from within. "Well, even if you're going to crawl under a carpet and pretend nothing was said, I'm pretty sure the board of trustees will have a different view." After taking a deep breath she composed herself and finished with, "Anyway, you have a job to do today. Go and put that pretty boy smile to use and mingle with the crowd. You can kick arse later."

*

AJ stood up and slowly headed back into the main exhibition area. With each step he took a longer stride and soon enough he began to walk at a confident pace which also brought with it a reassuring smile. Comments from exhibitors and the public recommenced as he walked back through the crowd.

"Looking good AJ."

"Great event."

"Come over and have a photo with us."

"AJ, would you like to make a comment for local radio?" A gruff-voiced younger man thrust a microphone in AJ's face. For a moment he panicked and thought he was referring to the comment about his disability but was soon relieved to learn he just wanted to discuss the expectations about the day.

"Yes of course! Follow me." He looked back and waved at Rani who was in the middle of her own broadcast but, nevertheless, acknowledged him with a thumbs-up.

It was time to get the show started.

CHAPTER 51:

SILENCE ISN'T GOLDEN

"Pick up the phone AJ. What's wrong with you?"

Olga was new in the role and had a long list of messages for her boss who had disappeared into hibernation for the last three days. She was a young finance manager originally from Russia and was efficient in every way. Balancing the finances was one headache which AJ left solely to someone who knew spreadsheets and formulae. He often commented that she was more powerful than he was in the business as she knew where the money was, which restricted his ability to spend.

Her last contact with him was his phone call late Sunday evening advising that he was taking some '*me*' time and to arrange any meetings for a couple of weeks later. The managers were asking after him, as was the Chair. Despite being new to the role, she was astute enough to state another reason for his absence. Nevertheless, if for no other reason, she still needed to check in to ensure he was OK.

"AJ, this is Olga. Hope you're OK. I'm building up a list of messages for you, some from managers, some from the board.

I'm sure you've had emails from them too. Can you give me a call as soon as you pick up this voicemail?"

He listened to the voicemail and turned his phone back off.

*

AJ stared at the mobile phone which was vibrating away on the coffee table directly in front of him. It was Olga, again. After several seconds it stopped. He noted thirty-nine missed calls on the screen as well as the need to urgently charge the battery.

He sat slumped in his armchair with the TV remote in his hand not really watching anything on the screen but it generated enough interest to lock him away from the outside world. However, the phone call was a distraction and prompted him to get some water. He noticed how dry his mouth was and even though he had been thirsty for more than an hour, he could not find the excuse or motivation to get up and make the short journey to the kitchen. *God bless you Olga. I'll have orange juice thanks to you.*

He stood up immediately, realising his legs and back were incredibly stiff and decided a couple of limb stretches should take priority. His pain was always enhanced when he was mentally unfit. Lightly holding onto pieces of furniture which he had arranged to double up as items to lean on, he headed towards the full-length mirror at the far end of the room. However, before he could begin the exercise as prescribed by his physiotherapist, the image staring back at him distracted him from any physical pain.

Facing him was a version of AJ on a par with the person with no direction in life who had lived in a flat all those years ago. His hair had no style. A patchy grey beard was growing without any purpose. His eyes looked as if they were being held up by the dark semi-circles beneath them. The fifty-year old CEO had let himself go once again. And right on queue, the inner monologue started up again.

How did this happen again? The fuckers have got to me. I'm weak. It's been ten months and I'm still affected by that fucking post. I need to draw a line under it.

Ten months had passed and despite AJ's board lodging a complaint with the local authority, the investigation had not been completed. Senior trustees were outraged and felt that such comments would deter disabled people from entering public service. AJ had given up on the Council's complaints procedure due to inaction over previous behaviour by the same opposition councillors. However, he wholeheartedly agreed that such an ignorant attitude towards disability and disabled people needed to be called out and supported the board's decision. The downside was that he was unable to address the accusation made in the post publicly until the process had been completed. The silence after ten months was distressing him royally.

Apart from a little outrage from his own party, AJ received little to no emotional support from any direction. The only therapeutic conversation was at each bi-monthly meeting of the trustees who asked for an update from the Monitoring Officer at Derby City Council. Each time the answer was the same: *We are still investigating the complaint and will be informing you of the outcome in due course.*

AJ looked once again at the mirror, sighed, and headed back towards the couch. He no longer felt thirsty and instead lay face down with his arm and leg hanging off the end. His eyesight was a little weaker than before but strong enough to note the urgent need for a vacuum.

Steffi had decided to take a few days off, which was usually the case when she recognised the usual pattern: her boss slipping slowly into depression. *"You just need a slap. Nothing wrong with you. You have everything and you're still sad. I come from a country where you have nothing and you are still happy."* She didn't understand AJ and therefore both agreed to maintain a temporary distance until he was back on his feet.

He focused on a peanut which must have fallen to the floor a couple of days earlier. A few feet away he saw a handful of crisps and could not recall how they had got there but accepted he must have dropped them too. AJ honed in again on the peanut.

That's me. I'm the peanut, all alone. The crisps fell but they fell together.

The description nevertheless was also absurd and the more he thought about it, he could feel a belly laugh escaping him. He looked at both crisps and the peanut and continued laughing. He felt a rush of tears down both sides of his face and soon began to cry softly.

A few seconds later, his mobile vibrated, indicating receipt of an email. It was from the monitoring officer. AJ immediately dried his eyes and sat up straight. He couldn't quite understand why he felt excited. He had been so upset for so many months that he hadn't actually thought about what a good outcome from the investigation would look like. He opened the email. It was addressed to the Chair of the charity.

It was only a few lines of text but that did not concern him at all. He jumped straight to the last paragraph which informed him that the Standards Committee had asked the offending Councillor to issue an apology online and in a letter. AJ let out his frustration by throwing his mobile phone across the room, fortunately it landed on the sofa opposite, which cushioned the impact.

A fucking apology in an online letter! That's it, and then I'm supposed to get over it?! Everybody's fucking happy!" He felt very agitated and restless. *"I need to get out of here.*

Heading upstairs towards the bathroom, he had a quick shower and put on some jeans and a sweatshirt, totally oblivious to the shooting pain in his lower back. Thirty minutes later, he found himself driving the streets of Derby without any planned destination. AJ drove for twenty minutes before it dawned on him that there should be a reason for him being on the road. He started to note the same pedestrians, recognising the car doing multiple laps.

If I'm stopped by the police, I won't have a reasonable explanation for repeatedly going up and down the same roads.

AJ decided to pull over at the first opportunity and found himself parked in a side street alongside a Gurdwara, a Sikh Temple. He switched off the engine and felt the need to get out of the car before he could question his motive.

As he stood leaning against his car, he watched a number of worshippers arrive, all of whom were greeted by a priest at the entrance. One by one they went in and disappeared into the main body of the temple. As the priest turned to join them, he saw AJ standing across the road and started walking towards him with a beaming smile. He was used to being recognised and wondered if he ought to have recognised the man walking towards him? The priest looked like he was in his late forties, dressed in traditional attire and a long grey beard with a few historical remnants of its original black colouring. After covering only half the distance, he called out to him.

CHAPTER 52:

DIVINE INTERVENTION

"Amraj Singh Rai, long time no see! How are you, sir?"

AJ projected a cautious smile but with enough confusion in it to prompt the priest. His English accent was perfect which ensured AJ would need to think a little harder about their connection.

"You don't recognise me? It's me, Tan. Tanvir Johal."

"Jees! Yes. Tan. How the fuck are....?"

AJ dropped his smile to a look of embarrassment with a hint of self-loathing. The last time he had seen Tan was thirty plus years earlier. Back then he was far from religious or spiritual in any way. Both would frequent the same pub and enjoy a drink together, often discussing flaws in world religions. Swearing in front of a 'Giani' was highly disrespectful.

"I'm so sorry. I didn't realise it was you. Shouldn't have used foul language."

"It's fine." Tan said with a wide smile, "Calm down. No need to panic. I'm a baptised Sikh but still live in the real world."

"When did you erm….?" he indicated the turban and attire.

AJ was still processing the shock of seeing an old friend who previously drank and ate meat but who was now clearly following a commendable lifestyle. His old friend, however, knew exactly what he wanted to ask.

"The Guru and I found each other just when my life was spiralling out of control. I was drinking so much that my wife left me. We're back together now. I became a danger to my family. Anyway, I was just listening to a *Shabad* one day, which intrigued me.

"I wanted to know what it meant and, once I learnt the meaning, I went on to the next stage. I wanted to know more about each line of text in the Shri Guru Granth Sahib. Before I knew it, I was no longer interested in any type of intoxication. Reading the Gurus' teachings quenched my thirst." He gave a full laugh and looked at AJ.

"You can't believe it, can you? In all honesty, when I look back, I don't recognise that person either.'

AJ's facial expressions had been changing throughout the conversation, switching between shock and admiration.

"Shocked is certainly an understatement." AJ just couldn't think of anything else to say and was pleased that Tan carried on talking.

"That's enough about me, my old friend. Your journey is far more impressive. I saw you on the TV a few months ago and pointed you out to my children. Told them you were an example of human resilience. Genuinely chuffed about your progress and achievements. Life wasn't too good for you all those years ago but you turned things around too." Tan looked exceptionally proud of AJ and the warmth and affection were almost palpable.

Unusually, AJ's ego wasn't enjoying the compliments and praise. The cocktail of emotions throughout the day were stripping him of any desire to reflect on himself. His face and posture appeared tired and Tan recognised a look of vulnerability.

"But what brings a politician to the house of the Guru? It's not election time is it?" Tan released a chuckle which had no effect on AJ. He could sense something was wrong. "Are you coming in?" Tan pointed towards the temple.

"No. No. I was just passing through." He wasn't going to admit his drive had been aimless and the Gurdwara was a good pit stop so he didn't look suspicious.

"Come on. There's a fresh batch of masala tea made. I know you can't resist that." Tan started gently pulling him towards the Gurdwara and, before he knew it, AJ was taking his shoes off and covering his hair with one of the head-coverings made available for visitors. The smell of fresh tea and langar was comforting, reminding him of his days as a small child accompanying his parents and grandparents to the temple each Sunday.

They both headed into the main hall where AJ went before the holy book, bowed, and sat at the back. The concept of being made to sit at the back on a bench because he was unable to sit on the floor was one of his bugbears but he had given up that argument many years earlier. After a couple of minutes. Tan gestured he should move out into the kitchen and langar hall.

AJ went straight for a table whilst his friend brought over two cups of tea and a plate of hot pakoras. The smells fired up his hunger as he tried to recall the last time he had eaten any hot food.

"So what's on your mind?" Tan was not one to beat around the bush. "The AJ I know doesn't turn to the Almighty for help." Tan's simple analysis was correct. In their youth, both discussed religion regularly and Tan recalled signs of a borderline atheist within his friend.

AJ wasn't sure whether it was the food and hot drink, but he found himself wanting to offload onto Tan. "I believe in a higher being or beings. I do. Honestly, I do. I've just not gone as far as making the ultimate commitment like you. I've had too much shi..." He paused again and lowered his head. He could feel his cheeks turn red with embarrassment. "In the house of God! I really do have a foul mouth."

Tan interrupted and put him at ease. "Let's park that conversation for now, tell me what's on your mind? Talk to me."

AJ raised his head and sat up straight. There was something strange about Tan's last sentence. Three very simple words, when put together, became a powerful reassuring request. *"Talk to me."* This was something very few people said to AJ. It was more common for people to discuss their own issues before showing the slightest, sometimes faked, interest in whatever was on AJ's mind. It was a strange feeling indeed.

"Just give me the outline of your problem, maybe I can offer some help or a different perspective?"

"I haven't got a problem; it's others who won't let me be," AJ started, struggling to convey the feeling of his own anguish and despair at the lack of support the last few months.

"Others? Is someone bothering you?"

AJ cleared his throat. Tan recognised the sign. Clearing his throat meant there was a lengthy conversation ahead. He sat back, broke a pakora in half, placed it in his mouth, and washed it down with some scorching hot tea, enabling AJ to launch into detail about the attack on his character.

For the next five minutes, Tan listened without interrupting, only grunting to acknowledge AJ's grievances, after which he grabbed another pakora, this time insisting AJ ate.

"So let me get this straight. We have a situation where an opposition Councillor could not attack you for your work and instead cast aspersions on your integrity, your character? And during the investigation, you needed to stay silent on the matter? But now, you've received an apology posted online and by letter?" Tan's summary really was accurate.

"Yes. That's right," AJ nodded with a mouth full of fresh food.

"Hmm." Tan began to stroke his beard into shape. "Do you want my take on it? It may not be the remedy you need to move on but could help."

"Yes. Go on. What do you think?" AJ felt a knot in his stomach. The few times he had shared, he had always been given advice that did not comfort him in the slightest. He was a little apprehensive of Tan's take on the situation.

"AJ, you're a Councillor. You are elected to serve the community as a whole. But you have been the voice of disabled people in this city for a far longer period. So let me ask you, what would the CEO of the Disability Rights Service do in this situation?"

AJ frowned, "I am the CEO...."

"Yes but all I've heard is the grievance of a Councillor." Tan was smiling. His teeth visible through his beard. "Now tell me what would a CEO do about it?"

"I don't quite understand," AJ admitted.

"You are a disabled person with a strong platform from which to raise awareness of what others are facing on a day-to-day basis. WaheGuru has given you that platform so use it. This is the time to use it and not just for yourself but for *Sarbat Da Bhala*."

AJ had heard the phrase before but had not really understood it. Tan must have seen his lost look and explained, "Sarbat Da Bhala, For the Good of All."

Comprehension dawned and AJ was starting to understand what Tan was talking about. He no longer needed to stay silent. For so long, he had been forced to conceal his thoughts on the subject and, more importantly, he had an obligation to ensure that other disabled people were not deterred from entering the political arena.

"I think I know what to do." AJ felt inspired.

"AJ, I don't need to know the details, just go and fix it. Everyone else will just go on with their lives. It was your integrity, your disability that was attacked, and only you can fix it."

AJ smiled at his old friend, "You're good, Tan."

With a small chuckle Tan responded. "No, I'm not. You just needed to talk to someone. Anyone would have given you the same advice. It's not your fault, AJ, we're conditioned as men not to talk about how we're feeling when we're hurt. After a while, it just builds up and we continue to suffer in silence. Our pain manifests in drinking, drugs, or other vices."

AJ was gripped by his learned friend's analysis. Tan on the other hand was more interested in catching up as his work was done; he wanted to move the subject on.

"Now shut up and let's have another plate of pakoras."

AJ felt energised and drove home mapping out a plan of action. As he pulled onto his drive, he reached for his phone, which had a new voicemail. The phone was still connected to the car speaker system. He rang his answerphone and expected another message from his assistant. On the contrary, however, the short message had been left by a very recognisable yet totally unexpected voice.

"Hi AJ. Hope you're well. I'm here if you need me."

It was Dr Sonia Khan.

CHAPTER 53:

MILK IN YOUR TEA?

"Mr Rai, your X-Rays and scans are showing increasing signs of deterioration in L1 and L2. Your discs are severely corroded, which is probably causing your back pain. I strongly suggest you avoid lengthy walks and use a stick for support when you're having a bad day."

AJ was at his yearly appointment with his Orthopaedic Consultant. Mr Patrick Hendry was himself reaching retirement and had been AJ's consultant since he was seven years old. He took great pride in letting all the student doctors know about AJ's success as an adult with Cerebral Palsy. Today, he had a serious tone in his prognosis.

"You need to physically slow down a little. Rest." He emphasised the last word, as if it were alien to AJ.

AJ had tried his best to mask his symptoms. He actually felt worse than he had described, not declaring half of the painkillers he was taking. Years earlier, the chance encounter with John Beard in hospital led to laughter therapy as an antidote to his pain. However, his condition had worsened to the extreme, much of which was self-inflicted. Painkillers were now his ally.

"Yes of course. I'll be putting my feet up for a couple of months. I've got loads of annual leave to take."

Mr Hendry knew too well AJ wasn't going to rest but went along with his patient's pretence. "OK, I'll see you in six months rather than a year. I want to keep an eye on your new gait. Take this sheet and hand it to the reception team on the way out. They'll book you in."

As he walked along the corridor towards the main exit, he noticed a woman who seemed familiar coming out of the neurology department. It took a few seconds for him to register that it was the very woman who had spent a short time as the one and only woman he had loved, Esha Kaur. He was hoping she wouldn't see him and so mixed in with a gathering of student doctors who were all heading the same way. However, the problem with Derby Royal was it only had one thoroughfare corridor connecting all departments. The exit was too far for him to reach without being seen. He kept his head down and continued, feeling his heartbeat increasing.

"AJ?" her voice was soft.

"Shit," he mumbled under his breath, there was no way he could get out of this without looking stupid. He plastered on a smile and turned round to face the woman who had broken his heart all those years ago.

"Hi Esha." She was still a very attractive woman with straight jet black hair and had aged incredibly well. She was a head shorter than him and dressed impeccably in a fitted navy coat over black trousers and heels.

"Of all places, I wasn't expecting to see you here, Esha." He kept his tone light and noticed the department she had exited from. It wasn't his place to question, as maybe she was here with her husband.

"I guess the world works in mysterious ways," she said with a smile. "It's good to see you, even here. I once saw you on the high street in your car a number of years ago, but you disappeared quite quickly."

AJ remembered the moment clearly; he had put his foot down pretty quickly but wasn't going to admit it to her though. Derby was a very small city and the fact they hadn't run into each other before now was a miracle. There was an awkward pause and he cleared his throat.

"Well, erm it's good to see you." He knew his display of haste would appear rude but he had enough on his plate and didn't want to add an encounter with her new family to his troubles.

"AJ, do you have time for some coffee?" She indicated Costa at the end of the long corridor. "It'd be great to catch up with you. I've not seen you in decades."

He couldn't think of anything to say to get out of it. Of course, he wanted to talk to her but another part of him wanted to run as fast as he could. The pain and anger he had harboured in his younger days had faded as he got older. His life had veered and taken on a course he had never expected and she had been pushed to the back of his mind. *I must be maturing,* he thought.

His brain felt frozen and his usual quips and excuses seemed to have deserted him. As he stood frantically thinking a way out of it, he knew it was pointless. *"Fuck It!"* All he was doing was creating a vacuum of awkwardness.

"Sure, yes. I have some time." She had a huge smile on her face and led the way to the coffee shop. The walk wasn't far but clearly silent and awkward for them both. He ordered their drinks as she found a free table and made his way over. His frozen brain began to thaw and thus initiated some self-berating. *All I had to say was I had a meeting. Idiot!*

She looked a little nervous as he sat down opposite her, as if she too regretted the invite. "I heard your track on the radio years ago. I recognised your voice immediately."

She was good; flattering AJ from the off was a way to get him to open up. He gave her a small, knowing smile, allowing her to continue.

"Your vocal tone has improved with age." Esha was trying to read his reaction. AJ displayed his poker face, usually reserved for business dealings.

"I suppose it's OK. I'm not really too bothered about singing again. It was just a phase. Anyway, how are you? How's married life?" He tried his best to hide his hurt but could not help but change his tone enough to demonstrate the slightest hint of sarcasm.

"I've been divorced for a few years now." Her smile disappeared as she took her eyes off AJ and looked deep into her coffee.

AJ decided he wasn't going to put her through anything which made her uncomfortable. It wasn't his business and thus he decided to do what he did best in any awkward conversation. Change the subject.

"You look exactly the same, Esha, you haven't changed at all. Whereas look at me. I'm overweight, have a massive forehead, and too many greys to count."

Esha laughed. AJ knew exactly how to make her feel at ease in any situation. He clearly still had a knack for it after all this time.

"You're not fat. In fact you're probably more slim than most men of a similar age. I often thought about you. We should have stayed in touch but I suppose it would have made things complicated."

AJ nodded. Their last conversation together was full of hurt and anger. It would have been impossible to have any relationship. The image of her walking away from him all those years ago was replayed in his mind and dreams more times than he wished. Esha could see his gaze slowly fall and this time felt the need to focus on happier times.

"Hey, do you remember when you and your friends played silly games to get my attention?"

He cast his mind back to teenage antics, which today he would probably not find amusing at all. She was right though. Both he and his old partner in silliness, Jags, would develop very unsuccessful plans to detract her from her studies to focus on a lovesick AJ.

"No, I can't remember much of those days." He tried to play it cool but the grin across his face gave away the truth.

"Liar!" She laughed. "I remember one time just to get my attention, you both staged a fake fight outside the entrance to the college. What was all that about?"

"Well, it didn't work did it? You just walked right past us!"

"So you do remember! Seriously. Why stage a fight?" Esha was now in hysterics.

"I don't know what you're talking about." AJ felt a little second-hand embarrassment for his younger self.

"Or what about the time you had twenty bottles of milk delivered to my front door?"

AJ definitely remembered this particular incident. Jags and AJ had gone for a late night walk and ended up on the street where she lived at the time with her parents. As they were walking past her house they could see a note inserted in one of the empty milk bottles. Jags crept up to the door and took out the note for them both to see.

2 pints tomorrow please.

The teenagers could not resist but added an extra zero instructing the milkman to leave twenty pints. AJ gave a nervous laugh. "Yeah I'm sorry about that. It was Jags' idea. I was dead against it."

"My parents were shocked to see a mini-dairy farm outside our doorstep the next day." She carried on laughing. "We gave the milk to the Gurdwara, so don't worry, it went to good use."

AJ sat in his chair feeling quite embarrassed, if not ashamed of himself. He had often felt guilty about the prank and today had an urge to apologise.

"I'm sorry. Really, really sorry. It was a stupid thing to do."

He was interrupted by Esha who had begun to laugh a little louder, which caught the attention of the staff at the cafe. He had forgotten about her infectious laugh. It started loud then faded into silence, always followed by a tear from her right eye which appeared right on cue. He was mesmerised, again.

As she calmed down, her face became cloudy and sad. She looked him straight in the eye and declared, "My husband left me AJ because I have MS." Her gaze instantly turned to that of a very tired person, as if saying it out loud had finally made it a reality. However, her proclamation had totally floored AJ who was once again lost for words.

"MS as in Multiple Sclerosis?"

"Yes, AJ, or more specifically, I have Relapsing Multiple Sclerosis."

Over the last three decades, AJ's day job had introduced him to many people with many impairments. He knew too well how MS affected people. He was desperate to give her words of comfort but he found himself becoming angry instead at the admission of why her husband left her.

"He left you? As in, totally deserted you because of your health? What the fuck Esha!"

"AJ, I don't want you to dwell on what's happened to me. I was diagnosed three years ago and I'm coming to terms with my new life and its limitations. I often thought about reaching out to you but just couldn't muster up the courage. But it doesn't matter really, we're here now."

"You know more than anyone else about backward views of the Asian community when it comes to appearance and health. Unless you're slim, light-skinned, fit, healthy, and have a high salary, you're a secondary citizen."

Esha had summed up AJ's life-long frustrations with the community. He looked up at her and noticed her smiling at him but she was also unsuccessfully trying to hide her pain. His mind once again shot back to their last encounter where they had decided not to elope because both sets of parents were against an inter-caste marriage — even more so between a disabled man and fit and healthy woman. Walking away from each other was the sensible thing to do as neither wanted to fall out and face the world without their respective families. Yet, here they were, years later sitting in a hospital, now both disabled.

"I don't know what to say Esha, and you know that's unlike me." He tried to inject some humour but it fell a little flat.

"There is nothing anyone can do."

"Yes there bloody well is!" AJ was keeping his anger at bay and could feel it rising in indication for her. "You've been suffering in silence. I know what that feels like. Well, no more, I won't allow you to suffer alone with this. So much life has already been wasted. We couldn't be together because of our own community and their backwards thinking mentality." He pointed at people walking in the corridor past the cafe, only to realise they were all white people.

"I mean backward fucking Asian society," he decided to point towards the main entrance hoping Esha would understand his gesture. Despite the seriousness of his tone, she let out a little chuckle. He really hadn't changed all that much.

"Look at us, thirty years later, sitting here both miserable. That lot out there are having a fucking whale of a time," he pointed back towards the corridor and allowed his finger to follow an elderly Asian woman innocently walking to her appointment.

"AJ, please calm down and lower your voice. Both our journeys needed to happen the way they did. I have no regrets. Look at you, you're a big-shot making waves in the charity and disability field. Everyone knows you. Do you really think you would have had the same love and respect as a two-bit singer? No. I don't believe you would have at all."

AJ paused and took a deep breath. Esha remembered too well how to distract him from whatever was annoying him, which involved annoying him about something else. "Two-bit singer? That was a bit harsh." He sighed and deflated back to a slump in his chair, defeated.

Deep down he knew she was right. Nevertheless, his anger needed a couple of minutes to catch up with reason.

"Anyway, forget about the crap stuff. Let's focus on the future. I'm going to give you my number and you're going to call me and ask me out. This time I won't take two years to give you an answer, I had to keep you waiting back in the day you know." She chuckled, hoping he would share the joke.

"A little confident aren't we? How do you know I'm not already in a relationship?" He quipped trying to call her bluff.

"You're not. You're such a plonker, you don't even know we're Facebook friends. I know you AJ — you would have updated your relationship status. I've been meaning to reach out but haven't had the nerve. It obviously wasn't the right time, and I wasn't sure how you would react to me messaging you, but I think God had other plans as we've bumped into each other today.

"What the fu...."

"Talking about Facebook, what are you doing about that idiot Councillor who suggested that you use your disability to get ahead politically?"

"How did you know? Right, yes *Facebook*. I give up." He had resigned himself to being the underdog in the whole conversation. "I'm on the case, don't worry, I'm definitely on the case and will get it sorted."

"Good. Like I said, call me." Esha stood up and walked over to AJ who just looked up at her, unsure what to do. "Get up and give me a hug, you idiot."

Stumbling out of his chair and being even more awkward than his teenage self, he stood up to give her an even more awkward one-armed side hug. A very Punjabi thing for him to do.

"By the way, keep the beard. It really suits you." She gave him a wink.

"Eh? What beard?" He reached for his phone and brought up the camera setting. "I've got a fucking beard!" He spent a few seconds wondering how he had let himself go enough to have grown such facial hair, which under normal circumstances he despised.

Esha walked off, shaking her head in amusement towards the exit, leaving AJ to sit back with a grin across his face and for the first time in many years, a slight hope for his future.

CHAPTER 54:

CASTE ASIDE YOUR DISABILITY

AJ stood outside Sonia's new clinic pondering on whether to stick with the appointment. Sonia had reached out to him for some unknown reason. He had missed her counsel and also hoped she was doing well but was afraid to engage.

He paced a few yards from one side of the building to the other. The meeting with Esha had left him feeling elated but had also led to many questions. Maybe Sonia could help him navigate through the multitude of emotions which felt ready to erupt at any moment.

"Bugger it. I'm going in."

He pushed through the double doors to find the layout of the reception area had changed, as had the personnel. *That's not Carole.*

Behind the desk sat a stern looking elderly woman who peered up at him as he approached the desk. She must have heard him muttering and looked up with a disappointed look.

"Yes?"

"Oh yes, sorry, I have a 1.30 appointment with Sonia. I mean Dr Khan."

"Have a seat. I'll inform her of your arrival."

AJ walked over to the seating area not overly impressed with the uninviting receptionist. He sat looking through the magazines which were mainly aimed at women. "Obviously don't get many men here."

After a few minutes, Sonia came out of her room with a much younger man. Despite being happy to see her, he could not help but notice the look on the face of the man whose frown overshadowed Sonia's smile. It was clear he wanted to exit the building as fast as possible.

AJ stood up and could not refrain from rushing over to Sonia. A familiar face was just the tonic he needed. However, the young man next to her had intrigued him and for some reason looked familiar to him. Before AJ could stop himself, he put out his hand to greet him.

The young man was not comfortable with the greeting and simply took a step back from him and walked towards the exit, glancing back, locking eyes firmly with AJ, and giving him a confused look.

"AJ. How are you? Come through."

"I'm fine, I feel like I know him, I'm sure of it." He was still trying to place the young man's face. It was often a source of amusement amongst his staff that he never remembered faces even after he'd met with people several times. He shrugged, thinking it would come to him sooner or later.

"AJ, please have a seat." Sonia was firm in her tone. She knew he had a tendency to get distracted and needed to rein it in early.

AJ looked around; pretty much all the decor had been refreshed. Nothing seemed familiar. In his subconscious, he had pictured himself sitting in his usual chair when he had received Sonia's text message a few days earlier. The only comforting item was a large bunch of yellow flowers placed in a vase on a corner table near her desk. He sat down on a chair which began to swallow him up by the second. "Great! I'm going to need a crane to lift me out of this thing!"

"I'm glad you returned my call; it's good to see you. I've heard about the work you've done over the years and get snippets of information from Carole here and there about your duties as an Councillor." She smiled with a hint of pride, as it was nice to see how far he had come from his first session with her. She had invited him to her office as she was now located between Derby and London. Her aim was to set up a new clinic and help more vulnerable young people. Her relationship with AJ had fizzled at a point when it looked like they could have been friends when she moved.

AJ was flattered she had kept tabs on him. He knew whatever relationship they had now would not be a fully formed friendship, as he had intended many years earlier; nor could they go back to how they were when they first met as client–therapist. It was a strange hybrid of the two. He was just happy to see her and that she had reached out. It came at a very poignant time in his life. *Divine intervention*, he thought to himself sarcastically.

"I saw the apology made by the opposition Councillor."

AJ sighed, "Everyone has bloody seen it, but I'm fine. It did get to me but I'm fine now."

Sonia wasn't convinced, "I did ring your office first and got the impression your staff were not entirely sure when you were back."

"No. No. I'm cool."

Sonia looked at him with real concern. He hadn't changed at all. His eyes were travelling around the room looking in every direction but hers. Any question about how he was feeling was answered initially with a defensive stance and she knew exactly what his next move would be.

"Anyway, how's married life?"

There it was, the ability to defer answering by asking your own question. His gaze stopped at the large new family portrait, which was settled on the mantelpiece behind her. Sonia was surrounded by three men, two of which must have been her sons and the other an older but well-built handsome man who had his arms around her. AJ smiled as if to show his pleasure at seeing her family.

"You guys look really happy. That's good."

Sonia joined him in admiring the portrait. Life had turned around perfectly for her. She was indeed happy. Both sons had graduated from university and begun their own careers. Her husband was attentive and caring. Despite pressure from her extended family to remain a widow, she was pleased she had taken the steps to restart her life. She still missed her first husband but was equally happy to have met the second.

"AJ, I'm genuinely concerned for you. The AJ I know will have been affected by such comments. I just wanted you to know that I'm here."

"You're what? His tone changed. He let out a chuckle. "You're here for me? You're kidding me right!?" He was laughing but it wasn't a real laugh, there was no humour in it.

"Nobody is there for anyone, Sonia. There was a time when you were exactly what I needed. A shrink on standby. But let's be honest, that's not how normal people live. It wasn't sustainable. Sooner or later, I had to go out and try on my own again, and guess what? It doesn't matter whether I'm successful in my job or as a politician. I'm still a delicate little flower that collapses from the slightest gust of wind!"

Sonia wasn't shocked at his response. She was experienced enough to recognise his slow release of built-up anger as very necessary and allowed, if not enabled, him to continue. Her facial expression showed no reaction other than that of complete interest in AJ's thoughts.

"I'm clearly an easy target. The Punjabi way is to deal with stupidity with the good old fisticuffs and these idiots know I'm not capable of any physical aggression. That's why they're so confident in attacking me and my character." He looked up at Sonia who this time could not disguise her concern about his comment.

"AJ, do you think you are the kind of person who would deal with matters with his fists?"

AJ knew she was right and realised it was almost an irrelevant comment to make but one which had crossed his mind. It was time to move the subject on.

"Anyway, you called me. Have you a solution to my problem or were you just looking to see if your old patient had what it takes to handle shit?"

"I genuinely just wanted to see if you were okay. Outside of work and politics, please tell me that you aren't always on your own?"

AJ's frown had intensified. Sonia realised she had definitely said the wrong thing. "Don't you remember what I said to you when we first met? No one in their right mind will give me their daughter. Of course I'm alone!"

"AJ, a lot of people have broken the mould of arranged marriages. Love marriages are all the rage."

"Love marriages?" AJ broke into uncontrollable laughter at Sonia's bemusement. "I've been invited to dozens of weddings which claim to be love marriages and let me tell you they are anything but. The scenarios are nearly always the same. Boy falls in love with the girl or vice versa, the boy does a background check on said girl. The same shit as before you know? Surname, family status, and of course, caste! I guarantee that, nine times out of ten, that's where it ends because one of those will not please the parents. If they tick all the boxes, then how can you call that a love marriage? All they've really done is arrange their own marriage."

Sonia was totally hooked into his thoughts and realised there and then she had missed him, particularly his often simple analysis of life. His theory was true. Over the years, many male and female patients discussed the trauma of being rejected at the first hurdle due to issues such as the curse of the caste system. Nevertheless, she felt the need to offer some balance.

"C'mon AJ. Caste has always been an issue, but it's a trend that is slowly dying with the new generation." Before she finished her sentence, she realised she had poked the bear even further as AJ stood up and walked towards the window and gestured she followed him. Sonia was intrigued.

"Listen. Can you hear it?" AJ's voice softened.

Across the road, he pointed towards a group of young men of Asian origin, who appeared to be in their early twenties, seated in a parked cabriolet car. They were enjoying Bhangra music which was loud enough to be heard in Sonia's clinic.

"Do you hear it?" AJ looked towards Sonia who was confused as to where the conversation was leading but nevertheless went with the flow.

"Yes, I hear a Bhangra song. I've heard it before, it's one of my favourites."

AJ shook his head in disappointment. "Sonia. Listen to the lyrics. Tell me what they mean." She was embarrassed. Like many, Sonia never actually listened to the lyrics but just enjoyed the sound and beat.

"Listen. Carefully," AJ insisted. After a few seconds she moved away from the window and went back to her seat. The doctor had realised AJ's point, and found it necessary to finish the conversation in the only way he could.

"That's right, just like that particular song, far too many songs feature a chorus which promotes the higher caste. The Jatt or Jatti." Sonia instantly tried to play back as many Bhangra songs as she could in her mind and had to agree. He was right.

"Singers and lyricists just don't realise what they're doing."
AJ seemed a little deflated. "They think they're celebrating
their roots by continually referring to a caste. All they're doing
is dividing future generations. Creating resentment."

"AJ, we're going off topic a little, don't you think?' Sonia
was finding AJ's statements quite uncomfortable and for some
unknown reason could not determine why.

"Okay. Let me put it another way." AJ was far too committed
to making his point and could not abandon his flow. "Imagine
listening to BBC Radio 1 to find that the lyrics of every other
song focussed on how white people were the best, how the
white person's way was above everything else."

AJ stopped to note a look of surprise across her face and
realised his point was made. "Every other community would
feel quite angry that — given that we're promoting equality,
community cohesion, and so forth — one community is being
promoted more than others. The British Asian community
would be up in arms. The same people who go around blasting
songs which may have a great dance beat would be quite pissed
off. Hypocrites!"

Sonia looked down at her pad wishing it was an actual
counselling session which she could steer better than in the
last few minutes. She sighed and decided she needed to guide
her old friend off his soap box.

"AJ, it's a disgusting system that needs to be changed and I
think will change over time. You and me getting upset about it
here today will not change it."

"Yes, it will change but only when they, out there, wake up."
He noted an increase in his heart rate. He needed to calm down

and as he had been pacing her office he sat back down in a chair in the corner next to the vase.

"And to answer your question, no I'm not married."

For a moment, he debated whether he should inform Sonia about the chance encounter with Esha but decided he would do so some other time.

"AJ, I really think we should have a couple of sessions to help you, if for no other reason than to get a few things off your chest." Sonia was hoping he would accept the recommendation. After just a few minutes in his company, she realised she cared about his well-being more than that of a patient. Somewhere in her subconscious in previous sessions over the years, she felt she was helping her deceased first husband.

"I don't know. Like I said earlier. I'm always going to be delicate. Sensitive. Maybe I'm just wired that way. What wouldn't bother others seems to floor me." He looked towards the vase. Sonia smiled.

"You converted me, I only like yellow flowers now. They have a way of brightening up your day and space even on the lowest of days." She had a fresh bunch delivered every week and thought about AJ each time she personally arranged them.

AJ gave a little chuckle. He too had not broken the cycle of fresh yellow flowers at home although he relied heavily on Steffi to display them in his kitchen.

"Let's do it, Dr Khan, book me back into counselling."

CHAPTER 55:

FIFTY-ONE COUNCILLORS

It was the last full council meeting before all political parties had to abide by the rules of purdah, the pre-election period. With the agreement of the leader of the group, AJ had managed to get a motion put forward. He had a strong feeling that he would lose in the forthcoming election and had mentally agreed with his own conclusion that he had entered politics at the wrong time. He had no fight left in him after four years of attack, from the moment he was elected to now, and accepted a need to be physically and mentally stronger to absorb the silly games played both inside and outside the council chamber.

AJ sat on the front bench of the opposition. His targets tonight were sat six rows behind in the far corner. The local media was in the chamber with notepads, cameras, and microphones too.

The Mayor of Derby started the meeting at 6 pm promptly. The chamber went through the usual items and eventually arrived at the motions which were put forward by parties to set or amend policy for the city.

AJ continually looked down at his paperwork. His speech was on his left and the motion on his right. His motion was listed as item number seventeen on the agenda. The very last item of the evening. This was his first and last major speech in the chamber and despite spending many long nights perfecting it, the troubled Councillor changed the whole thing at the eleventh hour.

He glanced down once more at the freshly printed document. A bead of sweat fell from his forehead onto the bottom right corner. AJ realised he was becoming anxious and took three long deep breaths and looked up at the Mayor who with remarkable timing looked across and invited AJ to present his item for debate.

AJ's thoughts dashed back to the chance meeting with his old acquaintance, Tan, who had nudged him towards this very moment. *Sarbat Da Bhala - For the Good of All.*

One of the officials sitting next to the Mayor read out the text which had also been circulated to everyone in the chamber.

"**Notice of Motion:** Equality and diversity training Moved by Councillor Rai, seconded by Councillor Emerson. The Council calls for all existing and future Councillors from May 2019 to receive meaningful and interactive workshop-based training with regard to all the protected characteristics under the Equality Act 2010 and any subsequent amendments to the Act. This training will replace the existing multiple-choice based e-learning modules."

The protocol was for Councillors to stand during motions and debates. AJ adhered and placed his glasses loosely on the end of his nose. He looked back at the Lib Dem team who had a sense of what was about to come. Many of the Councillors on his own side broke the tension with much needed words of encouragement.

"Go on, AJ. Don't hold back."

"Say it as it is, AJ."

A shout from the gallery added to AJ's confidence. "Top man AJ. Go for it."

AJ picked up the sheet of paper, cleared his throat, and then switched on the desktop microphone.

"Mr Mayor, there are a number of reasons as to why we have asked for this motion to be debated tonight."

"The first is that in this chamber there are 51 representatives of Derby elected from a variety of communities with varying skills and, most importantly, their own life experiences. Those communities have put their faith in us to vote on local policy, which will determine how they live and work in Derby. This is not only a huge honour but also a tremendous responsibility, as our actions in this chamber can have an effect on the lives of people for generations to come. We often receive detailed reports from officers to assist us with those decisions. Yet it is our life experiences and acquired skill sets which help us reach a conclusion on not only how we vote on budgets and policy but on how we behave inside and outside this chamber."

"Tonight we voted on the budget. Inside those budget papers were matters, which will affect people living in very difficult circumstances. But I ask everyone inside this chamber, before we cast that vote, can we put our hands on our hearts and say we truly understood the daily problems experienced by people accessing social care or the numerous problems parents of disabled children face? Even if we choose to vote on party lines, can we call upon a life experience to help make that choice? Not in every case."

"The second is that the existing *induction training* — and I use the word training very loosely — consists of nothing but being plonked in front of a PC/laptop or tablet to answer multiple-choice-based questions after reading a couple of paragraphs about each protected characteristic under the Equality Act. If we get answers wrong, we simply go back, do it again and again until it's right. Then the Council solicitors and insurers will be happy. But are the public happy or encouraged by this approach? Considering what I have already mentioned about understanding the needs of the communities we serve, we are not equipped with enough understanding by merely carrying out this training alone and I am confident in saying that the public will expect more.

"The third reason is that, whilst I've only been a Councillor for just under four years, in those four years I have unfortunately witnessed comments which confirm that we are in a period of UK history where we are *'taking our country back'*; we have also decided to teleport ourselves into the 1970s with sometimes sexist, borderline racist, and more recently disablist comments."

"Mr Mayor, you could ask me for an example of such behaviour. You probably won't but I'm going to give one anyway."

"In June last year, a Lib Dem Councillor felt that people on Facebook would benefit from learning that a Labour Councillor used his disability for political advantage, thus attacking his character. Making such an outlandish comment on social media is easy. But before making that comment, did he understand the journey I had taken as a disabled child from a minority ethnic group who was bullied and harassed all through school to where I stand today? Did he understand the discrimination I faced time after time in job interviews, including a job interview here in this building? Did he understand the constant pain and muscle spasms I endure just getting through the day?

Did he understand that by making that comment, he affected my family, my friends, and even my employer?

"Mr Mayor, no one inside this chamber knows this but I'll share it with you today. When I won my seat in 2014, I was approached by the Office for Disability Issues in Westminster who wanted to note my progress as a disabled person entering politics at a local level. Last week they emailed me asking for an update. I have not yet said anything but I ask this chamber, what do I say? That the barriers that I faced were not in my ward but came from inside this chamber?"

"It was my life experiences that pushed me into politics and I hope that people with experiences from all backgrounds make similar choices to enter into public office to serve their peers. But Mr Mayor, many who have much to offer will turn their backs without a second thought on entering public life if they witness examples of their disability, sexual orientation, ethnicity, or any other very personal characteristic targeted in this way."

"I'm not going to elaborate any further about that particular incident, Mr Mayor. However, I will say this. Had that comment been racist, sexist, homophobic, or dare I say anti-Semitic, the reaction both inside and outside the Council would have been much more condemning on the part of all parties, including the Standards committee. But hey, it's only disabled people — as usual, easy targets. The Equality and Human Rights Commission stated to me that this is classed as a hate-related incident and that I have options to consider. Derby City Council's website talks of a Tackling Hate Crime Together Protocol. But has Derby City Council extended any support to me once their investigation was over? No. I'll say no more on that issue. There's clearly a lot of work to be done here internally."

"Mr Mayor, the root of such views and comments rests in complete ignorance and a lack of awareness, which this chamber should not entertain. It now needs to demonstrate a desire to continually educate and develop not only its workforce and the citizens of Derby but also those who make decisions about the workforce and citizens of Derby.

"Every party here, and the Independents, will make statements about how they advocate a society in which everyone has an equal opportunity to live and work and that no one should be left behind. But when we are in office, we make decisions about those very people without a full understanding of how life truly affects them. The people have put us on a pedestal as their representatives. It is therefore primarily in their interests that we must have a basic understanding of the characteristics of the Equality law which protects them."

"Mr Mayor, in the motion we say 'meaningful' training. It needs to be interactive in workshop-based, or perhaps even placement-based, sessions and staggered over time. Each year at the Annual General Meetings, we divvy out roles such as Disability Champion, BAME Champion, etc. Why not give the people in those roles some teeth in facilitating training to Councillors? Just a thought.

"The existing level of awareness offered to Councillors is insufficient and if not actioned despite the very best legal advice by officers may lead to discriminatory decisions which will put people inside and outside this building at risk and should therefore not be acceptable to this chamber."

"Mr Mayor, I commend this motion to this chamber."

AJ sat down exhausted with a thump, with the feeling that every experience in his term as a politician had led up to and prepared him for this very moment.

The whole chamber, bar the Lib Dems and three of the Conservatives, erupted into a round of applause which AJ had not expected at all. The Mayor was not impressed. He needed to bring Councillors down to an acceptable level of decorum and switched on his microphone to remind all of the desired etiquette.

"Calm down everyone. You'll get your chance to speak. I'd like to ask if Cllr Emerson would like to speak now or later." The leader, Cllr Emerson, stood and asked to speak later.

AJ was now quite emotional. For ten months, he had bottled his hurt, anger, and mental pain. The speech he had just made was not only powerful in its message but was therapeutic. Strangely enough, he found himself thinking about his planned meetings as CEO the next day, as if he had stopped being a politician there and then.

I can't do anything else in this place, time to get back to the day job.

He looked up. One of the Conservatives, Cllr Willis, stood to comment but he looked directly towards AJ.

"Mr Mayor, I'm a gay man and much of Cllr Rai's speech resonated with me. I can confidently stand here today and say I'm gay because champions of equality such as Cllr Rai keep the conversation alive. I'd also like to say that I've been a Councillor for over twenty years and that was the best speech I've heard delivered in this chamber."

AJ looked across at Cllr Willis and put his right hand across his chest, smiled, and took a little bow. Before he could fully process the compliment, another councillor from the opposition took to the microphone. It was Cllr Anita Reynolds. Again, she directed her comment towards AJ.

"Mr Mayor. There's very little to add to what has just been said except to say that I admire your journey, Cllr Rai. You're an inspiration."

Further comments continued with his own side endorsing the need for better understanding about inequalities in the city. The Mayor was keen to bring the matter to a vote, which was passed unanimously.

AJ had changed council policy and could not contain his smile, which was beamed across the large screen in the council chamber. As he sat in his chair, he received his customary text message.

"Smashed it AJ. Smashed it." It was Salman.

AJ looked up towards the galley. Salman was with three other supporters from the ward who were all waving at him rigorously. After eye contact with him, they broke out into a silent Bhangra move.

"Only you could make something personal benefit others." His trusted accomplice was outraged by the original comment and could not hide his pleasure and pride in witnessing how AJ had handled the situation. AJ smiled and once again heard the echoes of the words recited by Tan.

Sarbat Da Bhala.

CHAPTER 56:

BORN TO BE HAPPY

AJ made the usual walk to Sonia's office from the car park, no more than a hundred yards, for his second appointment. He arrived at the entrance feeling strangely out of breath and decided he had only himself to blame as he had binged on nothing but takeaway curries and biscuits for the last few months. As he made his way over he was berating himself, and made fake promises of re-joining the gym from next week.

Before he entered, he could see the young man who he could not quite place exiting the building. He was in a hurry and made no eye contact with anyone around him, let alone AJ, who once again stood baffled. Years earlier, he had resigned himself to a poor memory.

Sonia stood smiling, watching him through the double glass doors.

"Have you worked it out yet?" She could tell he hadn't but felt the urge to tease.

"'No. He can't be that important, otherwise I would know who he is."

"Okay. Go through when you're ready. I'm just going to the little girls' room."

AJ made his way in, decided he wasn't going to sit in the sinking chair and instead made himself comfortable next to the vase again. As he sat down he felt a little shooting pain down his left arm and decided he must have overstretched a nerve in his shoulder. After a few seconds of stretching his arm out, it felt a little less stiff and he persuaded himself it wasn't really anything to worry about.

Sonia came back instantly noticing the strain on his face. "You okay AJ?"

"Yes. Yes. Just a bit of wear and tear in the shoulder. Getting old. I'm sure you know the feeling?"

"Zero tact as usual AJ. We need to work on your social etiquette. You should never refer to a woman as getting old!" She tried to be serious but looked at his face, which did not fit with his poor choice of words.

"You're roughly the same age as me, aren't you? Yes. Well, in that case, I'm old and you must be too."

She looked at him, shook her head and mumbled, "No wonder you're still bloody single. Anyway, tell me how you have been? I watched your speech the other day. Very impressive indeed." She had watched him in action with her children and husband who couldn't understand her infatuation with AJ but were impressed with the subject matter.

"Thanks. It needed saying. I've drawn a line under it now. Time to move on. I mean, don't get me wrong, I'll never forgive them for what was said about me. I spent my whole life trying to show people that my disability doesn't define who I am and with a few careless words on social media, they tried to define me. I had no choice but to retaliate. And I would do it again and again."

"Well, either way, it was well said. What's on your mind today?" Sonia had a plan for the session but wanted to give him the opportunity to initially control the conversation.

"To be honest, Sonia, I'm not sure why I'm here. I feel fine. In fact I feel great!" He did not feel good at all. He was tired and now started to focus on the pain in his shoulder.

"In that case, I'd like to try a little exercise which I do with quite a few patients now, if that's okay with you?"

"As long as it's not bloody role playing. I hate role playing and don't even think about asking me to be a tree or some other vegetable!"

Sonia could not help but laugh at his unwarranted fears and even after all this time his out of touch ideas on therapy. She reached for her trusty notepad and pen and began.

"Okay, I'm going to either ask you a question or make a statement or maybe even just say a couple of words. I then want you to give me your immediate thought on what I said but condensed to no more than one short sentence. I may ask you to expand. Are you okay with that?"

AJ scrunched his face for a second and nodded with a gesture from his hand to get on with it. Simply talking about the process was making him feel quite uneasy but he felt the need to entertain her request.

"Okay first word. Depression"

AJ looked straight up at her only to look away as the sun began to pierce his eyes. "Depression? Really? Going straight for the jugular, hey?"

"Come on, AJ, quick answers, otherwise this exercise is pointless." Sonia was firm as she looked down at him over her glasses.

"Depression. Hmm. It's mine, a part of me. I own it but every now and then it owns me."

Sonia began to scribble away but looking up at her patient and looking mildly impressed by his response. Within her patient list, his answer was the best one so far.

"Next one. Disability."

"Easy. It's in the eye of the beholder."

"Explain please."

"Well, I have a disability but it only becomes an issue when you make it an issue. For instance, I recall a meeting where the guest speaker described me as a very handsome man and asked me to come up to the front to assist her. As soon as I started walking, her facial expression wanted to take back her initial description. So, the truth is, I'm only handsome when I'm sitting down."

"Next one. Society."

"Society is like a flock of sheep. As for the social structures which make up society, for example, community, cultures, etc. well they can kiss my very fat ars..."

Sonia interrupted, "Next one. Older people."

"All older people have my utmost respect. Unless they are dickheads."

AJ was struggling to look at Sonia due to the sunlight and decided to stand up and walked towards the window. Sonia continued writing up his remarks. He tried to work out what she was writing but could only see something similar to shorthand.

"Next one. Revenge"

"Revenge. I never seek revenge. I simply sit back with my popcorn on standby."

"Elaborate please."

"Do I really need to elaborate? Just think back to all our conversations. It may take weeks, months, and in most cases years but whoever has upset me tends to cross paths with me, normally in a weaker state sooner or later. Even then, I don't take advantage of the situation. I just get on with things but will enjoy eating a few handfuls of popcorn whilst I watch their demise."

"Next one. AJ's demons."

He began to chuckle. "My demons are probably disabled too and if your follow-up is about angels the same answer goes for them."

"Next one. AJ's success"

"Whatever I am is down to ancestry."

"Explain please."

"Whatever I am today is due to a fantastic mixture of DNA from my ancestors and the sum of all their hopes and belief in a better economical standing for their descendants. Yes, I worked hard but only thanks to their work ethics." He sighed and appeared a little breathless.

AJ was also becoming a little tired of Sonia's experiment. He had been in the firing line many times in front of panels for tenders or interviews with journalists and even relished the challenge of questions which tested his knowledge on subjects close to his heart. However, he wasn't sure where Sonia was going with her questions about random topics, which he felt were better discussed in a pub over a brandy or two.

"How many more? This is becoming a little boring." As he spoke, he felt another twinge in his shoulder, travelling down his arm but just attempted to shake it off.

"Just one more, AJ. Happiness?"

He looked across to her family photo. "That looks like happiness."

"No. What makes AJ happy?"

"If I knew the answer to that, I wouldn't be here with you today. For some, it's marriage, kids, and a mortgage. For others, it's a carefree life. For me, it's, erm, it's. For me it's…" He was flummoxed. He looked around the room hoping for some inspiration without success.

"That's a stupid question Sonia. No one knows the answer to that question. Even Socrates, Confucius, or The Buddha will have struggled with that. You expect an idiot like me to answer this age-old question?"

"AJ. I need you to think. It's important. I've learnt a few new things about you today. Just one final answer to the question please." She was once again firm about the request with the slightest hint of desperation and excitement.

Unfortunately her hope for an engaging answer from her patient was in vain. AJ's concentration was split between her question and his nagging twinge in his arm.

"Are you for real? Okay, fuck it. Some people are happy; others strive to be happy. But I've reached one simple conclusion. Maybe I am not meant to be happy. Maybe those like me who are depressed were meant to be depressed. Do you know why? It's those who are not complicit with the concept of happiness who ask the difficult questions that challenge the norm, that want to improve on the status quo. Our road to happiness is never-ending. We have a different *raison d'être* from happy folk."

Sonia was almost glowing with his full-flowing outburst as she struggled to write fast enough to keep up with AJ's rant.

"Those of us who are depressed live to change the world. Charles Dickens, Abraham Lincoln, Winston Churchill, Mozart, Isaac Newton. Do I need to go on?

"Yes, I get pissed off. People piss me off. They can't help it. They're just being the way they are supposed to be. I can't get wrapped up with their stupidity anymore. It's taken me fifty years to realise it. My life, my journey, my path is for me to enjoy. Nobody owes me anything. I used to expect them to live by my code.

"I'm a plonker. My code." He laughed sarcastically at his own comment.

"My code is mine. They live by their own code which may even be right from where they stand, and that's where I need to change my ways. It's... it's happiness," he slowly looked up at Sonia.

"My code is my ... happiness," he concluded. He hadn't been sure of what he wanted to say and just rambled without fully knowing what was coming out of his mouth.

Sonia stopped writing, put her pen down, and began to clap her hands together. AJ could not fully comprehend the epiphany which had just presented itself. He locked eyes with Sonia and said it again, this time with half a smile.

"My way, my code, my chosen path is my happiness. Hmm, I see what you were doing. Very clever. Sneaky but clever. Someone has earned their stripes today."

Sonia had no desire to hide her satisfaction. She was indeed smug but also felt disappointed that she had not tried the tactic earlier.

"AJ, I'm smiling because today you did this all by yourself. I just steered the conversation but the words were yours."

"Yes okay. Let's move on before you start finally pinning me down for more stupid exercises." He chuckled as he headed towards the door. I'll see you next week."

"Good. Oh and by the way, you were wrong about one out of the three philosophers." She pointed towards a framed sketch behind the door which mainly consisted of text.

There is no path to happiness. Happiness is the path. — The Buddha.

CHAPTER 57:

S.O.S

AJ could not stop thinking about the session on the drive home. He flipped between an occasional smile and a frown. Sonia had worked her magic but also left him with a fear of what he should expect next.

He was definitely feeling good about something but just not quite sure what it was and decided he needed to share his experience. He gave the instruction through his car's voice command system to call Esha. They had both met up again for a meal the night before and had been text-messaging each other hour on hour ever since.

After a few rings, her call went to her answerphone. "Esha. Give me a call later. In fact, pop round. We'll get a take-away. I've had a cracking therapy session. Might have even made a breakthrough. Anyway, I'll text you my address. See you later."

As he disconnected, he was once again breathless. By the time he arrived home, he felt the return of the pain in his arm although this time it was accompanied with a slight tightening in his chest. "I need a brandy."

His legs felt heavier with each step from the car to the front door. AJ knew something was very wrong and looked up at the sky as he recognised the signs of a heart attack.

I finally found a little happiness and it's time for you to take me.

The bunch of keys from his hands slipped effortlessly to the ground, soon to be joined by their owner. At first, his right knee gave way which caused him to crash against the doorstep, followed by his full torso. The fall was painful but overshadowed by the chest pain. He lay sweating profusely with a view of his phone which had dropped a few feet away. It was ringing. Esha was returning his call.

A minute later, a neighbour who witnessed AJ's fall ran to his aid, simultaneously calling for an ambulance. He was an elderly man who kept his front lawn in pristine order. AJ would often joke about him putting his front drive to shame. However, today there was no banter. The old man was quite concerned about AJ clutching his chest and decided that it was best to keep him talking.

"AJ, old chap, don't worry. Paramedics are on their way. Do you take aspirin?"

"Yes. 75mg. There's a pack in my jacket pocket." Since his TIA he had been advised to take a low dosage on a daily basis as a precaution but had often missed tablets for weeks and months; he nevertheless kept them on his person habitually.

"75mg is nothing. Let's pop four of them in your mouth. Chew them up while I grab a drink of water."

"No need for water. I can just swallow them." The truth was that AJ didn't want to be left alone. *If I die, the old git will be the last image I take with me to hell. I want Esha.*

"Is there anyone you want me to call?" AJ pointed towards his phone with a look of hope and managed to give him his instruction before passing out.

"Esha. Phone ... Esha ..."

*

After a short period, AJ awoke on a hospital stretcher bed with a clear view of pandemonium around him in every direction. He recognised the Accident and Emergency unit, having brought his father in regularly with complications due to his Parkinson's. It was late evening and the department was beginning to fill up with older people with bad falls, younger people with too much alcohol in their systems, and middle-aged Chief Executives with too much of middle-age spread.

He could hear a sharp sound of air and noted it was coming from the mask attached to his face. Doctors had given him oxygen to help with breathing and further attached a multitude of wiring to significant parts of his body to monitor his heart rate and blood pressure.

His initial reaction was one of relief. *I'm not dead.* A tear made its way down the right side of his face. Ready for a full-blown breakdown, he was interrupted by the welcome sight of Toni and Shiny walking towards his bay. Both appeared visibly upset. His sister was holding a tissue in her right hand whilst the youngest sibling was clearly trying his utmost to hold himself together. They placed themselves on either side of his bed and his sister grabbed hold of his hand.

"AJ. Can you hear me? It's me, Shindy?" She was softly spoken. AJ nodded. "Are you okay? Are you in any pain?" One of the nurses came over to intervene, reminding them the patient needed to rest.

"It's okay. Don't talk. You're still with us. That's what matters." Toni made the calming statement whilst looking directly at his sister, gesturing at her to stop asking questions.

"Don't worry. We've not told mum and dad. You know what they're like. They'll hijack the first plane back!" Both siblings giggled, hoping AJ would share their little joke. He smiled enough to acknowledge the amusing prediction.

Their parents had been in India for the last four weeks. He would receive daily calls reminding him to eat properly, water his mother's many plants, and to go to the temple and pray for everything under the sun.

AJ's tears began again as he thought about his parents. It suddenly hit him that he was thousands of miles away from words of comfort and wisdom from his father and the loving ear-bashing he often enjoyed from his mother. The flow of tears had set his sister off too; she was now trying to hide behind what was left of a few strands of tissue paper. Once again, the younger brother gave his sister a stern look; she cleared her throat, smiled, and composed herself.

"Anyway, the doctor says you're going to be fine. It's just a little scare but nothing that can't be fixed." She squeezed her brother's hand a little tighter then let go thinking she might be hurting him.

"We're going to leave you to rest now. I'll call your office to let them know. We'll be back in the morning with some fresh clothes and toiletries." His brother was holding his keys. Apart from Steffi, he was the only other person who knew the alarm entry code to his property.

"Oh, by the way, there's someone else here to see you." AJ's sister immediately smiled as she moved away from the bed and gave a signal across the long corridor.

He waited a few seconds and could hear footsteps approaching until the silhouette of Esha was visible through the side-curtains. She looked towards him and smiled simultaneously, shaking her head to show disapproval about his predicament. Esha looked towards the siblings and gave a reassuring nod as they both left.

"I've got him from here."

AJ was exhausted but mustered up enough strength to sit up as much as he could without disturbing any wiring which connected him to the ECG monitor. However, during the shuffle, the movement had caused the canula in his hand to shift and he let out a painful groan. Esha grabbed hold of his hand to comfort him as she sat down next to his bed.

"If you want me to hold your hand, you don't need to go to these lengths."

AJ replied by gripping her hand as if it was the last time he would see her and his eyes were full of tears which sparkled from the bright hospital lights.

"Those green eyes won't get you out of trouble this time. I'm going to kick you into shape when they discharge you. No more crap food and plenty of exercise." AJ nodded in agreement and smiled. She was the only one who would insist his eyes were green whilst he always argued they were leaning more towards being hazel.

"There is everything to live for AJ but you have to want to live. I know you've had it bad all these years. We're all wrestling with our own demons." She began to look out across each bay which housed a patient. "They're all fighting their own battles just like you."

AJ decided not to join her in looking out towards his peers. He knew she was mad at him and hurt too. Receiving a lecture in being grateful for life from everyone who knew him was only to be expected. He had experienced a similar reaction from family members twenty-five years earlier.

"Time for a new approach to life AJ. I want to grow old with you. Did you hear that? I want to grow old with you."

AJ wasn't expecting such a revelation but was too tired to show his pleasure in hearing her words of hope. Before he had any time to ponder a future together, one of the nurses came across. She had a strong Nigerian accent.

"Mr Rai. As much as we are enjoying your company here, we need to move you to the Medical Assessment Unit. It's quieter there and the doctors will figure out what the plan is. Are you okay with that?"

AJ nodded as he struggled to keep his eyes focused. An earlier injection of morphine had now taken full effect.

"Is this your wife?"

The question was just the shot of caffeine needed. Both Esha and AJ began to shake their heads vigorously.

"No. No. Well, not yet. If he gets his act together, maybe."

"Do you hear that, Mr Rai? Better get yourself fixed up. A beautiful woman like this will get snapped up quickly. You're punching above your weight if you want my opinion" She laughed and turned with a wink towards Esha, who had begun to giggle while watching AJ, who wished he could disappear under the sheets.

"Anyway, while we wait for the porter to take him, can you start to complete some paperwork? Just some information on allergies, diet, and next of kin, etc."

"Okay. Next of kin, Esha Kaur."

CHAPTER 58:

WOMEN

Sonia returned to the present day via an interruption by Dr Kumar checking in on AJ's vitals. He called for the nurse out of the door and turned back to note a number of used tissues piling up on the bedside table. Sonia had not been able to hold back her tears. AJ wasn't an everyday patient. His connection to her was almost personal. In some strange way, she found his intermittent emotional crises a welcome test to her professional development and yet, inexplicably, felt his pain too.

"Dr Kumar, Mr Rai's next of kin is here." The nurse looked at Sonia as if to suggest she should leave, an idea that had also occurred to Sonia. She took a short look at AJ and stood whilst gathering her collection of tissues.

"Hello, you must be Esha."

The doctor's announcement startled Sonia, who felt a rush of blood straight to her head and without thinking just sat back in the chair. She looked across at the woman standing in the door. Esha was pretty, with shoulder-length hair and sharp but sleepy eyes. Sonia suddenly felt a little more enlightened about her patient. *She's very pretty. I see AJ's infatuation.*

Esha walked towards Dr. Kumar whilst glancing across at a slightly perturbed Sonia, who was trying desperately to hide two tissues which had escaped her earlier. Both acknowledged each other's presence with a smile and a nod.

For two to three minutes, the doctor and Esha discussed AJ's condition, with Sonia half-heartedly trying not to eavesdrop. The conversation was not much different to her earlier exchange with the doctor.

"Thank you, doctor. Is it okay for me to sit with him for a while?" Her face portrayed a number of emotions including hurt and helplessness.

"Yes, of course but I would ask you both to allow him to rest." He looked across to Sonia. She had sat beside AJ for almost an hour and could read Dr Kumar's expression as he left: he wanted her to leave too. Sonia stood and smiled at Esha and began what felt like an endless walk to the door.

"No, please stay."

She turned around and froze. Her insides were slowly knotting but only for a split second as she questioned her own reaction. *Why am I behaving this way? She seems nice. I am his counsellor but I am a friend too. I've nothing to fear.*

Esha came across and sat on the vacant seat next to where Sonia had held vigil. "We've not met before. I'm Esha."

"Esha. You are definitely Esha." Sonia had confidence in her statement. AJ had not devoted much time to describing the infamous woman but had disclosed her name and an outline of her looks.

"Yes but I'm embarrassed. I'm afraid I don't know you. I assume you are one of AJ's managers?" Sonia could not determine whether she had a soft voice or was speaking quietly due to their surroundings.

"No. No. My name is Sonia Khan. Dr Sonia Khan. I've known AJ off and on for twenty or so years. He's one of my..." She stopped, totally horrified at the thought of breaching any confidentiality codes. She was weary of how much the people in AJ's life knew about his therapy.

"Yes. Sonia. I've heard all about you." Esha smiled at her confusion. AJ had not mentioned any disclosure of their relationship to Esha. After a momentary and eerie silence, Esha realised Sonia would not be able to divulge any basis of her relationship with AJ and thus decided to relax the tension.

"Yes. He told me about having therapy sessions with you. I'm really pleased he was able to offload. As you will have deduced, he's quite a sensitive person, all for the right reasons." Esha looked across at AJ who seemed happy in a deep sleep.

"He's had to bottle up a fair amount of emotion. I wish I'd been there for him, sooner." Esha sighed as her voice went even softer.

"Despite the challenges and barriers, he's fought hard and clearly won many battles but even the strongest amongst us eventually break apart." Sonia was conscious of making only a generic statement rather than giving any specific detail.

"Yes. Yes. True. Quite true. But I think his issues are deeper than his personal battles. I asked him once whether he would still be so angry and driven about fighting injustice had he not been a disabled person. His reply, without any hesitation, was that he probably would be. He told me about his frustration at watching people walk away from their parents when they need them the most, which was something not connected to his disability."

Sonia nodded and reminisced about the story his grandfather told him which he later shared with her over a coffee.

"I suppose so. I think the remnants of pain are in our DNA as well as souls. We are taught to be compassionate to some extent but some of it's in our programming too." Sonia smiled as she recited this statement, which she had often used as part of presentations to her colleagues in her fraternity. She continued with her thoughts about her patient.

"Sometimes people channel their anger and frustration into helping others for the greater good whilst they're crumbling on the inside themselves. I'm genuinely encouraged by AJ's achievements as an influencer and change-maker." Sonia could sense herself becoming emotional as her voice began to tremble and was almost pleased with the interruption by Esha.

"I suppose people like AJ will always exist. You know, those who don't quite plug in to the system but run alongside it. Instead they are encouraging it to integrate with their own bespoke way of tackling change?" She began to smile. "He's a pain in the neck whilst he's conscious and a bigger pain unconscious. Look at us both. He's knocked out, probably delivering the speech of his life to a group of people who right now are trapped in his head with him."

Sonia was taken aback by Esha's comment but nevertheless laughed along with her, although both knew their reactions leaned more towards a coping mechanism for the shared-predicament theory.

"Do you think he'll be okay?" Sonia's tone turned serious.

"This one? Yes, of course. Don't worry about Mr Rai. He's as tough as Teflon. The doctor just told me he doesn't seem to be in any danger as the test results seem encouraging. In the meantime, come on, let's get out of here and grab a cuppa."

Sonia felt reassured by Esha's confidence and positive outlook and was happy to have met her. "Yes, great idea. I'm parched. There's a cafe downstairs near the main entrance?"

"I know it well." Esha smiled and they both walked towards the door. Esha looked back at AJ and whispered to him. "Don't worry. We'll be back to kick your backside into gear later." As they walked down the corridor she turned to Sonia. "Did he ever tell you about the time he tried to get my attention by trying to drown in a lake which was more like a puddle?"

Both women walked down the corridor and laughed together at Esha's accounts of AJ's failed romantic endeavours. Particularly the time he bought a bright yellow Ford to impress her and burned holes in their female classmates' clothing due to a leaky battery.

CHAPTER 59:

SECOND CHANCE AT LIFE

"C'mon Mr. Rai. Wakey wakey! Too much beauty sleep ain't good for anyone!"

AJ was already awake and just pretending to keep his eyes shut in order to avoid the annoying banter of the Australian nurse. It had been four days since his second minor attack and after the insertion of two stents, he was feeling a little stronger.

"Dr says you're going home today. I bet you're chuffed!"

AJ immediately opened his eyes. "Really? About time too!" AJ displayed a mixture of delight and frustration from having been caged in a side-room off the main ward for longer than he felt necessary. The news was very welcome.

"Have your breakfast and then I'll pop back later to go through your discharge papers. Is anyone available to pick you up?"

"Yes. I'll call my brother as soon as you're finished with me."

"No worries. Enjoy your fruit."

AJ looked at the tray in front of him. A glass of fruit juice stood proud alongside a plate of chopped oranges, peaches, and grapes with a little tub of yoghurt. "This isn't a fucking breakfast," he mumbled as he plotted a full fry-up as soon as he reached home. He sat up, scrunched his face when he attempted a spoon of fruit dipped in yoghurt, and soon switched to a look of satisfaction.

"Tastes better than the crap you normally eat, hey?" a soft and comforting voice made AJ look up. He saw Esha and Sonia walking through the door together; he reversed his expression to show dissatisfaction.

"Tastes like shit actually," he retorted, not wanting to admit she was right.

"Behave, Mr. Rai. You know too well we're going to sort out your haphazard diet and lifestyle." Esha was firm in her tone as AJ lowered his head mimicking a small child being scolded.

"I suppose eating this rabbit food is part of your new regime for me? Speaking of which, since when have you two become bosom buddies? I'm not sure how I feel about this!"

Sonia took one step forward and began to reset the flowers in his vase whilst adding her thoughts. "You might want to get used to it AJ. For the last few days we've been putting a plan of action together to make you strong again. Esha will be sorting out your diet and physical exercise plan while I'll be, let's just say I'll be looking after your mental well-being."

"What the fu..."

"And we're going to start with cleaning your mouth out. You swear far more than necessary. You're a smart, classy guy with a foul mouth. Time to sort your shit out!" Esha, joined by Sonia burst out laughing, realising the irony of her comment.

AJ retreated into his bed feeling defeated and overwhelmed by the two determined women. He began to picture his home turned into a boot camp and desperately wanted to find a way to take control of the situation. Meanwhile, Esha and Sonia were busy packing his belongings into carrier bags and discussing the benefits of juiced celery every morning. AJ wanted to change the subject but watching them both in their element, he just sighed and began to re-count the cracks in the ceiling. He was only too pleased to be interrupted by the nurse.

"Right mate, I've done your paperwork which just needs your autograph. Here are some pills to lower your cholesterol level and a letter for you to hand to your GP. As far I'm concerned, you're good to go! I'll send for a porter to wheel you down to the main entrance."

AJ looked almost horrified as he registered the speed of the discharge. "What? That's it? I don't feel right yet. Maybe I should stay another day or two. You know, just to make sure I'm fully fit?" He glanced through the corner of his eye at his two drill sergeants who didn't look too impressed.

"Mr. Rai, you were desperate to get out of here a few minutes ago!" the nurse was a little confused.

Sonia intervened. "Oh he's fine. He's just pulling your leg."

"His family is looking forward to seeing him today. And guess who's flying back from India tomorrow?" Esha couldn't help but giggle. She knew very well he wasn't looking forward to the smothering and lectures about how his heart attack had affected his mother. The nurse took a final reading of AJ's vitals and bid him farewell.

"Don't come back Mr Rai. Good health!"

AJ looked across at his two captors who were both performing the classic hands on hips pose, which AJ often experienced from his management when they were not too impressed with his behaviour.

"C'mon. Get up, get dressed." Esha began to lift the many layers of sheets above the fearful patient.

"Are you kidding me? Leave me with a little bit of dignity please. Unless you want to see me in my underwear!" AJ was visibly anxious of what lay ahead but felt getting dressed was one area where he needed to stamp his authority.

"Okay fine. Come on Sonia, let's give the little gentleman some space." As they were leaving his room, the porter came in with a wheelchair. He was a tall muscular man in his fifties.

"Mr Rai, I've brought your ride."

"I'm fine. I can walk and don't need the wheels."

"Hospital policy, old boy. I have to take you to the entrance. You can walk, run or dance as soon as you cross the barrier. Doesn't bother me."

AJ decided not to argue. Instead he reached for his trousers and began to slowly dress his aching and very stiff body. A few minutes later, he emerged from his room and sat in the wheelchair clutching at his belongings. Both Sonia and Esha walked a couple of steps ahead as he watched in dismay, trying to work out how so much had changed over a few days.

He was at the mercy of two women who were immensely important to him but not to the extent that they should dictate his lifestyle. *I'm a free spirit. These two are going to do my head in.* He looked up at the porter who had a cheesy smile and asked AJ an obvious question, which received an instant answer.

"Which one of those two is your better half?"

"Neither of them!"

Esha heard the little exchange and settled the discussion. "Me, if he behaves himself." She was joined in laughter by Sonia and they both continued their own conversation, which AJ had deduced was about sarees and tailors.

As they approached the entrance, AJ looked up again at the porter who could not help but chuckle as he was about to leave the gazelle with a couple of lionesses. As he walked off, he noted AJ's expression of helplessness.

"Right, Sonia, I'll fetch the car whilst you wait with Mr. Mardy Pants." Esha headed off to the car park, which was only a couple of hundred yards away.

AJ looked toward Sonia who smiled at him. "She's a diamond. You're in good hands. Make sure you're good to her. She's going through a lot too." Her tone changed back swiftly to one he recognised. It was almost comforting. AJ too slipped back into a familiar stance as he straightened himself up.

"Yes, of course. Goes without saying really."

Sonia took a step nearer to her old friend and gave him a hug.

"You had us all frightened, you know? You are needed. Much needed." She let him go and pointed ahead at an elderly man, standing behind his wife who was in a wheelchair.

"They need you, AJ. They need you to keep thinking two steps ahead of the game. Children need to see people like AJ Rai beat the odds. They want role models." AJ lowered his head and commenced his traditional gaze at the floor.

"You're an example of getting back up off the floor bigger and stronger than before you were knocked down."

It was not the first time AJ had heard such comments but somehow they resonated deeper than ever before. He was regularly told about his ability to inspire others but today was different. He felt it appropriate to fake a cough to lighten the mood.

"Do you know how much I hated coming to see you all those years ago? The amount of times I sat in your reception thinking about walking off before you came out of your office." He stopped and looked towards Sonia whilst his face broke into a little sweat.

"Are you okay, AJ? What's wrong?" Sonia had a little panic in her voice. He suddenly looked a little weaker. She was terrified she might have given him the talk a little too early. Yet she soon realised there was nothing physically wrong with him. Something had alerted him.

"That young lad I met coming out of your reception. I know who he is."

Sonia took a long breath full of relief. "Bloody hell AJ, talk about scaring me! Go on, how do you know him?" Her tone of voice was a mixture of relief and frustration but she couldn't hide the curiosity underneath it all.

AJ began to smile and sat on a bench a few feet away.

"He is me. That man is me. I was like that. He is me. Gosh!" AJ became increasingly pleased with himself for solving something which had aggravated him for too long. "That was one of his first sessions, yes?" He was making more of a statement than posing a question as he knew too well Sonia would not be able to answer.

"Anyway, you remember, don't you? I was a mess when I came to see you twenty plus years ago. Let me guess he needs some antidepressants too?"

Sonia wasn't impressed with his line of questioning.

"AJ, you know very well I won't divulge patient details to you and frankly I'm shocked at you for asking! Unfortunately, doctors are too quick to prescribe antidepressants now so patients don't get the type of support that you did. I'm afraid things have changed and not for the better." Sonia was serious but almost deflated in her tone. She was well aware of the increase in demand for counselling but the system was more rigged in favour of General Practitioners prescribing medication.

"Poor guy. I've been there. I know you can't discuss his case with me but here's an id..." Once again, AJ froze in mid-sentence. Sonia was adjusting to his new stop-start mannerism and simply allowed him the time to make his point.

"That's it! Dr Khan, you're great! Thank you!"

She was intrigued by what she had apparently done to deserve such applause from someone who only a few minutes earlier was quite agitated.

"Why are you thanking me, AJ?"

"You reached out to me. I came. I saw that young chap. He mirrors my own image twenty-five years earlier. I know what I need to do."

"AJ, I'm confused. What is it you need to do? I think you need to rest for a while, not take on a new project."

"Yes, Yes. I'll rest. Don't worry, I'll rest. It's just that I want to reach out to that young chap. In fact, I want to reach out to many more like him. To tell him that it will be okay and that I've been through something similar to whatever he is going through. That I talked to people like you, Sonia, and there's no shame in it. In fact, it shows character and strength, not weakness."

"This conversation needs to be wider. Not just between doctors and patients in enclosed rooms but in schools, universities, offices, shop floors, everywhere. If people know that I have depression, that I get down, very down and then I'm up, then maybe others will start to talk about whatever is on their minds. Maybe husbands and wives will talk more about emotions rather than yelling and blaming each other without understanding the underlying reasons behind it."

Sonia was pleased that AJ had wanted to go public with his story. Real-life examples of people fighting and beating depression were definitely a way to empower others to come forward. They saw Esha pull up beside them and she watched AJ drive off with her, a second chance at life.

Sonia went home with a smile and a final reassurance — and also with a sense of calm from the knowledge that her job with him was done.

CHAPTER 60:

FULL CIRCLE

"I'd like to now ask someone to the stage who, in all honesty, needs no introduction. As a champion of the rights of vulnerable and disadvantaged people, he doesn't hesitate in speaking on their behalf and shoots from the hip whenever necessary. In fact, I don't think he would disagree with being described as fearless.

"After twenty-seven years, he's one of the longest serving CEOs in the country with a CV which boasts over twenty-five million pounds in income generation. He even had a stint as a professional Bhangra singer, a politician, and a genuine all-round nice guy. He's been a strong force in the city and no matter what sector you work in, most have heard of his grit, sheer determination, and resilience. He's a local inspiration and a great person to have on your side."

"Ladies and gentlemen, please put your hands together for AJ Rai."

The introduction was made by Kelly Hamblyn, the Chairperson of the local Council for Voluntary Services. She had worked alongside AJ for a number of years on joint projects and was today awarding him with a certificate marking a quarter of a century as a CEO.

AJ headed towards the stage and glanced back at a room full of his family, work colleagues, peers, his friend Jags, and a few faces which he could not quite place. The applause from the audience lasted long enough for him to take his position at the lectern.

As he got closer, she leaned in and smiled, "Be nice, AJ."

"I'm always nice," he laughed and looked at the protruding microphone, hoping it had not picked up their exchange. He looked up at the smiling faces in front of him. After a quick calculation, he estimated an attendance of just under ninety people: nine rows with ten chairs in each. A few days earlier, he had been contacted by a local school's sixth form college who wanted to bring final-year disabled students to be inspired by AJ. He agreed and counted at least seven quite bored-looking individuals.

As he cleared his throat, he watched Sonia walk in with the young man AJ had seen at her office. They both took a seat on the back row next to Esha. She smiled at him with enough expression to include a virtual nudge to get on with it.

Over a three-week period, AJ had been nominated for local and national awards which were well-received but had sparked a thought in his mind that there must be a collective wish for him to begin his descent into retirement. It could be the only explanation for the nominations lately. Esha disagreed and quickly put paid to those notions by stressing that he was being acknowledged because he had so much more to offer. He was extremely grateful for her presence in his life.

"Friends, colleagues, and loved ones. I'm honoured and a little humbled to stand in front of you today. You have all taken time out from your busy lives to spend a few moments here with me today and I truly thank you."

"I will also take this opportunity to thank you for your kind and thoughtful messages which boosted my recovery from the recent spell in hospital. Over the last few weeks, I have had the opportunity to reflect on my life. It was either that or suffer at the mercy of daytime television."

AJ received a polite laugh from the audience at a comment which he knew was true and deep down not that humorous. It did, however, give him enough confidence to continue.

"I stand here before you, yes, as a long serving member of staff. Yet, the remarkable truth is, had I not been a disabled person, I can pretty much guarantee I would have been doing something else. This itself tells us what is wrong with us as individuals, as a society. We don't worry about disability until it directly or indirectly affects us. That's not a good thing. Disability is one of those things that will affect every person on the planet at some stage in life."

"You all think enough of me to have taken time out to be with me today and I'm very grateful too. Over the years, we've encountered each other at meetings, social events, and so forth. So many of you have commented on me being a controversial, forthright, and possibly challenging figure. Others see me as quiet and withdrawn and I remember accidentally overhearing a conversation in which I was described as *'strange'*."

"Those who see me more regularly know AJ Rai as always up for a laugh, a very dry and sarcastic person who has even been considered funny on occasion. And not to forget my very favourite being: AJ the evil genius always fighting for the greater good."

The room echoed with laughter and applause with many nodding in agreement with his latter comment as he had decided now was the time to go completely off-script.

"Those behaviours often stem from expectations, actions, or reactions, which all fit into agendas. I deduce that I became a chameleon. I just wanted to fit in, to please people. To make you think that AJ is more than a disability. Whatever I did, I did it to the extreme because I wanted to disappear into the cause rather than be the cause."

"If I sang, I wanted the song to be more successful than the singer. In the office, I wanted the project to be more successful than the CEO. Somehow, that didn't always happen. You're here celebrating my achievements, my service. Yet for so much of my life, I just wanted to be normal."

AJ's tone softened, causing everyone to listen more attentively. Apart from a cough from one of the middle rows, the room was silent. A glance at the back row showed a reassuring smile from Esha.

"Normal. Such an uncannily powerful word which can cause misery in so many lives. Most of us strive to be normal but no one knows what normal is. Yet the truth is that I've hidden a side to me which has personally affected me for too many years. In fact, it was only last week I decided it was time to begin to talk about it."

"I was just introduced as *fearless*. I don't know, maybe I have wrestled a few dragons and beaten them but the truth is that I've always been terrified. Every situation which I face frightens the life out of me."

"I was contacted a couple of days earlier and asked if these wonderful school leavers on the front row here could possibly take inspiration from my award today. I truly hope they do take something positive from this afternoon but I also hope they are prepared for the world outside these walls. A world which shows no mercy to people who do not fit in or look like the norm. A world desperate to label you, to pigeon-hole you, to keep you in your place."

The young adults on the front row were now alert and paying complete attention to AJ. They had been introduced to successful businessmen and women as part of their career lessons, yet nothing matched this straight-talking disabled man on the stage. AJ now talked directly to them.

"If you want to tick a box on the company's Equalities Monitoring Form, then get comfortable inside that pigeon-hole. If you want better opportunities for yourselves, then you have to be loud and proud of that impairment. You have to own it. That impairment, that disability, must not control you. You have to control it. The wheelchair is an important but inanimate object. It should not be a symbol of disability. I have Cerebral Palsy, but Cerebral Palsy does not and should not have me."

Once again, the audience erupted into a frenzy of applause. This time the youngsters joined in.

"But the harsh reality is, no one is going to help you. You are alone. Family and friends will be there if you call them but they have their own lives too. And If you're too busy battling with your own impairment, every opportunity will be grabbed out of your hands by others. You'll end up in constant overdrive expending every ounce of energy justifying your existence. And then you'll be left behind."

AJ was conscious he was now way off his original speech which was more upbeat and full of hope. He continuously scanned the expressions and reactions of the crowd. It was clear they appreciated his emotion and honesty and thus now decided to hone in on the young man sitting next to Sonia at the back.

"As I look out at each and every one of you, I know one thing for sure. You're all troubled by something right now in your life and you're hiding behind the sort of smile which has masked me too. Nobody is happy. We all have something that's niggling away at us.

"We struggle to tell anyone about it for fear of being seen as weak or even pathetic, but remember, sometimes the loudest one in the pub or the office is also the quietest one at home and quite possibly at risk."

An older man called out from the second row. It was his neighbour, the one who had seen him collapse and came to his aide. "You're as strong as they come, AJ. Not weak at all."

"Thank you for your confidence in my strength. And from that little boost, I'll admit it here today. Whilst you saw AJ Rai's seemingly comfortable journey from a singer, to CEO, a successful businessman and to a politician and cabinet member, AJ Rai was in therapy for severe depression for matters which he internalised throughout his childhood and teenage years. Therapy or counselling, they're words which strike fear and pity in many people. And that's why so many will distance themselves from the concept. But you don't always need to seek the path of a counsellor, you just need a non-judgemental ear. Someone who when you tell them what's bothering you will answer you by giving you an example of what's affecting them too. From there, a conversation starts."

AJ was interrupted with a short round of applause again but did not allow it to continue as he was in full flow. "Please don't take what I say next as a sexist comment but it needs to be said. Gentlemen, women have mastered those types of conversation for millennia. Let's face it, we are shit at it!"

A burst of laughter engulfed each row like a Mexican wave as the attendees nodded with approval, particularly from all the women as they looked at each nervous man sitting next to them.

"The conversation isn't manly enough unless men start by talking about football, cricket, or how much alcohol they drank over the last few days. Gentlemen, it's still a macho conversation if we start by saying, 'Guess what's pissing me off?'"

The room was now filled with slightly anxious men grunting and smiling enough as if to say, *"Point made, AJ. Move on."*

"My apologies. My next project is to seek help for my foul language." He glanced at Sonia and Esha who gave a thumbs up of approval with beaming smiles. "So, what's my point? Well, to say this: that the more we talk with our hearts, the less it affects our brains."

"Take me, for example. My own story is full of hurt and every time someone hurt me it got to me, deep inside my DNA, and I would mentally break. I wanted someone to reach out and fix me, yet I was the one who needed to make the first move. I had to be the one to ask for help and that wasn't something I was good at."

"In my younger days, it was rare to be prescribed antidepressants without seeking a counsellor first. Today, it's often a quick scribble on the prescription pad and Bob's your uncle! A life-long addiction to antidepressants awaits you. I was fortunate enough to be referred for counselling, where over time I offloaded about events, situations which affected me. I've been bullied, harassed, discriminated against, ignored, and judged, all without saying one single word."

"Just because a naive, young child was brought up to look for the good in people it hurt deeply when the reality kicked in: that not everyone had the same outlook. People obviously had other plans for me."

The room was silent. AJ could see tears rolling down the faces of at least three people. This was not his desired outcome but it was too late to change the tone of his speech.

"Without sounding like the beginning of a bad joke, apart from my therapist it was three priests — a Christian, a Muslim and a Sikh — who over the years talked to me when I was at my lowest. Maybe it's in their training to listen. I don't really know but their interventions at those precise moments could be classed as divine."

The silence in the room was incredible. Again, AJ softened his voice. His thoughts, however, rapidly targeted a single teardrop, which had started to build up in his right eye; this baffled him as he wasn't feeling overly emotional.

"My achievements over so many years are being celebrated today and that is nice. Anyone in a senior role will probably agree that it's a lonely and thankless job; our minds never switch off. Usually our critics outnumber our supporters and we're often firing on all cylinders whilst running on an empty tank. I'm tired. Really tired."

AJ stopped and joined the silence. His audience were too busy trying to determine if he was tired at that very moment or as a CEO in general. Within the crowd, his brother stood up along with his old friend Jags. Both began to walk slowly towards the stage. AJ watched them and again, turned his focus towards the youngsters on the front row, and decided to continue.

"It's a tough world out there. Today I'm being celebrated for generating over twenty-five million pounds over the years for projects for disabled people. I thought I had made a difference over the years, but whilst technology has made lives better for the young ones in front of me, the ignorance towards them out there thrives."

He gestured towards the ceiling and walls to indicate outdoors and society.

"It's more rampant than ever, particularly with the rise of social media, and I truly hope you fulfil your dreams and become CEOs like me, to make that change, become leaders in industry or commerce; don't just restrict yourself to disability charities and causes."

He turned towards the two men now standing at his side.

"These two have worked out that I'm about to cry like a little baby. That's why they've come forward. It's probably time for me to sit down; besides, you've only really come for the buffet hey?"

A round of applause followed by laughter rose from the room; many in the audience were wiping away tears. AJ turned his gaze to the back wall as if addressing something beyond the audience, into the street, and people's living rooms.

"Before I go, I want to thank you all once again; in one way or another, you have been a part of my journey. I want you all to talk and to keep talking, use whatever mechanism works for you as there is no off-the-shelf formula. You will all have an individual way of turning whatever's bothering you so much onto its head. Make sure you own it."

"I'll end with a quote from history. I can't quite remember who originally said it but that doesn't really matter right now. It has taken me over fifty years to understand it.

No one can hurt me without my permission."

Amo Raju

Amo Raju has spent more than half of his life creating and providing services for disabled people. However, as a disabled person, he also challenged mainstream expectations by becoming a semi-successful Bhangra singer, sector leader, and politician. His venture into writing has been mainly to provide hope, inspiration, and possibly a template for people who are affected by any type of disadvantage.

With thanks to:

To every single member of my family for being an absolute rock. I know I'm a pain in the neck, but I think you have all understood my reasons.

To Richard Shaw and the late Paul Matthews, for giving me that purpose in life. I was lost but you put me on the right path.

To my wife for pushing me that little bit more, for giving me that drive, and for simply tolerating me. Even I wouldn't live with me!

To every "Sonia" out there. I can only describe you as unsung heroes and heroines essential to every "AJ".

And to every "AJ". Do not give up. You are unique—not different. You are strong—not weak. And you are feared by those who do not want change.

Mani Hayre

Mani Hayre has been writing casually since 2016, with a blog born out of boredom and needing an outlet to share stories. An avid reader as a child, Mani grew up in a South Asian family, where becoming a writer wasn't considered a real career choice. She has a background in business development, training, and sales and graduated from the University of Lincoln with a BA (Hons) Degree in Business Studies.

Her venture into writing has been a natural progression. As she gained confidence as a writer and an online following who resonated with her stories on difficult subject matters (including mental health, depression, and social injustice), it was only a matter of time before she wrote her first book.

With thanks to:

To my parents, siblings, and friends—they know who they are—who have supported me throughout this process, encouraged me to keep going when I doubted myself, and propped me up with words of wisdom, laughter, and nights out. It meant more than you'll ever know.